# THE LIFE GUIDE FOR VICTORIOUS LIVING

*Daily Devotional New Believers*

BY

GIORON T. WILKINS, SR.

Watersprings
PUBLISHING

The Life Guide for Victorious Living: Daily Devotional for New Believers is published by Watersprings Publishing, a division of Watersprings Media House, LLC., P.O. Box 1284 Olive Branch, MS 38654.
www.waterspringspublishing.com

Contact the publisher for bulk orders and permission requests.

Printed in the United States of America.

ISBN-13: 979-8-9894494-1-5

# CONTENTS

# Praise for the Life Guide for Victorious Living

The Life Guide for Victorious Living is a fresh, innovative, and masterful approach to Kingdom truths that leave the reader with an overwhelming expectancy for more.

Minister Gioron's "common sense " writing style offers clarity, removing the guesswork from the "Why and how?" This devotional offers practical applications and disciplines to help you re-align yourself to Kingdom culture and truths.

The Life Guide for Victorious Living will strengthen the faith of the mature saint and is a beautiful introduction to the God of hope and transformation for new Believers.

This devotional fills you with joy and peace wherever you are in your spiritual walk because it will remind you of who you are in Christ.

*-Minister Jill Wilkins, Wilkins Ministries International Inc.*

# INTRODUCTION

Welcome to the journey through the sacred pages of the Bible, designed to bring clarity and inspiration to new believers of all ages. In this daily devotional, our goal is simple - to illuminate the profound wisdom of the Holy Scriptures and make it accessible to everyone.

Reading this devotional daily will bolster your faith and ignite hope within your heart. With a reader-centered approach, we address the everyday challenges we all encounter on our life's path. From healing our bodies to understanding the intricate makeup of our spirit, soul, and body, we delve into areas of life often left untouched by other devotionals. My aim is to equip you with practical insights that can be applied to your daily existence.

This 365-day devotional unravels God's original design for us, reflecting how He intended us to live from the beginning of creation. Each day, you will find a carefully selected scripture verse to guide you and provide the encouragement and teaching you need to live victoriously. It's an invitation to rise above adversity and find triumph in your faith journey.

Let's begin this transformative adventure as we explore the wisdom of the Bible, seek understanding in the ways of God, and embrace a life of victory over the trials and tribulations of our world. I'm rooting for you!

# *January 1*

# BRAND NEW START

*Isaiah 43:18-19*

*Do not [earnestly] remember the former things;*
*neither consider the things of old.*
*Behold, I am doing a new thing!*
*Now it springs forth; do you not perceive*
*and know it and will you not give heed to it?*
*I will even make a way in the wilderness*
*and rivers in the desert.*

It's a new year, it's time to forget those things that are behind us, and reach for the new things coming our way. We must be open for change, for even doing things differently than we have in the past. Change is indicative of growth in many areas of life. With new things comes new ways (2 Corinthians 5:17). We can learn the plan of God for our life by starting this year off with more time with Him. Clarity in knowing comes with committed to daily fellowship with God (Joshua 1:8). For starters, spending 10 or 15 minutes a day reading the Bible and praying is a great way to begin the necessary lifestyle required to know God's plan for our life. Now is a good time to start.

# *January 2*

# A CRY FOR JUSTICE

*Amos 5:24, NKJV*

*But let justice run down like waters and righteousness as a mighty and ever-flowing stream.*

We want justice when something happens that is clearly wrong, and when there is no accountability for the evil action done. Satan has so infiltrated our justice system to the point people are not surprised when evil-doers get off scott-free of the crime committed. Justice should run like a river, ever present, and should not be compromised. That is why Jesus prayed to God, that we may live above the evil in this world (John 17:15). The Word of God is conditional. We must be positioned properly in Him, in a place of refuge if needed, and strong in the faith, trusting Him for answers no matter what comes our way in life.

# *January 3*

# ATONEMENT REALIZED

*Romans 3:25*

*Whom God put forward [before the eyes of all] as a mercy seat and propitiation by His blood [the cleansing and life-giving sacrifice of atonement and reconciliation, to be received] through faith. This was to show God's righteousness, because in His divine forbearance He had passed over and ignored former sins without punishment.*

We have heard stories of how back in time, sacrifices were offered to the various gods that mankind would ignorantly serve and would try to please them through gifts, or offerings. This false, deranged idea of appeasing the gods to keep them happy was a diabolical and delusional deception from Satan himself. Any and everything Satan does is perverted; He has been trying to redirect the purity of the Almighty God's plan of atonement for the sin of mankind into something quite evil. Through the blood of Jesus Christ, our Lord, we have the remission of sin (as if it never existed), not a cover-up. The blood of Jesus covers all necessary sacrifices for wrongdoings from the beginning of time until the last day. All sin that has ever been committed and will be is under the blood of Jesus. We have atonement for our sins by accepting the salvific work of Jesus Christ at Calvary.

# *January 4*

## COME UP HIGHER

*Philippians 3:10-11*

*[For my determined purpose is] that I may know Him [that I may progressively become more deeply and intimately acquainted with Him, perceiving and recognizing and understanding the wonders of His Person more strongly and more clearly], and that I may in that same way come to know the power outflowing from His resurrection [*a*]which it exerts over believers], and that I may so share His sufferings as to be continually transformed [in spirit into His likeness even] to His death, [in the hope].*

To experience the mighty power that raised Him from the dead, we must suffer with Him, sharing in His death. Now that's not a literal command - "sharing in His death." To suffer with Him, can mean to "suffer" something said to you that was offensive or hurtful, and letting trivial, unnecessary confrontation go. To keep the peace in a bad situation could be a suffering moment. Suffering persecution for telling the truth is part of knowing you're on the right track (2 Timothy 3:12). Sharing in His death is indicative of Christians keeping the flesh under control. The flesh is your emotions, or inordinate appetites of the body, including overeating, unnatural sexual behavior, over indulgence in drinking alcohol, etc. Suffering with Christ is the next level up in Christian maturity. The Apostle Paul wrote this verse to the Philippians, he also wrote two thirds of the New Testament in the Bible. He yearned to be like Christ in every way. Are you eating meat yet (Hebrews 5:12), or are you still on the milk of God's Word?

# *January 5*

# HAS FEAR BECOME YOUR BFF?

*2 Timothy 1:3, NKJV*

*I thank God Whom I worship with a pure conscience, [a]in the spirit of my fathers, when without ceasing I remember you night and day in my prayers.*

Anytime you're experiencing fear, it is not from God. God has not given you the spirit of fear but of power, love, and a clear-thinking mind. Fear is a spirit, an entity of its own that seeks those who do not have a clear-thinking mind or who are estranged from any God-like character or attributes. A person well versed in the scriptures who knows the power of God in their own life is not easily affected by fear. There is a natural, healthy fear that tells us not to stand in the middle of the street when a truck is coming. The fear of God, which is a reverential fear, is good. The fear that cripples you, stops you from having a normal life is from the dark side. Do not be afraid. Do not allow fear to be your best friend.

# January 6

# HE SUPPLIES IT ALL!

*Philippians 4:19*
*And my God will liberally supply (fill to the full)*
*your every need according to His riches in glory in Christ Jesus.*

God supplies all of our needs according to the riches of His glory in Christ Jesus. That sounds like more than enough, and it is. Our basic need is for Jesus to save us from eternal damnation when our bodies die, and to have an acceptable quality of life here on Earth. Jesus did His part concerning the salvation of mankind and making it available for us to be in the family of God. Other needs are the basics for living. He supplies that above and beyond and has a never-ending supply for each of us. The Word of God is conditional. We should aspire to grow in every area of our lives, and that is God's prescribed way for us. The blessings of God are coming from a place of love and understanding. Your blessing can more easily find its way to you when there isn't the clutter of sin in your life, which can block God in general. Even if this is your situation, ask God for His mercy to help you. He supplies it all.

# January 7

# A CONFIDENT SOUL

*Psalm 56:3, NKJV*
*Whenever I am afraid, I will put my trust in You.*

Sooner or later, we all feel afraid. No matter what the issue is, it comes to us all, feeling alone even when we are not physically alone. The inner comfort we all seek knowingly or unknowingly, is the comfort of our souls. That kind of comfort requires a lifestyle conducive to the teachings and precepts of the Creator of our souls. The comfort of the world turns to drugs and alcohol, which masks the problem, but doesn't eliminate it. He's the only true genuine Father of comfort (2 Corinthians 1:3-5), and when He's on the scene peace comes, the fear leaves, and inner comfort which affects our entire life positively becomes a reality. We have our individual lifestyles, and we've been given a choice to pick whatever we want. This can be a dangerous thing if we don't have the basics of salvation operating in our lives. Your life must include God in at least the fundamental stage of salvation (Romans 10:9-10). Our lives can be a lot easier, more fulfilling, prosperous, and without the excessive fear if we simply trust God in our everyday lives. Your choices are your own, but not without consequence. Be confident in Him.

# *January 8*

# LEARN HOW TO FIGHT

*Romans 12:12, NLT*
*Rejoice in our confident hope.*
*Be patient in trouble and keep on praying.*

Suffering and tribulation comes to us all, there's no life without it. So, we must learn how to deal with it. Be joyful in hope, patient in affliction, and faithful in prayer. Hope is a seed of joyful expectation to our faith which keeps us until manifestation. Patience is necessary to wait on God's help. Through faith and patience we obtain the promises of God (Hebrews 6:12). Being faithful in prayer keeps God active in our need for help. Learn to fight the good fight of faith (1 Timothy 6:12). It's a good fight because we win, but you must be familiar with your weapons which are not carnal, but mighty through God to the pulling down of strongholds (2 Corinthians 10:4). The bottom line is that you want to get on the winning team of life and get the negativity of this world out of your heart, mind, and soul, to live the way you should - in victory.

# *January 9*

# PEACE, WE ALL WANT IT

*Matthew 5:9*

*Blessed (enjoying enviable happiness, spiritually prosperous—with life-joy and satisfaction in God's favor and salvation, regardless of their outward conditions) are the makers and maintainers of peace, for they shall be called the sons of God!*

A life of peace seems impossible in this world. But peace is available for those who want it and will do whatever it takes to get it. Blessed are the peacemakers, for they will be called children of God. Like anything else, something of great value is not normally handed over to you without a great price. Well, this bill has been paid by Jesus. To have the peace that surpasses all understanding, which only comes from God, a prerequisite must be met. We must first trust God and His Word. Getting our belief system up to the faith required to receive this peace is within a close and personal relationship with God. Knowing He has your back at every turn takes away worry. Once you stop worrying, doubting God, and running with the wrong people, peace has a better chance to come in. Get rid of the drama in your life at all costs. Clear out the natural garbage in your life, and then invoke your will to pursue peace, and it will manifest in your life.

# *January 10*

# STICKS AND STONES

*Proverbs 16:24, NKJV*
*Pleasant words are as a honeycomb,*
*sweet to the mind and healing to the body.*

"Sticks and stones can break my bones, but words will never hurt me." This well-known saying isn't true. When we understand the weight our words carry, there's another rule in affect. In the beginning, God said, "Let there be light." Don't you think as powerful as Almighty God is, He could have just thought creation into being? He was setting an example of the use, and power behind words. The demonstration of faith was given way back then for humanity to follow. God is in one realm of existence (spiritual), and we are in this natural one. So, faith is necessary for help from God. Being a child of God or not, your words carry power (Proverbs 15:1). When you blindly believe in something or someone, and you're constantly saying over and over what's in your heart concerning it, in time it will come to pass (Proverbs 18:21). Good or harsh words will manifest what you've been saying. Pleasant words are as a honeycomb, sweet to our mind, and healing to our bodies.

# *January 11*

## THE DEVIL EXPOSED

*John 10:10*

*The thief comes only in order to steal and kill and destroy. I came that they may have and enjoy life, and have it in abundance (to the full, till it overflows).*

The devil has always been in motion with his campaign against humanity since the fall of man in the garden of Eden. The devil formerly known as Lucifer, was God's right-hand man responsible for the praise and worship music in heaven before the creation of man. He got full of himself to the point he wanted to be like the Most High and ascend above God's throne. Once iniquity was found in his heart God kicked him out of heaven down to the Earth. Now he goes by the name of Satan, or Devil, which means the personification of evil. His way of getting back at God, is by coming after God's beloved creation, humankind. Because of this unseen being, we could follow this world's evil straight to hell. However, Jesus came to destroy the works of the devil so that we might have life and have it more abundantly. Therefore, a choice must be made by every living soul to pursue the get-out-of-hell-free card by accepting Jesus Christ as Lord and Savior of your life before leaving this world. A better life awaits us all. Live above the evil of this world every day through Jesus, He's the only way out.

# *January 12*

## LOVE'S POSTURE

*1 John 4:11*

*Beloved, if God loved us so [very much],*
*we also ought to love one another.*

The example for love was given to us by God our Father. God first loved us by sending His only begotten Son to die for our sin. Since Jesus lived a sinless life while on Earth, we can have a chance at loving each other God's way. Jesus destroyed the works of the devil, and freedom from habitual wrongdoing is available. We cannot love one another if we're bound by the sin nature. The love of God was shed abroad in our hearts by the Holy Spirit at the new birth (Romans 5:5). The ability is in us to love with the agape love of God. It's a selfless sacrificial love. When we can align ourselves with the teachings and precepts of the Lord. Love is like any other habit-forming entity, the more you love, the easier it is to do. It takes practice especially with unlovable people. But that seed of love was planted in you when you became saved. Now, it needs to grow like a tree, firm, and immovable, becoming a sure foundation ready for anything life throws at it.

# *January 13*

# UNFORGIVENESS HAS RISEN ITS HEAD AGAIN

### Matthew 6:14

*For if you forgive people their trespasses [their reckless and willful sins, leaving them, letting them go, and giving up resentment], your heavenly Father will also forgive you.*

I post on social media nuggets of my revelations of God's Word, and my fellowship with Him from selected scripture verses each day. So today, we're talking about unforgiveness. As we forgive others, God will also forgive us. Plain and simple. Forgiving an offense done to us is not so plain and simple. I can forgive a person and not be required to spend time with the offender. I can forgive them and not be friends with them. The straight and narrow way to offer forgiveness to someone, is to explain to them what they did and how it hurt. Decide to forgive them for what they did, and no longer allow them to have power over you for hating them for it. That confession alone will free "the hell" out of you. Whether they accept what's said to them or not, you will be free!

# January 14

# THE WAY, THE TRUTH, AND THE LIFE

*John 14:6*

*Jesus said to him, I am the Way and the Truth and the Life; no one comes to the Father except by (through) Me.*

Jesus is the way, the truth, and the life. He's the only way to Father God. He is the living word of God, which is the word of truth, and all life was created through Jesus. It could be said that Father God is the Chairman of the Board, the Son (Jesus) is the hands-on Entity, the Chief Operating Officer of Creation, and the Holy Spirit is the power behind the job of creation. Jesus is the key connection to God's creation of humanity. He became the mediator between humankind and God (1 Timothy 2:5), having lived as a man to demonstrate more intimately our struggles with sin and the evil in this world. After all He went through being on Earth, He has fulfilled the demand of justice for humankind's sin. There is no other name by which we are saved and no other way to heaven but by Him. The way of the Lord has been tried and proven true to provide the abundant life God promised His people.

# January 15

# WHAT YOU DON'T KNOW CAN HURT YOU

*Psalm 100:5*

*For the Lord is good; His mercy and loving-kindness are everlasting,*
*His faithfulness and truth endure to all generations.*

For the Lord is good, His mercy and loving-kindness are everlasting. God isn't out to get you, don't let that lie turn you away. His love for us keeps us wherever we go, and He's there for us when it counts the most. Justice must be satisfied because of sin, but God's not out to get you just for the fun of it. Many times, we bring trouble to ourselves by the decisions we make. We self-inflict because we lack knowledge of what's happening around us. When our parents watched over us as small children, they could see a dangerous situation coming towards us before it got to us, and we as children didn't have a clue. That's how God protects us as our Heavenly Father. There are enemies out there who cannot be seen with the natural eye (Ephesians 6:12). That's where God's help is available. To be more sensitive to the spirit realm, we must spend time knowing the light and leave the dark out of the picture altogether. Jesus is the light that lights the whole world for hope (John 8:12).

# *January 16*

# WHEN SORROW COMES

*Matthew 26:38*

*Then He said to them, My soul is very sad and deeply grieved, so that I am almost dying of sorrow. Stay here and keep awake and keep watch with Me.*

Did you know your soul can be overwhelmed with sorrow to the point of death? It is what Jesus said to His disciples before His greatest test of obedience. He even asked God if that cup of going through the crucifixion could pass from Him. Still, He said not My will, but Your will be done regardless of His feelings and fear (Matthews 26:39). Sometimes, we have to drink the cup of sorrow. Maybe to the point of death, but even though we walk through the valley of the shadow of death, we will fear no evil because God is with us (Psalm 23:4). God was with Jesus up to the point Jesus had to stand alone on the cross. But after the process was completed, Jesus overcoming the cross, death, and hell, He rose to a position with God of total victory and completion of the mission God gave Him. And now the entire world can access God and be a part of His family, if we choose to be.

# *January 17*

## YOU ARE THE BRANCH

### John 15:5

*I am the Vine; you are the branches. Whoever lives in Me and I in him bears much (abundant) fruit. However, apart from Me [cut off from vital union with Me] you can do nothing.*

We can do all things through Christ, who strengthens us, but apart from Him, we can do nothing worthwhile. Jesus is the Vine, and we are the branches. The Vine gets its nutrients from the foundation (God, the Father), and the branches get their nutrients from the Vine. The connection is real; as long as we stay connected to the Vine, we get the benefits from the Father. Staying connected means fighting the good fight of faith. Faith is the vehicle used for the nutrients to flow through to us. The greater our faith, the greater the measurement of nutrients will flow. The branches that don't fall are securely connected to the Vine. Are you the branch that falls, or stays connected? Pray that you remain connected.

# January 18

# DO YOU THINK YOU KNOW WHAT LOVE IS?

*1 Corinthians 13:4*

*Love endures long and is patient and kind; love never is envious nor boils over with jealousy, is not boastful or vainglorious, does not display itself haughtily.*

First, the word love in English has different meanings, unlike Greek or Hebrew, which defines the individual ways the word should be used. There's love for a friend or brotherly love. Then we say, "I love ice cream," which means you like it a lot. Then there's the romantic love between two people, husband and wife, a sensual love. There is also the love we have for a son or daughter. Many people use the words "I love you" for personal gain, but they really don't love you from the heart, only to get over on you. Love is a powerful word because God is love (1 John 4:8). When you tell someone you love them, and you don't, you are playing with a secret fire that will burn you eventually in life. Love is patient, love is kind, love does not envy, is not boastful or arrogant, and sustains the lover with self-control. So, when you say you love someone, what do you really mean? When we live and breathe God's (agape) love in our everyday lives, this is the highest level of love we can have. With this information today, do you truly love?

# *January 19*

# BE A ROCK LIKE YOUR FATHER

*1 Samuel 2:2*

*There is none holy like the Lord, there is none besides You; there is no Rock like our God.*

There's no one that can constantly rule and reign in love, joy, peace, kindness, patience, self-control, and the rest of the fruit of the spirit. No matter what circumstances are in the picture, God doesn't change. It is we who are subject to change when under the pressures of life. God does say, "Be ye holy for I Am Holy" (1 Peter 1:16). We have the potential to walk in holiness. The fruit of this godly quality was put in us at the new birth (Galatians 5:22-23). Fruit implies growth, and development is a must! When we become a Christian, sanctification is included. We were ordained to be in God's company and for His use while on Earth. In dealing with life's everyday struggles, sanctification is training ground to perfect Christians in the art of holiness. Many get caught up in their everyday affairs to the point of not even being mindful of the importance of this necessary attribute of the Lord. Be the rock in your circle of influence so that others will want what you have. The consistency in your Christian walk will win a person to God just as fast, in some cases even faster, then going to church and hearing the preacher preach or teach.

# January 20

## CHILDREN CAN BRING JOY AND PAIN

*Proverbs 23:24*

*The father of the [uncompromisingly] righteous (the upright, in right standing with God) shall greatly rejoice, and he who becomes the father of a wise child shall have joy in him.*

Parents want their child or children to do well. Training them up in the nurture and admonition of the Lord gives them a foundation of righteous stability in life (Proverbs 22:6). Communication with your children is the basis of life and helps develop a good relationship. Most parents don't have a clue what's on their children's minds. Today, the Internet is raising children, and we know the damage that can bring to a child if they're not supervised. Most parents want their children to do well in life. Not giving them the tools to be successful from an early age can be a problem, but with God all things are possible (Matthew 19:26). Training your child in the way they should go, implants an insurance policy, built-in to their spirits and minds so that later in life certain temptations won't stand a chance of your child yielding to it. The joy of the Lord is our strength, and the joy of a father is his wise and godly children.

# *January 21*

## SLOW DOWN AND BE STILL

*Psalm 46:10, NIV*
*He says, "Be still, and know that I am God;*
*I will be exalted among the nations, I will be exalted in the Earth."*

Being still before God isn't always an easy thing based on the busyness of life. But you'll never have time if you don't make time. We have free will, and that can get us into trouble if we're not careful with the decisions we make. One decision to make, which is investing in yourself, would be to acknowledge God in all your ways so He can direct your path in life (Proverbs 3:5-6). Spending time with God puts Him in the mix of our everyday lives. We as Christians must spend quality time in prayer, and God's Word, the Bible, it has all we need to live a victorious, abundant life of success on every level, socially, materially, with divine physical health, and healing (John 10:10).

# *January 22*

## CAN YOU BE STILL?

*Psalms 23:3*

*He refreshes and restores my life (myself); He leads me in the paths of righteousness [uprightness and right standing with Him—not for my earning it, but] for His name's sake.*

Sometimes we need to get off the boat and pull away from our daily routine to rest. Quality time with the Lord refreshes us. Pray and take time to read and meditate on His word. If we stay in His presence long enough, we'll be restored and have mental and physical strength released to us (Isaiah 40:31). Getting beyond our busy routine still puts us in the ballpark. Unfortunately, many of us can't sit still for two minutes. However, God's in that still, quiet, and easygoing realm where He can instill that rejuvenating spirit of hope and peace in us, but we must slow down. *"Be still and know that I Am God* (Psalm 46:10)," that is what the scripture teaches.

# January 23

# Change Your Life Now

*Proverbs 21:21, NLT*

*Whoever pursues righteousness and unfailing love will find life, righteousness, and honor.*

Our own righteousness is nothing, it's the righteousness that comes from faith in God that changes things. Earnestly seeking after and craving righteousness and love will bring us to Zoe life, prosperity, and honor. These are the attributes of truly living as God intended for mankind. Zoe life is the life of God allowed to thrive in us. This is another life option available for those who diligently seek after God. This life has grace and favor benefits necessary for living above the evil in this world. It is possible for those who believe to go beyond the natural limitations of the world system, and be all they're supposed to be. The kingdom of God is righteousness, peace, and joy in the Holy Spirit (Romans 14:17). If we could just see beyond our emotions and the distractions, and temptations meant to ensnare us, we'd be living on another level in life, unstoppable by anything or anyone in this world. Our business is our own, so go beyond what others think you should be doing and pursue these attributes of God, and change your life now!

# *January 24*

# DOING GOOD IS A
# COMMAND, NOT A CHOICE

### Hebrews 13:16

*Do not forget or neglect to do kindness and good, to be generous and distribute and contribute to the needy [of the church as embodiment and proof of fellowship], for such sacrifices are pleasing to God.*

In our everyday life we must be reminded to do kindness and good, be generous and distribute to those in need. This is most pleasing to God. Jesus said, you will always have the poor among you (Matthew 26:11). Lending to the poor gets us a return on our giving from the Lord. We are His hands and feet and mouthpiece in the Earth. Humans have been given the authority on Earth to rule. God cannot come in and take over our rightful position of authority, He'd be no better than the devil if He did. He would be going against His own master plan of man having dominion on Earth (Genesis 1:26). So when it's time for the Lord to use us to be a blessing to those in need, we should be available to do good works. When we put our hearts into helping others, there's always a return harvest of someone helping us when we need it most, because we planted the seed of kindness and goodness.

# January 25

# Fruit of a Different Kind

*Galatians 5:22-23*

*But the fruit of the [Holy] Spirit [the work which His presence within accomplishes] is love, joy (gladness), peace, patience (an even temper, forbearance), kindness, goodness (benevolence), faithfulness, Gentleness (meekness, humility), self-control (self-restraint, continence). Against such things there is no law [[a]that can bring a charge].*

These are the fruits of the newly recreated human spirit, not the Holy Spirit. When we are talking about fruit, that implies growth. The Holy Spirit is already perfect and does not need for growth. We must unlearn all that our flesh has learned from birth. Our flesh means our appetites and our emotions that have ruled us. All the fruit of the Spirit lay on the bed of love. Without love, none of them would have the power to be expressed or to shine. As we renew our minds with God's Word, we understand how all these things work together. It is a fight of faith we can win. Spirit against flesh has always been an internal battle we must conquer to be free, to be in a position to grow, and to live the victorious life the Lord has promised us.

# *January 26*

# GET YOUR HEAD STRAIGHT, THEN YOUR HEART WILL FOLLOW

*Psalm 19:14*

*Let the words of my mouth and the meditation of my heart be acceptable in Your sight, O Lord, my [firm, impenetrable] Rock and my Redeemer.*

Are your words and thoughts pleasing to the Lord? Aligning them with God's Word can make this a reality in your life (2 Corinthians 10:5). Though tempting thoughts may arise, when following Jesus' example, we can choose not to act on them (Hebrews 4:15). It's crucial to recognize that having a thought doesn't equate to sin; what matters is how we respond. By immersing ourselves in God's Word, we can overcome negative thoughts and ensure that our speech and meditations are acceptable to the Lord (Hebrews 4:14-15). Every area of life is dealt with in the Bible. Get that knowledge and live above your bad thoughts, then the words of your mouth and the meditation of your heart will be acceptable.

# *January 27*

# HE IS MIGHTY TO SAVE

*Zephaniah 3:17*

*The Lord your God is in the midst of you, a Mighty One, a Savior [Who saves]! He will rejoice over you with joy; He will rest [in silent satisfaction] and in His love He will be silent and make no mention [of past sins, or even recall them]; He will exalt over you with singing.*

The Lord is always present in our midst. He is omnipresent, meaning He's everywhere and in every place at the same time. It is not to be understood by the human mind, but to be believed by faith. Sometimes we go with the unseen because we have that gut knowing without ocular proof. God can and will save us from whatever we need saving from. He saves us from going to hell by receiving Jesus Christ as Lord and Savior. He saves us from harmful, detrimental situations that could alter our destiny and purpose in life. If He's our God, we have rights in the kingdom of God. We are joint heirs with Jesus and it's our inheritance (Colossians 1:12). Like any other inheritance, we must go after that which is ours, because our enemy will try blocking us from it. Jesus suffered walking the Earth (Hebrews 5:8). Father God saved Him from premature death so He could complete His assignment on Earth. He is mighty to save and because of this, we can rejoice.

# *January 28*

# IS GOD ON YOUR SIDE?

*Romans 8:31*

*What then shall we say to [all] this? If God is for us, who [can be] against us? [Who can be our foe, if God is on our side?]*

No one can successfully be against us when we know God's on our side. If you're not sure God's on your side, you're not using His full potential in your life. Since faith is the hand that receives from God, if your faith is weak, then the hand that receives from God isn't working properly for you. There's nothing that can successfully come against you when your faith to believe God is strong. When you trust God blindly, with all the conviction of knowing He'll come through on your behalf, leads to victory. Humankind has not been redeemed from the curse of the law if he has not yet accepted Jesus as Lord and Savior of his life (Galatians 3:13). We have been made more than conquerors in Christ Jesus (Romans 8:37). Once you've begun to understand your authority in Christ, you won't accept a lot of the garbage thrown at you in this world. Your dominion status has been restored in Christ. So, operating as a mere human (lower nature controlled), you are limited and normally will settle for less. Since God is for us, nothing can successfully be against us. We can live above the evil in this world by simply following the teachings and precepts of God. I get it, most of us don't want to study on a regular basis, no time, etc. (Joshua 1:8). If you want to stop getting beat up by life and people, do the work, and learn of God. He's on your side.

# January 29

# KEEPING THE FLESH UNDER CONTROL

*Galatians 5:24*

*And those who belong to Christ Jesus (the Messiah) have crucified the flesh (the godless human nature) with its passions and appetites and desires.*

Those who belong to Christ Jesus have crucified the godless human nature with its passions and desires. The temptation of these godless passions and desires will always be around. How we deal with them makes all the difference in our walk with God. We are not perfect in these bodies, and the Lord knows that, so there's a forgiveness for Christians who miss the mark in our everyday dealings. We do belong to Christ even though we have 'devilish' thoughts and even when our body reacts to those thoughts. However, we have not sinned until we act on those thoughts. Acting on those thoughts opens the door for trouble. The goal is to show our maturity in Christ by our lifestyle. Keeping the flesh under control is a never-ending task. Until death, it will not depart. However, we are more than conquerors in Christ, and we can do all things through Christ who strengthens us. Everything we need to survive is in Christ Jesus. Since we're in Him, we must learn of Him. We are destroyed from lack of knowledge. Jesus exemplified overcoming the flesh, which is our emotions, which takes the place of God's direction during crisis.

# *January 30*

# LOVE FINDS A WAY

*Philippians 1:9-11, NIV*
*And this is my prayer: that your love may abound more and more*
*in knowledge and depth of insight, so that you may be able to*
*discern what is best and may be pure and blameless for the day of*
*Christ, filled with the fruit of righteousness that comes through Jesus*
*Christ—to the glory and praise of God.*

L ove is the most powerful force in the universe. I say that based on the fact that God is love, as the Bible plainly states that in (1 John 4:16). The seed of God's love gets implanted in the heart of the newly recreated human spirit. We have the potential to let that seed of love in us grow. Once love becomes our motivation and not personal gain, we enter a new realm of reality. You begin to see people in a different light, understanding we are human, prone to mess up. The wisdom of love in us can discern another's intentions, good or bad, and can reply to those intentions accordingly. It is a walk of love that can help us live above the evil in the world. A sacrificial walk that can cause discomfort to our flesh, which is our soulish area, can mentally be challenging. Once we've got a handle on reprogramming our way of thinking to God's way (Romans 12:2), the battle will be easier to win. Everything of value has a higher cost. When a person gets to the point in their life where everyday life seems like a constant uphill battle, maybe it's time for change. Love finds a way.

# *January 31*

## TASTE AND SEE

*Psalm 34:8*

*O taste and see that the Lord [our God] is good!
Blessed (happy, fortunate, to be envied) is the man who
trusts and takes refuge in Him.*

We've heard things like, *"God's gonna get you for acting up."* Or *"God don't like ugly."* But do you have an informed opinion? Do you know the Lord for yourself? That is what really matters. Since we have a personal relationship with God, once we become a Christian, we must seek Him out for ourself, because opinions vary from person to person. Find out for yourself. Taste and see that the Lord is good. There is more to God than fearing He's going to get you for 'being bad.' Come to the Master for the truth about things, if you can handle the truth. Seek Him out for your own peace of mind. He is our refuge in times of trouble, He can make a way out of no way, He can and will turn things upside down to get to the person with faith-filled words of determination. He's good because He has our backs even when we don't realize it was Him that got us out of a jam. He prepared provisions for our lives before we were even born, taking care of that which concerns us. Taste and see for yourself that the Lord is good.

# *February 1*

# THE GOOD, THE BAD, AND THE UGLY

*2 Corinthians 9:6*

*[Remember] this: he who sows sparingly and grudgingly will also reap sparingly and grudgingly, and he who sows generously [that blessings may come to someone] will also reap generously and with blessings.*

The law of reciprocity, or seed, time and harvest, has been around since the beginning of time. What you sow and how you sow will come back to you. If you sow the seed of love to another, that's what you'll reap. Giving a little love to your neighbor brings back a little love to you. Sow a nasty seed of strife, and it's coming back to you. The same is so when you give away money. Give away a little, and a little will come back. The idea is to trust the system so you can be a blessing to others. Give to those less fortunate, and that same act of love with find you in your time of need. Be careful how you sow, because whatever you sow because it's coming back in time, the good, the bad, and the ugly.

# *February 2*

# THE WAY OF STRENGTH

*Philippians 2:13*

*[Not in your own strength] for it is God Who is all the while effectually at work in you [energizing and creating in you the power and desire], both to will and to work for His good pleasure and satisfaction and delight.*

When we allow God to do His thing in us, it's a win-win for us and God. He gets pleasure from it, and we'll prosper in all we do. His good pleasure means an abundance of good living for us. He goes before us and makes all the crooked places straight when we include Him in our everyday lives (Isaiah 45:2). Our own strength can wane after a while, but God's strength, working in us, is more than enough. How to get His strength on the scene is the same way we get anything from God - spend more time with Him in prayer and His Word. *"Meditate in this Word day and night, and you'll make your own way prosperous"* (Joshua 1:8). Those are God's words for success in life.

# *February 3*

# WHAT'S REALLY IN YOUR HEART?

*Luke 6:45*

*The upright (honorable, intrinsically good) man out of the good treasure [stored] in his heart produces what is upright (honorable and intrinsically good), and the evil man out of the evil storehouse brings forth that which is depraved (wicked and intrinsically evil); for out of the abundance (overflow) of the heart his mouth speaks.*

Whatever is in our hearts, our mouths will leak out. Out of the abundance of the heart, the mouth will speak. That is what the Bible tells us. Whatever we hear over and over again and again eventually drop down into our heart, our spirit. We program ourselves with whatever we're listening to a lot. That's why we must be careful of how and what we hear all the time. Keep listening to people's negativity, and we'll get used to it and begin to talk like them. We are clean slates, ready to be influenced and programmed by what we hear. Put positivity in your ears; your heart will be glad.

# *February 4*

# YOU CAN FORGIVE THAT PERSON!

*Colossians 3:13*

*Be gentle and forbearing with one another and, if one has a difference (a grievance or complaint) against another, readily pardoning each other; even as the Lord has [freely] forgiven you, so must you also [forgive].*

The example has been set. We all have faults that may rub someone the wrong way. We are still human with the tendency to mess up. None of us have reached the mark of being perfect. Even though someone got deep under your skin, finding a way to deal with it is vitally important. Don't be reactionary all the time. Walk away and know Jesus went through much worse than that for you. One of the hardest things to deal with in life is unforgiveness. Yes, the other person was wrong. Yes, they went too far this time, but you can shift that anger away from them to your real enemy, Satan. Come against him with God's Word and the name of Jesus concerning that situation. Practice working the Word of God in areas like preferring your brother before yourself (Romans 12:10). Focusing on the love of God that bears up under anything and everything that comes (1 Corinthians 13:7). Walking in the agape love of God will be like walking in a deeper dimension of understanding for that person who wronged you, and that will make it easier to forgive.

# *February 5*

# THE WINNER IN YOU

*Matthew 5:43-44*
*You have heard that it was said, you shall love your neighbor and hate your enemy; But I tell you, love your enemies and pray for those who persecute you.*

Back in the days of the law, the Old Testament, it was an eye for an eye, and a tooth for a tooth mentality. Today, we live in the dispensation of grace. In today's scripture are the words of Jesus. He fulfilled the law by keeping every commandment given to Moses on Mount Sinai. Jesus overcame this by using the Word of God (as we are to do now) and not by the divine powers He had before His Earth walk. It had to be done by working the Word of God, thereby giving us the example and legal passage to do the same to fight evil. This command from Jesus to love our enemies and pray for those who persecute us is based on the agape love of God. Fulfilling this command brings maturity to our fellowship with the Lord. The closer we draw to God, the more He'll draw closer to us (James 4:8). Without His teachings and our understanding, it could be difficult to love our enemies. Our position of love should not be predicated on whether we like or don't like someone, or what they've done to hurt us, etc. Our emotions cannot have any say in this task of keeping love first. The winner is in you; let him or her out!

# *February 6*

# ARE YOU REALLY FREE?

*Galatians 5:13*

*For you, brethren, were [indeed] called to freedom; only [do not let your] freedom be an incentive to your flesh and an opportunity or excuse [for selfishness], but through love you should serve one another.*

We as Christians are called to freedom, but that freedom should not be an incentive to indulge the flesh, the carnal nature, which doesn't acknowledge God in any of its ways. We should be led by our spirits, not by our flesh (Romans 8:14). Serving one another humbly in love is God's way. There is no humility in the flesh; it's all about me, myself, and I. Life on Earth can be busy to the point of serious distractions, side-tracking our destiny and purpose. We can be free from habitual sin. We don't have to do wrong all the time once we become Christians. That driving force of wrong-doing has no authority once we've accepted Jesus as Lord and Savior. He delivered us from the sin nature through the new birth. We have received the truth, and the truth (Jesus) has set us free, so be free.

# *February 7*

# GOD STANDS AT THE DOOR
# OF YOUR HEART

*Revelation 3:20*

*Behold, I stand at the door and knock; if anyone hears and listens
to and heeds My voice and opens the door, I will come into him
and will eat with him, and he [will eat] with Me.*

Jesus is standing at the door of your soul, knocking for you to open
your heart to receive Him. He will not force His way into your life
like the devil. The Lord wants willing people in His family. Answering
the call of God in your life is the most important decision anyone can
make because you must prepare yourself for life after death (Philippians
3:20-21). This world has our attention with so much of its distractions,
it's hard to easily hear His voice. The Lord wants communion with
His people, and He is ever-growing His family with those who are not
ashamed of Him. He is the good Shepherd of our souls. He brings
peace and comfort once we accept Him in our hearts. We have the
opportunity of a lifetime and beyond, by receiving Jesus as Lord and
Savior of our lives (Romans 10:9-10). He not only helps us become
more than conquerors now, but He prepares a place for us in heaven
after finishing our course in this life (John 14:3). Heed His voice and
open the door of your heart and let Him in. He's knocking.

# *February 8*

# HOW ARE WE DOING?

### *James 1:12*

*Blessed (happy, to be envied) is the man who is patient under trial and stands up under temptation, for when he has stood the test and been approved, he will receive [the victor's] crown of life which God has promised to those who love Him.*

A re you patient under trial? Can you hold your ground by being patient, and stand up against temptation? To persevere under pressure is the path to much success in life. If you can persevere, be patient in your endeavors, and not succumb to temptation, you will discover that these ingredients are vital for God's blessings and victorious living. With the greater One in us, we can be more than conquerors (Romans 8:37). The crown of life is a reward from God for our God-given accomplishments. We can do all things through Christ who strengthens us (Philippians 4:13). In God's eyes, the trial you face is only as big as you allow it to be in your mind, the fight is always spiritual behind the scenes.

# *February 9*

# A PURE HEART, IS THAT POSSIBLE?

*Psalm 51:10*

*Create in me a clean heart, O God, and renew a right, persevering, and steadfast spirit within me.*

David is speaking to God here about creating in himself a pure heart. What's a pure heart in a spiritually dead person's life? Before Jesus came and sacrificed His life for sin, no one had a truly pure heart in God's eyes. Now, David was the apple of God's eye, but he was not a born-again Christian back then. When we go through the heart change of becoming a new creation in Christ Jesus, we receive a new heart, spiritually alive to God. What was the pure heart David wanted God to create in him? It all comes down to sin and wrongdoings. David did some dastardly things before God, and he knew it was wrong. But God knew David didn't have the power to resist sin like we can today. A pure heart back in the day was different than a pure heart today after the work at Calvary. I believe David longed to walk uprightly before the Lord, but his struggle was constantly a bit much because he was still spiritually dead to God. Because of the sinful nature of humankind in the Old Testament, they could never have what we have today, thanks to the sacrifice of Jesus Christ our Lord. You can have a pure heart.

# February 10

# GET WISDOM, WE NEED IT

*James 1:5*

*If any of you is deficient in wisdom, let him ask of the giving God [Who gives] to everyone liberally and ungrudgingly, without reproaching or faultfinding, and it will be given him.*

To receive God's wisdom, we must have a humble attitude. If we think we know it all, that's an indication we need God's wisdom. God's wisdom controls the knowledge we've obtained over the years. The Bible says to ask, and it will be given to you (Matthew 7:7). The wisdom of God helps us operate above the worldly challenges we face. Our shortcomings are often due to our need for wisdom. How to apply knowledge on any given subject is done by wisdom. God's wisdom is winsome, pleasant to our souls, and will make understanding anything much simpler. However, much knowledge can puff us up with pride. God's wisdom operating in our life will help us understand when we must be brought down from a prideful state because of the knowledge obtained. Wisdom understands we must go through trouble to build strong faith. Wisdom gives us the bigger picture, not just insight into an immediate fix. Ask, and it will be given to us with no strings attached. Without wisdom, intelligence is lacking on every side.

# *February 11*

# HIDDEN IN YOUR HEART

*Psalm 119:11*
*Your word have I laid up in my heart,*
*that I might not sin against You.*

The way to prevent us from sinning against God is to hide His Word in our hearts. We must know and understand His Word to the point that it becomes a part of us. Meditate on His Word day and night, and you'll make your way prosperous (Joshua 1:8). If we sin against God, we have a mediator between God and man, Jesus Christ, who can relate to our struggles and shortcomings. Our understanding must be enlightened to the Word of God to the point that we have renewed our minds in how we think and react to crises or calamities. You become comforted with this new way of thinking based on the Lord's teachings and precepts. Jesus is the Living Word of God. During this time on Earth, He became a living sacrifice for our sins. He kept His sinless nature because God was His Father, and He never yielded to the temptations we all deal with. In doing so, He led the way as an example to us of what it is to hide God's Word in our hearts. He overcame sin by using the Word of God. He left His deity in heaven, no superpowers to fight Satan, only God's written Word (which is all-powerful and effective against Satan and his crew). Hide His word in your heart; it'll be there when trouble comes, and it will keep you from sinning against God.

# February 12

# The Power Twins

*Psalm 9:1*

*I will praise You, O Lord, with my whole heart; I will show forth (recount and tell aloud) all Your marvelous works and wonderful deeds!*

To praise God with all your heart, taps into the Lord's soft heart. He loves praise from His people. The Father desires to be worshiped in spirit and in truth (John 4:24). Praise and thanksgiving are the power twins for entrance into the presence of God (Psalm 100:4). Praise the Lord with your whole heart, it's real. Praising Him when our heart isn't in it, is like an unacceptable offering. We may start off praising God and our emotions are not in it, but starting out by faith will bring our heart and soul into alignment with the Spirit of God. Giving thanks to God is an acknowledgement of His existence and our appreciation of Him which will bring favor to our life. Give thanks to the Lord, and praise Him with all your heart.

# *February 13*

## DO YOUR FEELINGS RULE YOU?

*Ephesians 4:2*

*[...Living as becomes you] with complete lowliness of mind (humility) and meekness (unselfishness, gentleness, mildness), with patience, bearing with one another and making allowances because you love one another.*

B eing completely humble and gentle is possible for those of us who are not by nature easy going. The seed of humility, kindness, and gentleness were deposited in our new recreated human spirits when we got saved (Galatians 5:22-23). The decision to grow those seeds may be another situation we're not willing to do. The Bible speaks of allowing the entire leaning of our personality on Him (Colossians 1:4, AMPC). We can all change, but we may not want to because our flesh is too strong, our feelings rule us. To be patient and bearing with one another in love is the goal. Make the world a better place and chillax in Christ.

# February 14

# THE LOVE THAT COUNTS

*Galatians 5:14*

*For the whole Law [concerning human relationships] is complied with in the one precept, You shall love your neighbor as [you do] yourself.*

J ust imagine, if everyone loved their neighbor as they love themselves, the world would be in much better shape. Unfortunately, the world rule system is built on the devil's agenda. He came to kill, steal, and destroy (John 10:10), with no love in his plans for us. So as Christians, we are fighting an uphill battle living in this world. However, we can overcome evil with good, but it's a fight we must be prepared to enter into. Our relationship with God must be cultivated, and then our fellowship with Him will draw from Him what is necessary for obtaining the victory. Once we have come to know God on this level, it will be a downhill battle because we'll have the high ground with God on our side. Some folks, we must love from a distance because we are not mature enough in our love walk yet to be in their face without wanting to hurt them. That is real, and so is the strength and power of love. Since God is love, we have all the help there is to have.

# *February 15*

# THE GLORY OF GOD, WHAT IS IT?

*Habakkuk 2:14*

*But [the time is coming when] the Earth shall be filled with the knowledge of the glory of the Lord as the waters cover the sea.*

The knowledge of the glory of God is the knowledge of God's manifested presence. As the waters cover the sea, so shall the glory of God be known in the Earth. His glory has been the reason we are Christians today. Jesus was God's manifested presence on the Earth over 2000 years ago when He walked it. Miracles ride on the back of God's glory to bring us that impossible help. He makes a way out of no way and can create something out of nothing if necessary. The shekhinah glory of God is the strongest dose we can handle without it killing us. When Ministers minister underneath it, they can hardly stand up while praying for others (2 Chronicles 5:14). It's a corporate anointing situation that God uses to reach more people at one time who are gathered at a service. The glory of God, once tasted, will change your life forever. You will know for sure that there is a living God who cares about you.

# *February 16*

# THE MERCY CARD

## Luke 6:36

*So be merciful (sympathetic, tender, responsive, and compassionate)
even as your Father is [all these].*

Our Heavenly Father is merciful and we are His children reflecting His nature of love. Without love, how can we be merciful? Mercy is not giving someone the punishment they deserve based on the offense committed. When another person wrongs you, do you automatically react with a reprimanding response, or do you wait and try to understand this person's dilemma? In most cases, they were already pissed about something else but released their frustrations on you. There are other times when some people are just straight-up nasty or mean. The latter needs your merciful kindness more than most. Being sympathetic, tender, responsive, and compassionate are the true traits of mercy's character. We don't get there overnight but through much heartache, trouble, and crisis we begin to understand. The training room of trials and storms in our lives is where we cultivate this mercy and we will have experienced the need for mercy ourselves by not giving up. Mercy swoops down to bail us out. Sow the seed of mercy to others, you never know when you might need that same harvest in your life.

# *February 17*

# THE POWER OF LOVE

*1 John 4:7*

*Beloved, let us love one another, for love is (springs) from God; and he who loves [his fellowmen] is begotten (born) of God and is coming [progressively] to know and understand God [to perceive and recognize and get a better and clearer knowledge of Him].*

A better and more precise knowledge of God will come when we love one another. Why? Because love springs from God, and we are children of a God who is love (1 John 4:8). We can love one another in diverse ways. Caring for your brother or sister in Christ should be our purposeful intent. It does not come naturally at all. Even as Christians, we must work on being a doer of God's Word in thought, purpose, and action. Giving ourselves over to leaning our entire personality upon Him will help get self-centeredness out of the picture. Our old sinful nature will try and rear its head up if not brought into subjection regularly. As we love our brothers and sisters, the agape love of God will develop in us. We must practice the love walk every day, knowing the Lord's hand of approval is upon that. Show the world you have been born of God and know Him.

# *February 18*

# WHO WILL ANSWER THE CALL?

*Isaiah 6:8, NKJV*

*Also I heard the voice of the Lord, saying, Whom shall I send? And who will go for Us? Then said I, Here am I; send me.*

The Lord needs laborers to go out into the fields to reap the harvest which is ripe. God cannot physically carry out His plan for humankind without humans. Humans has dominion in the Earth, not God (Genesis 1:26-31), it was given to us in the garden with Adam and Eve. He needs us to get the job done. So, who will answer the call? Who will stand up for the Lord and help fulfill His plan of reconciliation? We need God, but He needs us as well. Using His word, the Lord expects us to exercise authority over our trials, crises, and bad situations. We must work the Word of God in every situation and circumstance of our life. Stand up for what's already been given to you by God. Learn to fight, learn how to stand during troubled times. It will make you fit for God's army. Can God send you?

# *February 19*

# ARE YOU POOR?

*Matthew 5:3*

*Blessed (happy, to be envied, and spiritually prosperous—with life-joy and satisfaction in God's favor and salvation, regardless of their outward conditions) are the poor in spirit (the humble, who rate themselves insignificant), for theirs is the kingdom of heaven!*

God blesses those who are poor and realize their need for God, for the Kingdom of heaven is theirs. God is always aware and responsive to those who realize their need for Him. When we really trust Him to come through for us in times of need, He can't help but respond. Through faith and patience, we obtain the promises of God (Hebrews 6:12). He is true to His Word; we are not always true to ours. Because we live in an imperfect world, there are many situations that can take us off our game of truth and honesty. As we learn to totally trust Him in all areas of life, we begin to see His faithfulness toward us. The poor are mostly humbled because of their circumstances of lack, being in this state of mind keeps pride at bay, which is a prayer blocker. Sometimes a good crisis in our life can bring us right where God needs us to be, so He's more easily found. God blesses those who are poor, those who are emptied of pride, hate, lying, gossip, backbiting, etc. Blessed are the poor.

# *February 20*

# ETERNAL LIFE, DO YOU HAVE IT?

*John 5:24*

*I assure you, most solemnly I tell you, the person whose ears are open to My words [who listens to My message] and believes and trusts in and clings to and relies on Him Who sent Me has (possesses now) eternal life. And he does not come into judgment [does not incur sentence of judgment, will not come under condemnation], but he has already passed over out of death into life.*

These are the words of Jesus our Savior. His message is that of hope, and life. Jesus is the way the truth and the life, no man gets into heaven except by Him (John 14:6). He became the Savior of the world by paying the price that justice demands because of humankind's sin. We were born with the sin nature in us, helpless. All have sinned and fallen short of being in right standing with God (Romans 3:23). Jesus was born on the Earth without the sin nature being passed on, because God is His Father. So, Jesus was the perfect sacrifice for sin since He lived a sinless life (Hebrews 4:15). When you called on His name and you were saved, and able to enter into the Kingdom of God, and therefore obtain eternal life.

# *February 21*

# THE PEACE MAKER

*Romans 12:21*

*Do not let yourself be overcome by evil,*
*but overcome (master) evil with good.*

When a person is cursing, harassing, giving you unjust drama, before you react with the same level of intensity, and cutting words, in that moment try to respond with a soft kind reply. It will deescalate the situation because you're not giving the other person any fuel to continue their campaign against you. If we can exercise the fruit of self-control, we will not be easily offended, and not be reactionary to the nonsense. Since this world is evil, we must find a way in our everyday lives to deal with it. People won't expect you to respond with good when they come with malicious intent. It'll throw their plan of attack sideways. Overcome evil with good, can you do it? God says you can.

# *February 22*

# THE TRUTH ABOUT THE DEVIL

## James 4:7, MSG

*So let God work his will in you. Yell a loud no to the Devil and watch him make himself scarce. Say a quiet yes to God and he'll be there in no time. Quit dabbling in sin. Purify your inner life. Quit playing the field. Hit bottom, and cry your eyes out. The fun and games are over. Get serious, really serious. Get down on your knees before the Master; it's the only way you'll get on your feet.*

After submitting yourself to God, you can resist the devil, and he'll flee from you. People have said, "the devil made me do it," which solidifies the fact that you don't know who you are in Christ Jesus. Once you find out who you are in Christ Jesus, you can speak commands with the authority rightfully belonging to you, and the devil WILL leave you, running as if he is terrified. What a role switch! You, ordering the devil out of your life. Many people don't believe he exists while he's running havoc in their lives. Temptations are a part of life. What you do with them when they come can either make you stronger by not taking the bait, or it'll open the door to something that will bite eventually. The devil is very real and will steal, kill, and destroy if you let him. That's the truth.

# *February 23*

# WHOSE SIDE ARE YOU ON?

*Proverbs 13:6*

*Righteousness (rightness and justice in every area and relation)
guards him who is upright in the way, but wickedness plunges into
sin and overthrows the sinner.*

Righteousness guards the path of the blameless, but the evil is misled by sin and wrongdoing. If you're trying to be right with God in your everyday life, there's an extra protection from God that goes along with it. But those who refuse to do the right thing in life will be misled by their sinful ways and wide open for Satan's attacks. This world has two basic sides, good and evil: God or the devil. And in no way is the devil a suitable or able contestant to come against Almighty God victoriously. But until this world has passed away, the devil runs it, but God owns it. The time is soon coming for the return of Christ, which will eliminate Satan's rule of the Earth once and for all. Until then, we are in a battle with evil. Make sure you're on the winning side before the end.

# *February 24*

# ASK ACCORDING TO HIS WILL

*1 John 5:14*

*And this is the confidence (the assurance, the privilege of boldness) which we have in Him: [we are sure] that if we ask anything (make any request) according to His will (in agreement with His own plan), He listens to and hears us.*

If we ask anything according to His will, He hears us. Anything isn't asking Him to help you rob a bank or have someone else's spouse. This passage is written to Christians, and the message is clear as to praying or asking for anything according to His will, which is His word, which is the Bible. When we pray or ask according to God's will, He definitely hears our words (1 John 5:14-15), because we're praying back His words to Him, and that gets the job done on a higher level of return. Being in agreement with God's plan for your life puts you in the upper echelon of God's very important people for His service, and the abundant life for us that goes along with it. We must know the Lord's will before we can pray or ask according to it. *"Meditate on His Word day and night, that you may observe to do all that's written there in, and you will make your own way prosperous"* (Joshua 1:8). He is a rewarder of those who diligently seek Him. Seek, and you shall find, knock, and the door will be opened. Ask, and it will be given you (Matthew 7:7-8). You have not, because you ask not, and when you ask, you're asking for personal unrelated gain not in line with your purpose in life, so the answer isn't coming.

# *February 25*

# CLEAN UP YOUR SPEECH, IT MATTERS

*Ephesians 4:29, NIV*

*Do not let any unwholesome talk come out of your mouths, but only what is helpful for building others up according to their needs, that it may benefit those who listen.*

Is your speech seasoned with foul or polluting language? What we say and how we say it can uplift or crush another person. Some people have sensitive ears when it comes to curse words. For those of us that are world-class cussers, every other word out of the mouth is an "F" bomb or any other four letter word that cuts straight to the heart and soul of another, there's hope for us too. First we must decide that we want to stop with the foul and polluting language. If the people we associate with have a potty mouth too, we won't easily stop cussing because of their constant input into your life. Without the invoking of our will it won't work. Being a truck driver in the past, my language needed some help. It takes practice and help from God. You can start in a natural way by substituting certain curse words with the word goodness. Try it, instead of the F bomb or four letter word in moments of frustration or hurt, say goodness! The other spiritual way involving your heart and soul, which helps sustain your clean speech, is by renewing your mind with the Word of God (Romans 12:2). Clean up your speech, you'll get better friends because of it.

# *February 26*

# GET OUT OF YOUR HEAD, FOLLOW YOUR GUT

*Proverbs 16:9*

*A man's mind plans his way [as he journeys through life],*
*But the Lord directs his steps and establishes them.*

In our hearts, we plan our course, but the lord establishes our steps. Because we walk by faith and not by sight, God can lead us through the path of least resistance. But the path of resistance will sometimes be used to help develop our faith. Every step we take should be towards our destiny and purpose. We are here for a reason, not just to exist. In our hearts are the undeveloped plans of God. He wants to lead us into victorious living and purpose. Our sensitivity to God's leading is vital to fulfilling our God-given purpose. Many are living that reality now, they have found the God connection between their heart, mind, and soul. This keeps us in step with the right way to go without effort, but the opposition will be our portion from time to time, with God, we will go right through it.

# *February 27*

# THE HUMAN SPIRIT

*2 Corinthians 4:16, NLT*

*That is why we never give up.*
*Though our bodies are dying, our spirits are*
*being renewed every day.*

Our death-doomed bodies are not here forever, but our spirit never dies. God is eternal, and whatever He makes is eternal. He won't destroy Satan, who at one time was His right-hand guy (Lucifer). That's why God created hell. It was initially for Satan and his crew, but as humanity follows the evil in this world, they'll have to take the eternal punishment that goes with it. Our bodies are for this realm, on Earth. But when we die, we lose these bodies and take on a different form, pure spirit, the real you. Our body grows weaker, but our spirits grow stronger every day. We often come to that point of knowing the spirit is willing, but the flesh is weak. Wee must go beyond our feelings to press in for the high calling in Christ Jesus and really live.

# *February 28*

# WHO'S REALLY IN CHARGE?

*Psalm 24:1*

*The Earth is the Lord's, and the fullness of it,
the world and they who dwell in it.*

The Bible tells us the Earth is the Lord's and everything in it, including the world, and all who live in it. After all, He made it, and mankind, and the animals, etc. The lordship of this world's system and authority was handed over to the devil after Adam and Eve dropped the ball by obeying Satan and eating the forbidden fruit (Genesis 3:2-6). Once your Creator tells you not to do something, and you go with your feelings (the temptation), your bad thoughts, or anything going against the command of God, you've lost your right of authority over that thing. Jesus restored the authority back to man at Calvary. Our job is to follow God's voice again like Adam and Eve did before the fall and live above Satan's Earthly rule.

# *February 29*

# TO NEVER GIVE UP, IS TO NEVER LOSE

## Colossians 4:2

*Be earnest and unwearied and steadfast in your prayer [life], being [both] alert and intent in [your praying] with thanksgiving.*

Many have prayed to the Lord and said that it didn't work. Most of that attitude exemplifies a lack of faith and mostly patience. The Bible says through faith and patience, we obtain the promises of God (Hebrews 6:12). It's like a farmer planting seed for a harvest but expecting, after a few days and maybe a week, for the harvest to come. It doesn't work that way. When you've prayed for something, there has to be a waiting period, and there's always the possibility of an on-the-spot miracle. During the waiting period, God's lining things up for the manifestation to come, and it is a time of our faith being tested. Being watchful and thankful as we devote ourself to prayer. We are expected to be earnest and unwearied and steadfast in prayer. We take the first steps, not God. If you never give up, you will never lose.

# *March 1*

# ARE PEOPLE TREATING
# YOU RIGHT?

*Matthew 7:12*

*So then, whatever you desire that others would do to and for you,
even so do also to and for them, for this is (sums up) the Law and
the Prophets.*

In everything, do to others what you would have them do to you.
Here we see the law of reciprocity, that you reap what you sow. This
law (seed, time and harvest) has been around since the beginning of
time. What you plant with your mouth or actions toward others, after
the passing of time, your harvest of good or evil is on its way back to
you. The last commandment Jesus gave, which is the fulfillment of the
ten commandments, is to love your neighbor as yourself. Some of us
don't love ourselves. Low self-esteem, insecurity, and being a victim of
abuse, can take the love of self out of our life. Seek the Lord like your
life depends on it, because in your situation, it does. The Bible says,
give and it shall be given again unto you, good measure pressed down,
shaken together and running over... ( Luke 6:38).The amount of love
you show to others, is the amount of love to be shown back to you.
We write our own destiny with our thoughts and actions. Handle the
game of reaching for success without bringing others down, or you
won't stand for long.

# *March 2*

## FOLLOW THE KING

*Hebrews 13:8*

*Jesus Christ (the Messiah) is [always] the same, yesterday, today, [yes] and forever (to the ages).*

We change because circumstances or situations are out of our control. Certain pressures in our lives can test us. Those life pressures can keep some of us from keeping our word, our promise, or commitment to something we are expected to keep. In this life, to get ahead and be successful, you must be a man or woman of your word. Be honest, people know when you're not truthful. The Lord Jesus kept His course and commitment to God as promised. He is Lord because He kept Himself free from committing sin while walking the Earth as a man (Hebrews 4:15), not using His deity from heaven to overcome trouble. He worked God's Word, as we are expected to do. Our spirits may be willing, but even Jesus said, the flesh is weak. But we can do all things through Christ who strengthens us (Philippians 4:13), and we are more than conquerors through Christ. Because Jesus won't change, we can count on Him, not like a human who has the propensity to suddenly change up. If you need stability in your life, look no further. Follow the King.

# *March 3*

# God's Direct Helpline

*John 14:26*

*But the Comforter (Counselor, Helper, Intercessor, Advocate, Strengthener, Standby), the Holy Spirit, Whom the Father will send in My name [in My place, to represent Me and act on My behalf], He will teach you all things. And He will cause you to recall (will remind you of, bring to your remembrance) everything I have told you.*

The Spirit of God is our helper. That may sound a little spooky to some, but it's a thing. We are spirit, soul, and body, the Godhead is Father, Son, and Holy Ghost, or Holy Spirit. We, like God, are three-part beings. For the Holy Spirit to be our helper, we must become sensitive to our spiritual self. When our spirits have the ascendancy of our makeup, allowing us to be led by God, it brings us into a whole other realm of existence. And that's part of how the Spirit of God is our helper. He will teach us all things and remind us of everything Jesus said when He walked the Earth. He also knows the future. He will guide us step-by-step to take paths in the life of unnecessary detour not conforming to our purpose and destiny.

# *March 4*

# IS HE YOUR ROCK?

*Psalm 18:2*

*The Lord is my Rock, my Fortress, and my Deliverer; my God, my keen and firm Strength in Whom I will trust and take refuge, my Shield, and the Horn of my salvation, my High Tower.*

When a Christian says that God is my rock, in whom I take refuge, He's my shield and the horn of my salvation, it means that person has experience in God keeping them from harm allowing them to walk in safety in their everyday life. We need to try God, see that He is good and how His mercy is boundless toward helping us. He is whatever we need, in the way we individually need Him to come through for us. If you don't trust Him, you'll never know Him as your rock or shield. When the bill is due, God can push back the due date if you're really trusting Him. Help from God always manifests in His timing, not when we expect it, nor how we think He should move on our behalf. Living for God becomes a lifestyle. Until we live for Jesus, we'll never experience all that God has for us here and now. He's our Rock, our Sword, and our Shield. He's our wheel in the middle of a wheel, and He'll never let us down. If you are living for Jesus and experience troubling times, understand that you are experiencing growing pains. Trust God while you are waiting for your answer, it will be worth the wait.

# *March 5*

# THE MAKING OF A PROVERBS 31 WOMAN

### *Proverbs 31:25-26*

*Strength and dignity are her clothing and her position is strong and secure; she rejoices over the future [the latter day or time to come, knowing that she and her family are in readiness for it]!*

*She opens her mouth in skillful and godly Wisdom, and on her tongue is the law of kindness [giving counsel and instruction].*

The Proverbs 31 woman is a fine example for all to see. She has structure and total control of her day. She has her hands full in between raising children, running the household, and being a wife. Dignity in how she performs her day is also her portion. She rises early in the morning to take charge of all she does. She speaks with wisdom and faithful instruction on her tongue. Her love for the Lord is her motivation, and it fuels her day to perform in excellence. It almost sounds too good to be true and challenging for today's woman. If you can laugh at the days to come, with confident expectation that everything will work out, you are a woman of faith and understanding and have been empowered by God because of your constant seeking of Him every day. All excellence comes from spending quality time with God. We can do all things through Christ who strengthens us (Philippians 4:13), but we can do nothing of great value and worth without Him (John 15:5).

# *March 6*

# WHAT KIND OF LOVE IS THIS?

*1 Corinthians 13:7*

*Love bears up under anything and everything that comes, is ever ready to believe the best of every person, its hopes are fadeless under all circumstances, and it endures everything [without weakening].*

Love never gives up because God is love. He never gives up working in and through us. Love has different qualities, as life has various aspects to deal with. Sometimes, we need to flow in tough love as some people find it harder to reach the truth of their situation. Sometimes, we need understanding and love and allow the other person to vent while we just listen. Do not refute their point, even if they are in error. But love will eventually tell that person the truth about their wayward behavior. A mother's love for her child is a strong bond, but it's natural, which isn't bad but limited. The love of God goes beyond limitations to the throne of God. Showing sacrificial love is for the Christian who wants a higher level of living for God no matter what challenges come. Love overrules any and every law. That is when you are walking in the agape love of God, you're blameless (Romans 13:10). The fruit of our newly recreated human spirits all lie on the bed of love. You can't be kind without love, you can't genuinely be patient without love, you can't be joyful without love or understanding, etc. God so loved the world that He sent His only begotten Son. Love moved God and should be the moving force in our lives.

# *March 7*

# WHEN HIS NAME IS PRAISED

*Psalm 113:3*

*From the rising of the sun to the going down of it and from east to west, the name of the Lord is to be praised!*

Everywhere from east to west, praise the name of the Lord; that's the message David proclaimed. David found out that praising the Lord, especially through trouble, brings God to the scene of our issues to help. What happens behind the scenes in the spirit world is very real; there are enemy entities that can't stand being in the presence of God (Ephesians 6:12). When we praise and worship the Lord, God inhabits the praises of His people, so when His presence manifests, the devil and his crew leave as if in terror. Praise is one of the weapons of choice for Christians in battle (2 Chronicles 20:21). Praising God regularly keeps back many bad situations or circumstances that may bring us harm. Many of us have avoided seriously bad situations simply by praising God in the moment. His name is above every name. It is the name and faith in the name that can make us whole (Acts 3:16). Thank God for the name, another weapon of choice for battle.

# *March 8*

# YOU'RE GONNA LEARN TODAY?

*Proverbs 1:7*

*The reverent and worshipful fear of the Lord is the beginning and the principal and choice part of knowledge [its starting point and its essence]; but fools despise skillful and godly Wisdom, instruction, and discipline.*

The best way to realize a fool in your midst is when that person despises skillful and godly wisdom, instruction, and discipline. When we become unteachable and uncorrectable, we are at the door that reads; all fools enter here. The fear of the Lord is the beginning of knowledge (Proverbs 9:10); the reverential fear, having a deep respect for God, opens the door for knowledge to walk through. We must be in an attitude of living a life of deep respect for the Lord. Then, all of life's concerns and challenges get filtered through the knowledge and wisdom of God so that clear understanding can rule our dilemmas and unexpected troubles. "My people are destroyed for lack of knowledge" (Hosea 4:6).

# March 9

# ARE YOU A GIVER, OR A TIGHTWAD?

*Proverbs 11:25*

*The liberal person shall be enriched, and he who waters shall himself be watered.*

The liberal or generous person will prosper. As you bless others, you will be blessed. Thank God our blessings from God are not dependent on selfish, tightwad people, although the Lord can use the devil to deliver a blessing to you. Give and it shall be given back to you, whatever it is, good or bad (Luke 6-38). To him that has, shall more be given. We are to be like rivers that flow through an area, allowing the overflow of blessings in our lives to help others. We can't out-give God when it comes to helping people without Him rewarding us more. As we learn to hear the voice of God more clearly, we can give in a more fertile area to someone's life, at the exact time God wants it done, which yields a better return to us.

# *March 10*

# DRAMA-FOLK OR PEACE?

*Philippians 4:7*

*And God's peace [shall be yours, that tranquil state of a soul assured of its salvation through Christ, and so fearing nothing from God and being content with its Earthly lot of whatever sort that is, that peace] which transcends all understanding shall garrison and mount guard over your hearts and minds in Christ Jesus.*

The soul that is assured of its salvation, meaning you know you're not going to burn in hell after you die, is the foundation of having peace today. As we understand this truth our subconscious is more at ease, knowing the worst-case scenario happening to you will bring you to your reward in heaven. This is far better than what this world has to offer (Matthew 5:12). But while we're down here, seek peace and stay clear of 'drama-folk.' Drama-folk never have peace, and if you are around them, you won't either. The Bible says don't be anxious about anything (Philippians 4:6) but bring all your requests to God with thanksgiving, and the peace of God which passes all understanding will guard your hearts and minds in Christ Jesus. Jesus said before He left the Earth, He leaves His peace with us, but we can't live like the devil, and expect God's peace. It's all connected.

# *March 11*

# THE HIDDEN REALITY
# OF THE TEMPLE

*1 Corinthians 3:16, ERV*
*You should know that you yourselves are*
*God's temple God's Spirit lives in you.*

W e are the temple of the Holy Spirit. We are a spirit, have a soul, and live in a body. Our bodies are where the Spirit of God dwells. More specifically, He lives in our new recreated human spirits, which happens after we become Christians. It is important to become God inside-minded to reap the benefits of His presence in us. He's not a freeloader, just hitching a ride around the planet in us. He is our Helper, our Teacher about life and all things, our Comforter and a very present help in times of trouble. Once we come to the point in our Christian walk of understanding that God's not just a Sunday morning feel-good experience we can begin to put Him to work to solve our everyday human struggles. That is part of His purpose for living in us. We belong to God, and He desires to be involved in our daily lives. He will never force Himself on us like the devil does, but God allows us to make the choice on our own, to want His help. Keep your temple in order, and find out what makes things tick and how. There are many hidden mysteries exposed to the person who diligently seeks after the Lord. His Spirit in us reveals all truth about everything concerning us.

# March 12

# WHEN ALL HELL BREAKS OUT

*James 1:2-3*

*Consider it wholly joyful, my brethren, whenever you are enveloped in or encounter trials of any sort or fall into various temptations.*

*Be assured and understand that the trial and proving of your faith bring out endurance and steadfastness and patience.*

How do you consider it pure joy whenever you face trials of many kinds? Well, it's knowing without a doubt that the testing of your faith produces perseverance and helps develop the seed of patience in your newly recreated human spirit. When we have the assurance that our faith is being developed through the trouble we face, the test will be a welcomed purpose that must be endured. As we go through the fiery trials of life, we must know God is with us. God was with the three Hebrew boys in the fire (Daniel 3:16-18), Daniel in the lion's den (Daniel 6:16-21), and countless other stories of how God goes through trouble with us. He doesn't remove the trouble but allows it to come to us to help develop our trust in Him. When He brings you through your crisis, especially in a way you did not see coming, the boost you get in your faith is exhilarating and fulfilling beyond words.

# *March 13*

# TO LOVE ONE ANOTHER

*Romans 12:10*

*Love one another with brotherly affection [as members of one family], giving precedence and showing honor to one another.*

We, as Christians, are children of a loving God. Our natural demeanor should be easily approachable, inviting, and open to peaceful ways. There's a precursor to walking in and demonstrating love to others. Our knowledge of God must be at an acceptable level to begin walking in love toward others. We, like soldiers, must go through basic training to really be able to take a hate punch and not respond to it on that level of hostility. The love of God operating in His children's lives must be practiced every day for development. The Holy Spirit sheds the love of God in our hearts at the Christian new birth when we get saved (Romans 5:5). The seed of love is in us all. To allow it to grow and mature gets us in the VIP section of God's elite soldiers who can take a punch and repay that person who offended us with kindness. Kindness will convict the offender in most cases. Otherwise, they will reap what they've sowed eventually if they don't repent (to turn away from the wrongdoings).

# *March 14*

# ARE YOU ASHAMED OF THE GOSPEL?

*Romans 1:16*

*For I am not ashamed of the Gospel (good news) of Christ, for it is God's power working unto salvation [for deliverance from eternal death] to everyone who believes with a personal trust and a confident surrender and firm reliance, to the Jew first and also to the Greek,*

The Gospel is God's power working to people getting saved from eternal death. Eternal death means life after death without God. Life after your body dies, leads to one of two places, either with God in the happily-ever-after nice place, or you go down to another place that's quite the opposite. So, to be ashamed of sharing the gospel or living the life of a closet Christian, there's zero power working on your behalf for helping to save people from that other place when they die. When the saints go marching in, make sure you're in that number, and be bold about your faith. There's nothing worse than a lukewarm person (Revelation 3:16). Be either hot or cold, because being on the fence leaves you powerless.

# *March 15*

# FOLLOWING THE LIGHT

*John 1:5*

*And the Light shines on in the darkness, for the darkness has never overpowered it [put it out or absorbed it or appropriated it, and is unreceptive to it].*

The darkness represents everything wrong, demonic, without hope, and devilish in nature. The light is the Lord Jesus Christ. He is the light that lights every person (John 8:12). The light is the life of men and women. We have no existence without the light of the Creator (John 1:4). The force of God's light will never be held back by the darkness in this world. The light of God can and does shine right through the darkest areas of our lives. When we find ourselves in a low place, darkness gets in. The degree of darkness in life varies from person to person. Some areas of darkness in our lives may not even be detected until we've said something that clearly represents it. Or our actions have demonstrated our position and it's subtle in many cases. Our words always paint a picture of our heart's motives. *"In Him was life, and that life was the light of men"* (John 1:4). The less of Jesus in our life, the better chance for darkness to do its thing in us.

# March 16

## GOD MISSES YOU

*Joel 2:12*

*Therefore also now, says the Lord, turn and keep on coming to Me with all your heart, with fasting, with weeping, and with mourning [until every hindrance is removed and the broken fellowship is restored].*

When you return to the Lord with all your heart, fasting, weeping, and mourning, broken fellowship will be restored when every hindrance is removed. He doesn't move from our start position with Him because of circumstances and life pressures; we do. It is our responsibility to keep close fellowship with God. It's the only way we can maintain balance in life (James 4:8). It doesn't matter what caused you to stop trusting God or depending on Him for help. You can make things right today. Wholehearted repentance works for God every time. If you don't mean it, don't bother faking it. However, the door is always open for new converts of Christ, and Christians wanting to make things right again.

# *March 17*

# THE HARVEST IS PLENTIFUL, SO GO GET 'EM

## *Matthew 28:19, ERV*

*So go and make followers of all people in the world. Baptize them in the name of the Father and the Son and the Holy Spirit.*

Herein lies the great commission of God, sharing the good news, which is the Bible. Jesus made disciples of the twelve who followed Him. An example has been given for us to go out and do the same. People won't follow you if there's no attraction to what you're saying. Having the Holy Spirit in times of not knowing what to say and how to say it is vital for effective ministry. We must exude the righteousness, peace, and joy of the Holy Spirit in our lives because this is the way of God's Kingdom. People know fake when they're around it. The wisdom of God operating in your life will help make you approachable with a sense of being blameless to the person you're going after for discipleship. They may not be ready to receive Jesus as Lord and Savior at that moment, but you will have planted the seed of the Gospel in them. Then, God will send another person to water that word you planted to help confirm the witness you provided first. And then God gives the increase, in which He'll send another person to lead them to the Lord by the sinner's prayer. We are laborers together with God, but without Him, we can do nothing. The harvest is ripe, but the laborers are few.

# March 18

## TRUST IN THE NAME

*Psalm 20:7*

*Some trust in and boast of chariots and some of horses, but we will trust in and boast of the name of the Lord our God.*

To trust in the name of the Lord is a sure sign of maturity in the things of God. We often put our trust in uncertain things, bad situations, or people who turn against us later. Everything in and of this world is temporary, fleeting, in the process of passing away (2 Corinthians 4:18). The only true stability in this life is Jesus Christ, the same yesterday, today, and forever. Once we've come to a place of reverence and trust in the Lord, we will begin to trust in the name of Jesus. The fullness of the Godhead resides in that name (Colossians 2:9). It is the name above every name. When a Believer utters that name with faith, the temporal things in and of this world must obey. We can come against all evil using that name (Philippians 2:9). Demons, sicknesses, and situations gone wrong will bow down and cease to exist because Jesus conquered the world's evil a long time ago. Because He did, Father God made His name above all and filled it with all power to correct and disperse evil coming against us. Trust in the Name!

# March 19

# GOD CAN BE GANGSTER

*Lamentations 3:22-23*

*It is because of the Lord's mercy and loving-kindness that we are not consumed, because His [tender] compassions fail not.*

The sin nature that was passed on to humankind from Adam and Eve's transgression in the garden has contaminated us and alienated us from the presence of God. We'd hear God's voice very clearly if it weren't for the sinful nature in our flesh. Even though we're born again, having a new, recreated human spirit, our bodies have other ideas not conducive to God's ways. God's loving-kindness stays the hand of God's wrath on us because justice must be satisfied. He's a loving God, but He's also a God of justice (Isaiah 30:18). He is faithful to His Word and won't take us out prematurely. Because we're born into sin, God's plan of redemption has saved those who want it (Romans 5:12). In the old days, there was no grace when you messed up, boom! You're dead from God's lightning strike from heaven or something. Today, because of His loving-kindness, we live in the dispensation of grace to give time for the call of God to come into His family. Make no mistake, there's a time coming when we will have to answer to God.

# *March 20*

# THE NEXT LEVEL UP

*1 Corinthians 10:31*

*So then, whether you eat or drink, or whatever you may do, do all for the honor and glory of God.*

In all things, we should honor God with our actions and motives. Making God proud of you is the desire of the mature Christian. It's not even for the benefits that go along with the deeper dimension of the Christian walk but because you love the Lord. You can reach this point by invoking your will to seek Him as your life depends on it, and it does for total victorious living. Honoring God is a way of life once you understand how it all works together. Your conformity to God's Word in thought, purpose, and action brings clarity and meaning to your everyday life. Everything becomes plain, and there's less life-clutter of busyness. In all honesty, the Christian walk is a costly lifestyle. Anything of significant value costs! There's no greater value than God having His way in humanity to bring him to a place of prosperity and blessings beyond thought or imagination. "...He is able to do exceedingly abundantly above all we can ask or think" (Ephesians 3:20-21). So willingly honoring God puts us in a position to receive the cup running over with blessings.

# *March 21*

# LET THE SPIRIT OF TRUTH GUIDE YOU, WE ALL NEED HIM

*John 16:13, NIV*

*But when He, the Spirit of truth, comes, He will guide you into all the truth. He will not speak on His own; He will speak only what He hears, and He will tell you what is yet to come.*

The Spirit of truth has come to set things straight. Since we can't always know or understand everything, this is where the Spirit of truth comes in and sets things right in our lives. Truth overrides facts because Jesus is the way, the truth, and the life. He walked in the law of the Spirit of life while on Earth, thereby defeating the law of sin and death. All facts of the Old Testament commandments have been fulfilled or superseded by the new commandment Jesus gave of loving your neighbor as yourself. The Spirit of truth working in you will guide you into all truth. In this world, the facts about many things in life have been a lie. The news or 'fakebook' on social media is often deceptive. Without knowing the truth in every situation or circumstance of your life, the evil one (Satan) in this world can have a foothold in your decision-making and most of your thoughts, where he begins to work on you with lies. Let the Spirit of truth guide you. We all need Him.

# March 22

# WE LOVE THEM THROUGH IT

*2 John 1:6*

*And what this love consists in is this: that we live and walk in accordance with and guided by His commandments (His orders, ordinances, precepts, teaching). This is the commandment, as you have heard from the beginning, that you continue to walk in love [guided by it and following it].*

To obey God's commandments is to love God. All His commandments can be summed up with the last one Jesus gave after the ten commandments, love your neighbor as yourself (John 13:34-35). If everyone loved each other, there would be no stealing, killing, hurt, pain, or anything that makes us sad or feel defeated in life. If everyone would at least try to walk in love towards everyone else, the world would be unrecognizable for the better. Loving each other becomes easier when the underlying motive for trying to understand one another is rooted in truth and honesty. When we have truth, honesty, and understanding working in our lives, there is nothing we cannot handle or go through victoriously. The force of love is very strong in the life of a person when integrity, character, and understanding come together in unity. We begin to see things more like God does concerning others. Always be mindful that people are not perfect and prone to mess up, so we love them through it.

# March 23

# THE GREATEST LOVE OF ALL

*1 John 4:19*
*We love Him, because He first loved us.*

The Lord sowed us the first seed of love by sending His only begotten Son to die for our sins on the cross. His only begotten Son means God used the virgin Mary, a human being, but God Himself overshadowed Mary by the Holy Spirit to put the seed of love in her, producing Jesus Christ our Lord. And God feels no different than we do about allowing His child to be killed for someone else, but because He so loved the world, He gave His only begotten Son as a sacrificial lamb so that justice could be satisfied. Only the blood of Jesus, a sinless man, could accomplish obtaining our freedom from wrongdoings. We can now choose to be free from habitually doing wrong. Love was given to be passed on. Once we come to a saving knowledge of the truth, we can love God because He first loved us. There is no greater love than this that a man would lay down his life for another.

# *March 24*

# DON'T GIVE UP NOW

*Galatians 6:9*

*And let us not lose heart and grow weary and faint in acting nobly and doing right, for in due time and at the appointed season we shall reap, if we do not loosen and relax our courage and faint.*

We all can get weary in doing good. During times of needing refuge from the struggles of life, there is help. The Bible says come to me all of you that labor and are heavy laden (Matthew 11:28-29), and the Lord will give you rest. Our struggles and battles in life are not unknown to the Lord. When He says let us not become weary in well doing, that means we can do this. But not so easily without God's help. All soldiers get tired from the battle and must recoup and regroup but not give up or give in. Our strength comes from the Lord (Isaiah 40:31); to utilize that help, we must spend quality time with Him. In those quiet times alone with the Lord, He can instill in us what is needed to carry on in the fight of life. Once tapped into the Lord and His power, we can do all things through Christ, who strengthens us. He leads us beside the still waters of peace and quiet. Once we've gotten what we need, it's time to continue the good fight of faith. Our work is not in vain. The Lord sees our good works and our effort in staying steady in doing good. "Lift up your heads, O ye gates; and be ye lift up, ye everlasting doors, and the King of glory shall come in" (Psalm 24:7-10, KJV). Stay encouraged. God has got your back!

# *March 25*

# YOUR WAY, OR GOD'S WAY?

*Psalm 143:10*

*Teach me to do Your will, for You are my God; let Your good Spirit lead me into a level country and into the land of uprightness.*

D avid asked God to teach him His will. God's will is in the Bible, and it's all there. You may need help understanding it clearly, but that's His word in a book. God's Word is His will. He can be counted on never to change as humans do from the pressures of life. To do the Lord's will takes trials and much error to develop us into God's outward image and likeness. We are made in His image and likeness from the beginning. But after sin was introduced into the world, we did not act like God. We must be taught or, really, reprogrammed from creation to be like the Lord. This world is all about your feelings, being gratified, and having your way 24/7. Because of this, there's a discipline of self-control that must be mastered. We are in this world as Christians but not of this world at all. Born on Earth, subject to the governing rules of the land, we must live life from the perspective of the kingdom of God and its rules that can supersede this world's natural laws and rules with truth. Learn His will for yourself and live as God intended for you to live.

# *March 26*

# THINK BEFORE YOU ACT

*Philippians 2:3, NLT*
*Don't be selfish; don't try to impress others. Be humble, thinking of others as better than yourselves.*

There's no need to make a move when you're feeling any of this. We all have our moods, some more funky than others, but wait for a calm state of mind before you act. When we are prompted by conceit and empty arrogance instead of a true spirit of humility, the outcome of our deeds will turn rotten; it may bite us in a tender area of our body that leaves us bruised physically and or emotionally. When our funky mood contaminates our motivation, self-inflicted hurt will be coming our way. *"...let each regard the other as better than and superior to himself (thinking more highly of one another than you do of yourselves)"* (Romans 12:3). This will help our pride issues if we practice it. The plumbline of advice here is, since we are responsible for our actions and words spoken, why not think about what you're about to do before you do it. Don't let the heat of the moment control you. Step back, take a breath, or a day to calm down, then handle your business from a humble state of mind.

# *March 27*

# ARE YOU CONNECTED TO THE VINE?

### John 15:2

*Any branch in Me that does not bear fruit [that stops bearing] He cuts away (trims off, takes away); and He cleanses and repeatedly prunes every branch that continues to bear fruit, to make it bear more and richer and more excellent fruit.*

Jesus is the vine. We, Christians, are the branches. The fruit develops on the branches, and the nutrients are supplied by the vine. Our fruit-bearing are works we, Christians, are doing for the Lord. The plan of reconciliation is for and commissioned to every Christian (2 Corinthians 5:18-19). Witnessing and sharing the Gospel with the world is the great commission. As we draw our spiritual help from God, through the Vine, Jesus Christ, we can bear much fruit. He removes and or prunes us to bear more fruit. Pruning isn't comfortable but necessary for growth. Like the fig tree Jesus cursed because it wasn't giving the fruit it was intended to (Mark 11:12-14, 20), He will never curse us, but He will remove those not bearing fruit because our purpose now has been lost. Staying connected to the vine is a lifestyle, not a once in a while thing.

# March 28

# FOLLOW THE LIGHT, THEN BE THE LIGHT

*Isaiah 60:3*
*And nations shall come to your light,*
*and kings to the brightness of your rising.*

We are the light of the world as Christians because of Jesus, and He lives in us. The light of God's Word expels darkness from our bad situations and gives clarity to the Believer. Nations are made of people that are attracted to the light. Light has always represented good, while darkness has always stood for evil. Most people have a longing for the light by nature, but this fallen world has made many insensitive to the goodness behind the light. Our make-up was based on God's image and likeness, God is light, and we are His children. All things positive and right, with integrity and good character, come from the light. You are the light and are due to shine for the Lord as bright as possible. As light expels darkness, we should be able to instantly walk into a room and brighten the atmosphere.

# March 29

# THE ACT OF GIVING

*Matthew 6:3*

*But when you give to charity, do not let your left hand know what your right hand is doing,*

Basically, when we give to the needy, we shouldn't go around boasting how we were the one that helped them out, so all can see our generosity. Pride will never win God's approval no matter what you've done to help someone. It is the motivation behind your giving that gets the Lord's attention, and that should be from a place of love, and compassion. It's better to give without thought, in the sense of not being concerned about your own needs, but from your heart's reaction to their need. The law of reciprocity is always in effect, what goes around, comes around. Seed, time, and harvest are still working. Give and in time, the harvest of your giving will come. God will not be mocked, whatsoever a man sows that will he reap (Galatians 6:7). He loves a cheerful giver whose heart loves to give. The feeling we get after giving to someone (without expecting anything in return), is the best feeling in the world. Especially when the person was hurting badly from the lack in their life. If each one of us will help one another, this world would be a much better place.

# *March 30*

# WHEN YOU PRAY

*Matthew 6:7-8*

*And when you pray, do not heap up phrases (multiply words, repeating the same ones over and over) as the Gentiles do, for they think they will be heard for their much speaking.*

When you pray, heaping up phrases, multiplying words, and repeating the same words is unnecessary. We don't want to follow some theologians with the idea of big words being the only way to get to God in prayer. Simply talking to God like you'd talk to another person will do the job. He honors heartfelt, genuine prayer, not the slickness of fancy words. That's why God comes through for many people when they're desperate and don't know where to turn for help, and He answers that prayer. When we pray according to His will, we know He hears us, and since we know He hears us, we know we have the petitions we've asked of Him (1 John 5:14). He knows what you need before you pray. Our part is to pray from the heart, believing we've received the moment we pray. After you've prayed, watch your words; they must align with what you've prayed for, or you negate the prayer. Faith is the hand that comes from God. Pray in faith and believing, and you'll get it. Sometimes, the answer is slow in coming, and that's where patience is most necessary. Still pray.

# *March 31*

# THE WISDOM WALK

*Proverbs 13:20*

*He who walks [as a companion] with wise men is wise, but he who associates with [self-confident] fools is [a fool himself and] shall smart for it.*

Walking with the wise keeps you wise. Being a companion of fools makes you a fool, as per the Bible. Just as by law, you are guilty by association hanging with a criminal. We must think about who we are spending time with constantly. Is that person good for us, or are we the one always giving, and giving out, bleeding ourselves dry if we let them? Associating with the wise is better because the wise person already knows that their character and life-giving words of wisdom and experience are valuable, and they won't jeopardize that position by trying to get over on us. Wisdom is more precious than fine gold. We'd stay out of so much trouble by using it.

# *April 1*

# ALL HAVE FALLEN SHORT

*Psalm 85:2*

*You have forgiven and taken away the iniquity of Your people, You have covered all their sin. Selah [pause, and calmly realize what that means]!*

All of our wrongdoings (sins) have been forgiven and taken away. Once you've repented for messing up, ask God's forgiveness, and you mean it, and you are forgiven (1 John 1:9). We must know this truth for ourselves. So once we ask God for forgiveness, the devil can't harass us into condemnation over our mistake. We walk by faith not by sight in our dealings with the Lord (2 Corinthians 5:7). It's a lifestyle of faith that positions us into a posture of always receiving from God. We have all fallen short of the righteousness of God, without God. Our self-righteousness doesn't get us to heaven but the righteousness of God in Christ Jesus will. We're in Christ once we've become a born again Christian, at that point we have been sanctified and put in right standing with God. You are a king in your own right once you've become a part of God's family. We are kings of whom Jesus is King of (Revelations 19:16), we are lords of whom Jesus is Lord of and over. There's now no condemnation for those in Christ walking according to the Spirit and not the flesh (if your emotions rule you, condemnation will be close by). If you don't have a peaceful feeling when you think about what might be wrong in your life, there could be room for repentance, if you desire God's unlimited blessings.

# *April 2*

# GOD ALWAYS HAD A PLAN TO SAVE US

*1 Timothy 2:5*

*For there [is only] one God, and [only] one Mediator between God and men, the Man Christ Jesus,*

There is one God and one mediator between God and humanity: Christ Jesus. The One who created heaven and Earth is the only living God, and Jesus is the way to Him (John 14:6). Jesus stands in the gap for us when we mess up. We will mess up because we have yet to be made perfect like Jesus. In the next life, we will have glorified bodies like Jesus. We will be changed in the twinkling of an eye if we're still alive when Jesus comes back to get us. He is faithful and just to forgive us of wrongdoing if we confess it to Him. Until we are totally changed in spirit, soul, and body, we are imperfect beings needing a go-between who understands the struggle down here. Jesus, the mediator, keeps us from the strong arm of justice's rightful punishment for sinning against God. Without Jesus, we would be jacked up forever. Go with the God that's alive, and live for the real purpose He placed in you from birth.

# *April 3*

# HE'S OUR ALL AND ALL

*1 Chronicles 29:11*

*Yours, O Lord, is the greatness and the power and the glory and the victory and the majesty, for all that is in the heavens and the Earth is Yours; Yours is the kingdom, O Lord, and Yours it is to be exalted as Head over all.*

The Earth is the Lord's and everything in it (Psalm 24:1). He created the heavens and the Earth from nothing visible (Hebrews 11:3). He is great, powerful, glorious, splendid, and majestic. He is to be reverenced and honored as King of kings, and Lord of lords. We are the kings He's King of, and the lords He's Lord over. He is the Lilly of the valley, and the bright morning star. He is the life giver of all living things. The First and the Last. The Beginning and the End, and the Author and Finisher of our faith. He is our all in all, and better understood by meditating in His Word (Joshua 1:8). We can't even begin to understand the ways of God without reading the Bible and it helps having someone you trust help you understand it. The Spirit of God is the Teacher who helps us get revelation, knowledge of the scriptures, and brings to light many mysteries of the faith we may not understand. Almighty God is head over all, and Satan's days are numbered.

# *April 4*

# THE LOVE CONNECTION

*Romans 8:38-39*

*For I am persuaded beyond doubt (am sure) that neither death nor life, nor angels nor principalities, nor things [a] impending and threatening nor things to come, nor powers, Nor height nor depth, nor anything else in all creation will be able to separate us from the love of God which is in Christ Jesus our Lord.*

In this text, Paul speaks to the Romans about his experience with God and His loving kindness. Nothing can or ever will separate us from God's love for us. We are precious to Him in every way. Our nature has been altered since He created us, but God always has a plan. His love for us is unparalleled by anything we can comprehend. Unlike humankind, God has no obstacles or pressures in life that could change Him. He's the same yesterday, today, and forever. We may get close to something detrimental, but His love will not allow us to fall and stay down. We have a part to play in connecting to the Lord's love to complete the love circuit that undergirds our faith. Faith works by love, and everything about our relationship and fellowship with God is by faith. We may forsake God, but that's not in His nature to do it to us. Nothing can separate us from God's love, so count on it and know He's got you.

# *April 5*

# WHEN THE FIGHT GETS TOO HOT

*Psalm 91:2*

*I will say of the Lord, He is my Refuge and my Fortress, my God;*
*on Him I lean and rely, and in Him I [confidently] trust!*

G od is our shelter from pursuit, danger, or trouble. He is a military stronghold, and there is a strongly fortified place of safety in Him. It's called the secret place because, for the most part, only more mature Christians find it. We can trust Him, as He is not susceptible to outside influence or disturbance. If you have trust issues, there is one who is not a man that He can lie, so if you're in trouble and fearing for your life, go to God, who will receive you no matter what you've done or didn't do. Those of us who have tasted and seen that the Lord is good already know of God's trustworthiness (Psalm 34:8). The fight is always on its way to your doorstep, so fight the good fight of faith (1 Timothy 6:11-12), and when you need a break, go to the secret place of the Most-High God.

# *April 6*

# YOUR JUSTIFICATION WITH GOD IS FREE

*Acts 2:38*

*And Peter answered them, repent (change your views and purpose to accept the will of God in your inner selves instead of rejecting it) and be baptized, every one of you, in the name of Jesus Christ for the forgiveness of and release from your sins; and you shall receive the gift of the Holy Spirit.*

We must turn away from our wrongdoings and consciously decide to do the right thing in life. We are imperfect beings prone to mess up because of our human nature. That's why we must turn from our wrongdoings and seek, willfully going after, the right thing in every life situation. Make it a habit to change your old way of doing things in general. If you've been stuck in life and wondering why you're not where you want to be, start with you. Many times, the afflictions we experience in life are self-inflicted. What you think you're doing in secret that no one sees, the laws of God are, in effect. They apply to saints and sinners alike. God's no respecter of persons (Romans 2:11). The bill comes due for your wrongdoings sooner or later. Each of us must repent and be baptized. If you don't change, nothing about your life will.

# *April 7*

# THE WAY TO ENTER IN

*Psalm 100:4*

*Enter into His gates with thanksgiving and a thank offering
and into His courts with praise! Be thankful and say so to Him,
bless and affectionately praise His name!*

Approaching the Lord with thanksgiving is the first step, and then, as we approach His courts, we give Him praise. Even hell has gates before you enter. "The gates of hell shall not prevail against the church" (Matthew 16:17-18). So there's a protocol before entering in. At one point in our Christian walk, we should have the mindset of going to God simply to bless Him, not with "gimmie gimmie gimmie my name is Jimmy." He knows what we have need of before we ask (Matthew 6:8). We invoke our will over our flesh (emotions) to give thanks even though we don't feel like it. Then we go into praising God to complete our entry into His presence. In the Old Testament, God's people would bring offerings to Him to cover their sins. Today, we live in the dispensation of grace, and our sins have been totally washed away by the work at Calvary Jesus finished. Now, instead of physical offerings, we bring the sacrifice of praise into the house of the Lord. It has been said that thanking God is great to do when you're in need of a miracle. Thanking Him means you believe He's there, which is your faith in action, and that brings God to the scene of your trouble.

# *April 8*

# A MESSAGE OF HOPE

*Romans 10:10*

*For with the heart a person believes (adheres to, trusts in, and relies
on Christ) and so is justified (declared righteous, acceptable to
God), and with the mouth he confesses (declares openly and speaks
out freely his faith) and confirms [his] salvation.*

If it were difficult to be right with God, not many of us would be. It
is about the willingness of a person to choose God for themselves.
Our words and our belief behind the words we speak, is where the
power lies (Mark 11:23-24). God said in the beginning, "Let there be
light." And He believed what He said would come to pass, hence the
example given to us as His children. God could have thought existence
into being but gave us the example of confessing with our mouth
and believing in our hearts. The power on our lips of confession can
change the world. We don't have unlimited power like God for obvious
reasons. Your power will increase, as your knowledge and commitment
to serve the Lord increases (2 Peter 3:18). Once you've gotten hold of
this principle and the law of reciprocity concerning the power of your
words, you will be unstoppable. For now, if you haven't yet, follow the
instructions at the beginning of this message and live saved, get right
with God. Your eternal life depends on it!

# *April 9*

## YOU GOT THIS,
## AND GOD'S GOT YOU

*Deuteronomy 31:6*

*Be strong, courageous, and firm; fear not nor be in terror before them, for it is the Lord your God who goes with you; He will not fail you or forsake you.*

The command is for us to be strong, courageous, and firm. Be determined to be strong, courageous, and firm in life, knowing the Lord will never leave you or forsake you. If He commands us to be these things, we can be. Overcome fear with faith. The two will not operate at the same time in a person. Perfect love, mature love, drives out fear, and our faith works by love according to the Bible (Galatians 5:6). Living a life of faith in God's Word for yourself keeps fear at bay. Healthy fear tells us to move out of the way of the tractor-trailer truck coming down the street. Crippling fear stops us from doing what's necessary to live the abundant life the Lord has promised each of us. We must move forward in life knowing God has our back. The battlefield of our intentions and desired manifested actions begins in our mind, but fear can and will alter the results of what we originally wanted. Your enemy isn't that strong. So be strong and courageous; you got this, and God's got you.

# *April 10*

# GO GET 'EM!

*Mark 16:15*

*And He said to them, Go into all the world and preach and publish openly the good news (the Gospel) to every creature [of the whole human race].*

The great commission is to be carried out by every Christian today. Until this is completed, the return of Christ cannot happen. Every living being will have an opportunity to choose or reject the Lord Jesus Christ (Matthew 24:14). In the end, every knee shall bow, and every tongue confess that Jesus Christ is Lord to the glory of God (Philippians 2:10-11). We are to follow the example of Jesus. Jesus went into the places that were considered the most sinful and worldly areas (today, we'd call them clubs or bars). Nevertheless, He knew they needed to hear the Gospel regardless of the opinions of the church-world judging Him for doing it. When we become too heavenly-minded, we become no Earthly good toward helping others. There must be a balance in living in this world but not being a part of it (John 17:14). Jesus didn't care what the religious folk of the day had to say, He knew His assignment. Your God-given purpose may rock the church world's religious way of doing things, but your calling is your calling, and no one is to stop you from fulfilling it. Go get 'em!

# *April 11*

# THE LORD BLESS YOU NOW!

*Numbers 6:24-26*

*The Lord bless you and watch, guard, and keep you; The Lord make His face to shine upon and enlighten you and be gracious (kind, merciful, and giving favor) to you; The Lord lift up His [approving] countenance upon you and give you peace (tranquility of heart and life continually).*

The Lord will bless and keep you, turn His face toward you, and give you peace. The key to it all is faith. Like anything else, the more time you spend with a person, the more you understand them, and the more you'll believe in them as they show you, you can trust them. Fellowship with God is vital to all the promises of God coming to pass in your life. Through faith and patience, we obtain the promises of God (Hebrews 6:12). The good news is He loves blessing His children, especially those who are always in His face. The Lord desires a relationship and close fellowship with us. Once His face has turned toward you, He gives you peace. We write our own ticket concerning our involvement with God. Meaning we do the work of fighting the good fight of faith. Everything is done by faith in God. We must believe He's there even though we can't physically see Him. That, my friend, is faith. May the Lord bless you now!

# *April 12*

# MY REDEEMER LIVES

## *Job 19:25*

*For I know that my Redeemer and Vindicator lives, and at last He [the Last One] will stand upon the Earth.*

I know my redeemer lives. Until we have a relationship and fellowship with the Lord, there's no way we can know Him for ourselves, and it is all about a personal relationship. Once we know for ourselves that He lives, like the song says, "I can face tomorrow." We have been redeemed from the curse of the law. The curse of the law has to do with us not being in right standing with God, or hell bound as the ol' church mothers would say. It can be hard sometimes with the struggles we face in this life to stay Christ-centered. The Word of God must govern our thoughts, not our circumstances or feelings. Once we accept God's Word as truth, which overrides facts, we raise above the boundaries of this world's limitations. We know we have been redeemed without a shadow of a doubt once the hunger for right standing with God dominates our thinking and actions. Jesus, our Redeemer, is alive and well. His desire is that we live the life He died for. This standard of life requires spiritual sensitivity to the Lord and His living Word. Once the believer of God takes hold of this lifestyle, an awareness comes upon them, that not only is Jesus alive today, but the life we now live we live by faith in the Son of God. You cannot see Him with your physical eyes, but it does not mean He's not there.

# April 13

# THE MESSAGE MUST PREVAIL

*Matthew 10:16*

*Behold, I am sending you out like sheep in the midst of wolves; be wary and wise as serpents, and be innocent (harmless, guileless, and without falsity) as doves.*

Jesus sends us out to help fulfill the plan of reconciliation (share the Gospel). As we go out, we should know the wolves of this world are those trying to oppose the message of the Gospel. For our safety, we are to be wise as serpents and innocent as doves. We may go out like sheep, but we have the backing of the Godhead to handle the wolves. Once we know our authority in Christ, we stop allowing many unnecessary attacks to overtake us. No weapon formed against us will prosper (Isaiah 54:17). The weapon may form against us, but it won't prosper to our purpose's detriment or demise. We're in a war down here, and hopefully, we know Satan's devices. He has nothing new under the sun (2 Corinthians 2:11). He comes with deception, strong temptations, inordinate desires, delusional thoughts, and mind-binding spirits to attack our thought life, and that's where the battle starts, in your head. So renew your mind with the Word of God, think like Him, and wolves will know you know God, and then they'll back off.

# *April 14*

# YOU ARE ROYALTY IN CHRIST, ACT LIKE IT

*Matthew 5:6*

*Blessed and fortunate and happy and spiritually prosperous (in that state in which the born-again child of God enjoys His favor and salvation) are those who hunger and thirst for righteousness (uprightness and right standing with God), for they shall be completely satisfied!*

If you hunger and thirst for right standing with God, you shall be satisfied. You became blessed to be a blessing. We are the righteousness of God in Christ Jesus (2 Corinthians 5:21). Then, we renew our old way of thinking with the Word of God so we can be more of a blessing to others (Romans 12:2). Your right standing with God comes at the new birth when you get saved. But increasing quality fellowship with God brings us to a new level of blessings. He's a rewarder of those who diligently seek Him (Hebrews 11:6). Live for Christ and show this world who you really are. You are royalty.

# *April 15*

# TO HONOR YOUR NOT SO HONORABLE PARENTS

*Ephesians 6:2-3*

*Honor (esteem and value as precious) your father and your mother—this is the first commandment with a promise—*

*That all may be well with you and that you may live long on the Earth.*

To honor your father and mother is a command from the Lord. When we do, we will live long on Earth, which is promised by God Himself. What about when your parent or parents aren't honorable? That's when your development in the love of God is necessary. We live in this natural world and have to deal with natural things that can affect our emotions, which can affect how we see another person, totally human. Some parents have gone through some unbelievable life experiences that could wreck anyone, and your parents never got a break, so they are broken and considered damaged goods, and then you were born under that. But we are called to live above the evil in this world and, in so doing, respect our unlovable parents. There's a way; you may need God to help you, but it's doable by faith. So honor your parents so it may be well with you in life (Ephesians 6:3, NLT). No matter what your parents or parent has done to you, there's always God's way to approach them. The challenge is, whether or not you will take the way of escape God provides during the issues concerning your parents. Honor your parents!

# *April 16*

# GOD'S GREATEST WORK

*Isaiah 25:1*

*O Lord, You are my God; I will exalt You, I will praise Your name, for You have done wonderful things, even purposes planned of old [and fulfilled] in faithfulness and truth.*

We praise God's name because He has done great things. You might say, what great things, well let's start with it's a great thing that air comes back into your lungs after each time you exhale. Or that you woke up this morning. Yes, I know we take it for granted and expect that to happen every day, but some of us didn't wake up this morning, or others may have serious lung issues, etc. Ultimately, we praise Him for Jesus dying on our behalf, being the sacrificial offering for our sins, now that's the greatest work of God. He repositions situations and circumstances so that, in the end, we benefit from them. He moves impossibilities around so we can bear a thing we're dealing with; you just don't always realize it's God behind the scenes at work for you. He's willing and working to do His good pleasure in you.

# *April 17*

# HIS WORD IS A LAMP

*Psalm 119:105*
*Your word is a lamp to my feet and a light to my path.*

God's Word is a lamp for our feet, and a light on our path. If something does not line up with God's Word that you come across, it is to be refused. We have two basic ways of knowing when something is wrong. We have that intuition, that feeling inside that something is wrong, and there's the knowledge of God's Word that clearly points out evil, confusion, and danger. If everything we do in life was to pass through the understanding of God's Word first, before we do it, we would live a perfect life. Not a life without trouble or tests, because that helps you grow up. The light of God's Word will keep us on the path that leads to prosperity and peace.

# April 18

## PRAY CONTINUALLY

*1 Thessalonians 5:17*
*Be unceasing in prayer [praying perseveringly].*

These are important instructions in receiving answered prayer. The prayer of Thanksgiving should be our prayer once we've prayed in faith concerning a thing. To pray again for the same thing as if you didn't believe God heard you the first time isn't good. The persistence of a Believer always gets the prize. Our hearts must be in our prayers. Do not pray with unbelief or with a lackadaisical attitude. You must invoke your spirit, soul, and mind in the execution of your prayer. God needs to see the burning desire of your prayer; heartfelt prayers get His attention. When you pray, believe you received at the moment you prayed. Don't give up because it's taking a long time for the answer to come; keep praying!

# *April 19*

# THE BODY

*1 Corinthians 12:27*
*Now you [collectively] are Christ's body and [individually] you are*
*members of it, each part severally and distinct [each with his own*
*place and function].*

We are all a part of Christ's body and have a role to play for the kingdom of God, a unique part that only we can do. There's work to be done in the kingdom here and now before the return of Jesus Christ can happen. You were born with a purpose and that God given purpose is to be used for kingdom building. Some of us are harvesters, leading people to Christ through the sinners prayer. Some sow the seed of the Word of God, and others water (1 Corinthians 3:6), encouraging others to accept Christ. Every part is necessary. We are God's extended hands in the Earth to get the job done. Since man has the dominion in the Earth, given to us by God, the Lord needs us to act on His behalf (Genesis 1:26). He will not go over our heads concerning decisions because He gave us free will. We have dominion in the Earth, use it.

# *April 20*

# WHEN YOUR ENEMY'S DOWN, KICK HIM?

*1 Corinthians 13:6*

*It does not rejoice at injustice and unrighteousness, but rejoices when right and truth prevail.*

Today's verse is referencing the agape love of God. Many of us are delighted when something bad happens to someone who wronged us. But that's not love's way. The law of reciprocity is always in effect; what goes around comes around, good or bad, depending on what seed you planted. The love of God is a sacrificial love, a love that can handle disrespect, unrighteous behavior, and betrayal when it has matured in us. It is not easily angered and pays no attention to a suffered wrong done to us. When you associate with evil people regularly, the love of God will not shine on you. We can be products of our environment if we don't guard our hearts (Proverbs 4:23). Because we live in a potentially harmful, demonic world, everything about it is geared toward you, not operating in the love of God. It's a day-to-day practice of walking in the love of God. As we do, there's no law that can come against us (Galatians 5:23); you'll be blameless, and karma will never be a problem. Love does not delight in evil, so when we do, God's love takes a step backward.

# *April 21*

# WE MUST HAVE HONOR

*Ephesians 6:2-3*

*Honor (esteem and value as precious) your father and your mother—this is the first commandment with a promise—That all may be well with you and that you may live long on the Earth.*

Honor is another step toward having a longer life. Honoring your father and mother can be difficult for some. If you've grown up in a family that has no honor about or in anything, honoring anyone is a problem. You've learned how to be dishonorable as a lifestyle growing up. Maybe your parents were not honorable people. But all of our negative backgrounds, bad environments, and upbringings in general can be remolded into an honorable life with the Lord's help. The teachings and precepts of God won't change because you're too lazy to work the Word of God in your life. There is always a way of escaping all of life's struggles by living the life God intended for us to live. But it takes some work on our part. The constant warring between our flesh and spirit will not end until death. It is vital to learn how to fight using the words of the Bible. Therein lies the power to resist temptations and gain the strength to triumph over being hurt. We must honor our father and mother to have a long life.

# *April 22*

## RECHARGE

*Nahum 1:7*

*The Lord is good, a strength and stronghold in the day of trouble;*
*He knows (recognizes, has knowledge of, and understands) those*
*who take refuge and trust in Him.*

When we are weak, then are we strong. So when we feel weak, the Lord is good, a strength, and stronghold in the day of trouble. He knows those who take refuge in Him; most importantly, He understands. The Lord God Almighty is the only one who can and does understand everything. He is omniscient and omnipresent, which means He knows it all, and He is everywhere simultaneously (Don't try to figure that out; believe it). Nothing goes unnoticed before God. When we come to Him for refuge and/or strength, He already knows why we came and what we need from Him. Times of trouble can be a blessing in disguise as we mature. Without trials and crises in our lives, we'd never grow to the potential deep in our hearts. Trouble makes us reach down there for dear life. Life's struggles will always yield the harvest of strong faith if we don't give up or give in to our situation. You are strong in the Lord and in the power of His might. Come to Him now for everything. He's an ever-ready help in times of need.

# *April 23*

# TIME TO WAKE UP!

*Philippians 2:7-8*

*But stripped Himself [of all privileges and rightful dignity], so as to assume the guise of a servant (slave), in that He became like men and was born a human being. And after He had appeared in human form, He abased and humbled Himself [still further] and carried His obedience to the extreme of death, even the death of the cross!*

Jesus stripped Himself of all privileges and rightful dignity so as to assume the nature of a servant being made in human likeness and becoming obedient to death on the cross. The worse death on Earth was to be crucified. In becoming a man and experiencing everything good and bad we go through, this makes Jesus the mediator between us and God the Father (1 Timothy 2:5). Because of Jesus, God the Judge, can more clearly understand with detail, the evil we deal with on a regular basis. Jesus left His deity, and supernatural power in heaven when He came to Earth to be just like a man who has no deity status or Godhead power. Jesus came to destroy the works of the devil as a human would, using God's Word to overcome life's problems, victorious in every area of life (1John 3:8). He did this while never committing sin, thus making Him the perfect sacrificial lamb to get rid of our sins justifying us with Father God.

# *April 24*

# LIVE AT PEACE WITH EVERYBODY

*Hebrews 12:14*

*Strive to live in peace with everybody and pursue that consecration and holiness without which no one will [ever] see the Lord.*

The Bible says that we should make every effort to live in peace with everybody. It should be easier to live at peace with our fellow Believers in Christ, but we must handle things the same way concerning living in peace no matter who the other person is. We are all at different levels in the Lord. Some of us are more mature than others. However, the scary part is, that some people who are still novices, think they are all grown up in the Lord, but don't have enough faith to believe their way out of a paper bag. Without holiness no one will see the Lord. Being holy is practicing living a life based on the fruit of your newly recreated human spirit: love, joy, peace, patience, self-control, are the other fruit. Be holy because God is holy, and peace will be your portion.

# April 25

# HELP ONLY GOD CAN GIVE

*Psalm 23:3*

*He refreshes and restores my life (myself); He leads me in the paths of righteousness [uprightness and right standing with Him—not for my earning it, but] for His name's sake.*

Only God, the creator of our soul can refresh and restore our souls. Sometimes we can't help ourselves and that's when the Lord will reign supreme in doing so. When our mind is sick, things are not as easily corrected. We usually need psychological help from specialists in this area. A demon-possessed person cannot deliver himself from that stronghold. It will take a person who knows his authority in Christ Jesus to deliver you. They call them exorcists. But, it only takes a person who has regular rich fellowship with the Lord that KNOWS God, and He knows, and can trust you with His power to deliver others. Overworked, and overburdened people need this refreshment from the Lord. To restore your soul or your life to what it's supposed to be, is just as easy thing for Him to do. Seek and you shall find, knock, and God will open the door to your victory.

# April 26

# THE REQUIREMENT

*Micah 6:8*

*He has showed you, O man, what is good. And what does the Lord require of you but to do justly, and to love kindness and mercy, and to humble yourself and walk humbly with your God?*

Doing what is right to other people, being kind to others, and living humbly. Those were the words of the Lord from the Old Testament that He still expects of us today. God gave us dominion in the Earth, and He won't supersede His own law. The goodness of God is all throughout the world, it has been partly hidden by this world's system run by Satan, who got the authority following Adam and Eve's disobedience. But Jesus came to Earth and fixed the authority long ago. We're in charge now, but if you don't know it you won't act on it, and you're still in bondage to this world's way. As we learn to be kind to others and live in humility, we can live above the evil in this world because God is with us. If you're not kind to others, and are full of pride, the devil's just hugging you a lot tighter, and God can't hear your prayers, which are now blocked by the sin in your life. Do what the Lord requires from you instead.

# *April 27*

# WHAT IS FAITH ANYWAY?

*Hebrews 11:1*

*Now faith is the assurance (the confirmation, the title deed) of the things [we] hope for, being the proof of things [we] do not see and the conviction of their reality [faith perceiving as real fact what is not revealed to the senses].*

Faith is taking God at His word. Acting on what He has said in His Word is trusting Him to bring to pass whatever we confess with our mouths and believe in our hearts; it is the basis for and heartbeat of Christianity. Without faith, it is impossible to please God (Hebrews 11:6). Faith is knowing without seeing, touching, smelling, hearing, or tasting. Faith does not, nor cannot, depend upon this world's natural ways. This world is subject to change, and God is the same yesterday, today, and forever (Hebrews 13:8). Since faith comes by hearing and hearing by the word of God (Romans 10:17), we can have strong faith, ever-increasing faith, or we can be weak in faith, or have little faith which limits God's ability to release the abundant life He promises us. We can write our ticket with God by our faith. The choice, as always, is ours to make. Do the work of studying God's Word and become all you were created to become in Him. Meditate in His Word day and night, and you'll make your way prosperous (Joshua 1:8).

# April 28

# DO YOU NEED HELP?

*Psalm 121:2*

*My help comes from the Lord, who made heaven and Earth.*

Can you say your help comes from the Lord, or are you mostly doing things in your own strength? The Lord is your strength and shield; your heart should trust in Him, and then help comes. Without trust, you're doing things your way, which may not always be a good idea. Things may be good, but they can always be better with God in them. The maker of Heaven and Earth wants to help us all the time for everything we do in life. Most of us are too busy to slow down and get it. When sickness comes, or injury keeps us from physically getting around, that's when God gets our attention. Help is available, but we must know how to get it and act on it regardless of our feelings. Through faith and patience, we obtain the promises of God (Hebrews 6:12).

# *April 29*

# TO CARRY EACH OTHERS BURDENS

*Galatians 6:2*

*Bear (endure, carry) one another's burdens and troublesome moral faults, and in this way fulfill and observe perfectly the law of Christ (the Messiah) and complete [b]what is lacking [in your obedience to it].*

As we help carry the burdens of others, we are fulfilling the law of Christ, which is basically to love your neighbor as yourself. Your neighbor is anyone you come into contact with. The big picture is each one is to help one. This attitude is like the familiar phrase, "It takes a village." We often come into situations that present a choice; how you respond to that choice should be independent of the level of offense in the situation against you. As we become stronger in our faith (which works by love), we learn how to live above the offenses against us (1 Corinthians 13:5, AMP). Jesus prayed to God while He was on the Earth, *"Father, I pray You to help them live above the evil in the world."* In your mind, your thinking is telling you that's not possible, but as your love for God grows, so will your resilience against those special people sent to help develop your love walk. Allowing the process will bring you to a place in God that seems unreal to most people, but the process never fails to mature as long as we man up and stay the course. You can't carry someone else's burdens while yours is too heavy. There's always a reward for those who walk in the love of God regularly. God is love, allow more of God in your life, and everything gets better. Don't try it; live it!

# *April 30*

# GOD'S EYES

*1 Peter 3:12*

*For the eyes of the Lord are upon the righteous (those who are upright and in right standing with God), and His ears are attentive to their prayer. But the face of the Lord is against those who practice evil [to oppose them, to frustrate, and defeat them].*

God's eyes are on those in right standing with Him (the righteous), but His face is against those who do evil. When His face is against those who do evil, it's to oppose them, to frustrate, and defeat them. That's what the Bible says. His ears are attentive to the righteous when they pray. When you are in right standing with God, meaning you're a born-again Christian, there are graces, and favor bestowed upon you that help make life a little easier than the sinner, a person that hasn't received Jesus as Lord and Savior of their life. In other words, He takes care of His kids, those in His family. Yes, we are capable of messing up, just like a sinner, but Jesus stands in the gap for our failures (1 John 1:9).

# *May 1*

# A WORD FOR THE POOR

*Proverbs 19:17*

*He who has pity on the poor lends to the Lord, and that which he has given He will repay to him.*

When we have pity on the poor and give anything to help them, that gets the Lord's attention. When we help the helpless, we are acting in God's stead. Sometimes we change a person's entire outlook on things by showing them kindness. God shows His love many times through people, He uses people to get things done because we have the dominion on the Earth (Genesis 1:26-27). He'd be like the devil if He were to force or make us do anything, that's the devil's way. Most people don't know or truly understand they have the authority on Earth to rule and reign in total victorious living. Satan knows if you don't know and uses your words against you (2 Corinthians 2:10-11). The power is in your faith-filled confession and your words of belief, good or bad. That's why we must be deliberate in our choice of words. Our thoughts form words of encouragement or discouragement. Don't allow the negative out of your mouth. Give to the poor when you can. Even a strong word of encouragement, if it comes from your heart, the power will be there to help.

# *May 2*

# CHARACTER AND INTEGRITY

*Romans 5:3-5*

*Moreover [let us also be full of joy now!] let us exult and triumph in our troubles and rejoice in our sufferings, knowing that pressure and affliction and hardship produce patient and unswerving endurance. And endurance (fortitude) develops maturity of character (approved faith and tried integrity). And character [of this sort] produces [the habit of] joyful and confident hope of eternal salvation. Such hope never disappoints or deludes or shames us, for God's love has been poured out in our hearts through the Holy Spirit Who has been given to us.*

Romans 5:3-5 is truly full and impactful. Let's begin with endurance (fortitude) which develops maturity of character which is approved faith and tried integrity. To walk in the dream career of your life, there has to be an acceptable amount of character and integrity already operating in you, recognized by others, and helping you move ahead successfully in this world. Your degree from college isn't always enough to get the job. Another person with the exact education, degrees, and credentials that you have will get the job before you, because of their character and integrity. So, rejoice in the sufferings and troubles of this life, character and integrity are being developed in you.

# *May 3*

# THE PRICE IS RIGHT

*Ephesians 2:8-9*

*For it is by free grace (God's unmerited favor) that you are saved ([a]delivered from judgment and made partakers of Christ's salvation) through [your] faith. And this [salvation] is not of yourselves [of your own doing, it came not through your own striving], but it is the gift of God; Not because of works [not the fulfillment of the Law's demands], lest any man should boast. [It is not the result of what anyone can possibly do, so no one can pride himself in it or take glory to himself.]*

The gift of God has been given to all mankind. Since we have free will, we must choose the gift - God's plan of redemption. Many won't choose Him as Lord and Savior thereby condemning themselves to pay the price for their own lifetime of sins, which is forever. You see, justice must be satisfied concerning humankind's wrongdoings. If we don't receive Jesus Christ as our personal Lord and Savior, we will have to personally go and pay the price of sin. It is by God's grace we are saved (Ephesians 2:8). The price of sin has been paid by Jesus. He died on the cross, taking our sins to hell, where He left them, on our behalf. Without Jesus in our life, the price can never be paid otherwise. Those that call on the name of the Lord shall be saved. Don't delay any further, hell's gates are open to sinners. Jesus paid the price so you don't have to.

# *May 4*

# YOU HAVE A CHOICE

*Romans 8:6*

*Now the mind of the flesh [which is sense and reason without the Holy Spirit] is death [death that comprises all the miseries arising from sin, both here and hereafter]. But the mind of the [Holy] Spirit is life and [soul] peace [both now and forever].*

There are two minds the scripture talks about. The mind governed by the flesh is death, but the mind governed by the spirit is life and peace. The way we think, our thought patterns, or our normal way of reasoning is influenced by either our emotions being in charge of our reactions, responses, or what the Bible says we should do in times of trouble. Our imperfect environment can influence us if there's no other influence allowed to have the last say in our decision-making. Once we understand the ways of God, which are above our natural way, we can have an abundant life of peace and comfort. The battleground is in our mind. It is the central system where commands are carried out. Being human, we will act upon either of the two minds we are influenced by: the mind ruled by our flesh (our emotions) or the mind ruled by who God says we are. We have a choice.

# *May 5*

# GOD SAID IT, BELIEVE IT!

*Matthew 6:34*

*So do not worry or be anxious about tomorrow, for tomorrow will have worries and anxieties of its own. Sufficient for each day is its own trouble.*

Worrying about tomorrow is forbidden in the law of faith. Faith believes God has things under control no matter what comes. God's saying to us, do not worry or be anxious about tomorrow. As a child, there's no concern about tomorrow or anything because we know our parents will provide, protect, comfort, and console us anytime needed. Worrying about something in the future is a sure sign of a lack of faith. You can doubt in your mind but not in your heart. So, the Word of God should only come out of your mouth during a crisis or anything out of your control. Find the right scripture for your dilemma and stand on it until victory. Once you've prayed, and the following words out of your mouth are, "I don't know what I'm going to do," you're doubting in your heart, and there's zero power working on your behalf. God said it, believe it!

# *May 6*

# KINGSHIP AT LARGE

*Luke 19:38*

*Crying, blessed (celebrated with praises) is the King Who comes in the name of the Lord! Peace in heaven [freedom there from all the distresses that are experienced as the result of sin] and glory (majesty and splendor) in the highest [heaven]!*

The King who comes in the name of the Lord is King Jesus. He has proven to be the King of kings and Lord of lords (1 Timothy 6:15). We are the other kings of whom He is King. We were adopted into the family because King Jesus was victorious in His Earthly walk, and never committed sin, becoming the perfect sacrificial lamb so we could be forgiven and be seated in heavenly places with Christ Jesus to a royal priesthood position. We are royalty to God and should conduct ourselves as such while we are still here on Earth. The King is blessed forever, and we are with Him because He said so. Walk with the King and be a blessing.

# *May 7*

# THE BOY WHO CRIED WOLF

*John 10:11*

*I am the Good Shepherd. The Good Shepherd risks and lays down
His [own] life for the sheep.*

A true shepherd or overseer will protect and guide that which is
his. The life of Jesus Christ, in us, will bring us to a realization of
His great stewardship over us, His people. He takes care of that which
concerns us and is always ready to help us in a time of need. Just like
sheep in the field, there is always a chance of a wolf coming in to kill,
steal, or destroy our life. The enemy can disguise himself as a sheep
before the kill. Beware of false prophets, which come to you in sheep's
clothing, but inwardly they are ravening wolves (Matthew 7:15). This
message is for anyone dealing with people or a particular person that
you may have an uneasy feeling about in your gut, knowing something
is off about them. It could be a wolf in sheep's clothing out to get you.
Very stealth in their approach, talking the right talk, and seemingly
walking the right walk. But they're still a wolf, whether the person
realizes it or not. From such, turn away for your own survival. Anyone
coming against God's anointed for any reason will answer to God, no
matter who you are, God's not a respecter of persons. Recognize the
wolf and treat Him accordingly.

# May 8

# A MESSAGE FOR WORRIERS

*Proverbs 12:25*

*Anxiety in a man's heart weighs it down, but an encouraging word makes it glad.*

Anxiety and worry are the bad boys of hope. When we are dealing with thoughts that go against the Word of God, it can throw us off course. The Bible says, bring every thought into captivity to the scrutiny of God's Word concerning you (2 Corinthians 10:5). If that thought doesn't line up to what the Bible says about you, then it's from the dark side of influence. As we re-program our thought processes with God's Word, we begin to move into a faith-led lifestyle which doesn't include anxiety. All the "What-ifs" or "Suppose this happens," mentality will be moved back to the forefront of our decision making, because faith doesn't care about tomorrow's troubles. Anxiety weighs down the heart if you let it, but a kind word cheers it up. We must protect and guard our hearts at all costs. Out of the abundance of the heart, the mouth will speak. If we are allowing bad conversations, with drama-folk to be in our lives, then worry, and anxiety aren't far away. What we constantly hear drops down into our hearts, and with much input of whatever we're listening to, you will begin to speak it out of your mouth, good or bad (Matthew 12:34). Through this door anxiety can enter. There are many ways we can be tempted to worry, but it all starts with what's being heard. Hanging around the right people can make a world of difference in our lives concerning not having anxiety and worry.

# *May 9*

# DON'T LOOK BACK

*Isaiah 43:18-19a, NIV*

*Forget the former things; do not dwell on the past. See, I am doing a new thing! Now it springs up; do you not perceive it?*

*I am making a way in the wilderness and streams in the wasteland.*

Many of us wish certain things in the past that we've done, and are not proud of, would just never come back into our thought life. Yes, it happened. Yes, you've screwed up like everyone else in one way or another has. We can't go back and change it, but we can guard against it happening again. Isaiah 43:18-19 speaks more specifically about not dwelling on the former things so you can be in tune with what's to happen now and in the near future. When our minds are caught up on past bad experiences, we can't clearly discern the God-given plans for us that will position us for greatness. Forgetting those things that are behind and start reaching for the high calling of God which is in Christ Jesus for your life (Philippians 3:13-14). There's a plan, destiny, and purpose that you can't afford to fall behind schedule on. As we continue being caught up with the past, our best future is slipping away. Once we confess our wrongdoings to God, and ask forgiveness, that's it! (1 John 1:9). Your sin is in the sea of God's forgetfulness, so stop bringing it up again and again (Micah 7:18-19). You're building a wall of darkness that God has already torn down by the blood of Jesus. Leave your past there, your future demands all of your attention.

# May 10

# HE SAID WHAT?
# BECAUSE YOU'RE YOUNGER?

*1 Timothy 4:12*

*Let no one despise or think less of you because of your youth, but be an example (pattern) for the believers in speech, in conduct, in love, in faith, and in purity.*

If anyone despises you as you fulfill the purpose of God for your life because you're young, then Houston, we have a problem. And the problem isn't yours. It's the person treating you with less respect because of your age. The element of pride is very present in such cases. The Bible encourages older men to come alongside the younger men to help them along the way in their God-given destiny. Things can be done differently than our former leaders that led the way. The world is constantly changing, and the body of Christ must be flexible in this area. No minister or ministry has exclusive knowledge of how the Lord will lead us individually in getting the Gospel out. Without the youth, there is no tomorrow for the next seasons of life to flourish. This is why it's so vital to be able to hear from God for yourself. You don't need to hear that still, small voice to have the conviction to go forth in confidence. You may be the type that has a sense you're doing it the way you're supposed to, your gut feeling. As we become more knowledgeable of God's Word, we develop the boldness of the purpose He has put in us. Go with God and be a blessing; chin up, you got this.

# *May 11*

# THE BOTTOM LINE FOR PEACE

*Romans 5:1*

*Therefore, since we are justified (acquitted, declared righteous, and given a right standing with God) through faith, let us [grasp the fact that we] have [the peace of reconciliation to hold and to enjoy] peace with God through our Lord Jesus Christ (the Messiah, the Anointed One).*

To have peace with God, we must be justified by faith. Accepting the finished work at Calvary gets us justified. Justified could mean; Just-As-If-I'd-Never-Sinned. Our sins have been remitted, not just covered up, but washed away. Having peace with God is knowing you're in right standing with God based on what His Word says about the subject. Your only enemy is condemnation, that feeling of being unworthy. The reality is Jesus took your sins and dropped them off in hell. Everyone would have to go to hell for doing the bad things we've all done. But submitting to the plan of salvation and becoming saved, or born again, takes us out of the kingdom of darkness and transports us into the kingdom of Jesus Christ (Colossians 1:13). This is where God is waiting with open arms to receive you. You have not been justified for approval into God's kingdom until you receive Jesus Christ as Lord and Savior of your life, bottom line. Know God, know peace. No God, no peace.

# May 12

## WE ALL MESS UP, GOD STILL ACCEPTS US

*Psalm 139:23-24*

*Search me [thoroughly], O God, and know my heart! Try me and know my thoughts! And see if there is any wicked or hurtful way in me, and lead me in the way everlasting.*

In the Bible, David told God to search me, know my heart, try me (that means through trials or testing trouble), and know my thoughts. God knows our hearts and the thoughts we think. But are you willing to ask God to do that to you? If you're not hiding anything because we know our faults, why not? Because conviction and condemnation have gripped us so strongly, we shy away from God. David asked God to see if there was any hurtful or wicked way in him, and he said, "lead me in the way everlasting." If you know David, he was messing up left and right, and God still said about him, "He's the apple of my eye" (Psalm 17:8). David had done stuff not cool with God, but he was quick to repent, stop doing wrong the best he could. If you want to do better, ask God if there is anything you need to correct in your life, then do it.

# *May 13*

# NOTHING CAN STAND AGAINST THE POWER OF LOVE

*Philippians 1:9-10. NIV*

*And this is my prayer: that your love may abound more and more in knowledge and depth of insight, so that you may be able to discern what is best and may be pure and blameless for the day of Christ,*

Did you know your love can abound in knowledge and depth of insight? To have a more comprehensive discernment, you will be able to understand where a person is coming from. When walking in the agape love of God, you have the proper discernment to deal with people where they really are concerning their motives or intent (it's like you pick up an extra awareness by loving harder). Our love grows as we love others more and more. To love the unlovable is a true testament to your love level. Anyone can love someone else who shows love to them first. But to love a person through offense, disrespect, or just straight-up nasty, takes patience. Allow love (God) to abound in you, and you won't recognize yourself. Nothing can stand against the power of love.

# May 14

# YOU'RE GONNA SERVE SOMEBODY, OR SOME THING

## Matthew 18:3-5

*And said, Truly I say to you, unless you repent (change, turn about) and become like little children [trusting, lowly, loving, forgiving], you can never enter the kingdom of heaven [at all]. Whoever will humble himself therefore and become like this little child [trusting, lowly, loving, forgiving] is greatest in the kingdom of heaven. And whoever receives and accepts and welcomes one little child like this for My sake and in My name receives and accepts and welcomes Me.*

These are the words of Jesus Christ to His church, Christians. We must humble ourselves and become like little children, trusting, lowly, loving, and forgiving. The person conforming to this way of living is the greatest in the kingdom of heaven (Matthew 18:1-5). That's what Jesus said to His disciples, which applies to us today. Basically, we want to give Satan no place in our life. The devil has a hold on us when we operate in falsehood, pride, not trusting, unforgiveness, and doubt. The rules and laws have been put in place since the beginning. Being human is one thing; who's influencing you is another. We are made to be free to choose who or what we will serve. We may think we are serving one master, but in reality, we're serving another unaware. Invoke your will to serve the kingdom of God.

# *May 15*

# BE STRONG AND COURAGEOUS

*Joshua 1:9*

*Have not I commanded you? Be strong, vigorous, and very courageous. Be not afraid, neither be dismayed, for the Lord your God is with you wherever you go.*

The Lord wouldn't command us to be strong and courageous if we weren't able to, or didn't have the knowledge to do so. His command is based on our understanding of the power we have within us. Being strong in the Lord and the power of His might is our portion as Christians (Ephesians 6:10). We can overcome fear by walking in a greater dimension of the love of God planted in us at the new birth. Perfect love or mature love drives out fear (1 John 4:18). We are in the Lord's army, which indicates being soldiers; battles are always coming. Learning how to fight is vital to our survival and to advance the Kingdom of God on Earth. Our enemy, the devil, searches throughout all the Earth to seek who he can devour. He knows those who are prepared for battle and those who are not. But we have a Champion to follow who already gave the devil a Holy beat down in hell. Learn how our Champion Jesus fought the devil and follow His lead (Matthew 4:1-11). Knowing He lives in us gives us confidence to be strong and courageous.

# *May 16*

# GOD IS GREAT, AND SO ARE YOU

*Psalm 105:1*

*O give thanks unto the Lord, call upon His name, make known His doings among the peoples!*

Part of sharing the Gospel is telling of God's greatness. We were made in His image and likeness, so we can understand how receiving a little praise once in a while is a great encouragement. We were created for God's pleasure, someone for Him to have fellowship with on His level. The angels and all the angelic creatures in heaven were not created in God's image and likeness, we were. We are His handiwork, created to do good works. As we give thanks to the Lord and proclaim His greatness, we unlock blessings from heaven that others won't receive. You may think, I don't feel like I'm in God's image. The job of the evil one on this planet is to keep you feeling, thinking, and believing you're not made in God's image. Although, because of the constant struggles of life we deal with, we're kept at bay concerning using the supernatural help we're born-again with. You can and must break that cycle. God is great, and so are you!

# *May 17*

# DRY PLACES NEED WATERING

*Isaiah 40:3*

*A voice of one who cries: Prepare in the wilderness the way of the Lord [clear away the obstacles]; make straight and smooth in the desert a highway for our God!*

As we live on the Earth, we are to make way for the Gospel to go forth. John the Baptist cried out, announcing the coming of the Messiah and declaring to repent of our sins. That was John the Baptist's calling. Once we know our calling and begin to walk in it, we will follow the great commission to go out into all the world and preach the Gospel (Mark 16:15). Preach to the dry places of the land where people haven't heard of the Gospel of Jesus Christ. Dry places are just lands where the Gospel has not been heard. Every Christian has this commandment from God. We are not of this world as it is now, but we will be once the end comes and God sets up camp after Satan is locked up. For now, go into all the world and share the Gospel with every living creature so the end can come. The Lord needs access to all people; we are the vehicle He uses to get it done.

# *May 18*

# THE ETERNALS

### John 3:16

*For God so greatly loved and dearly prized the world that He [even]
gave up His only begotten (unique) Son, so that whoever believes
in (trusts in, clings to, relies on) Him shall not perish (come to
destruction, be lost) but have eternal (everlasting) life.*

God loved the world so much, He gave His only Son to die for our sins, that whoever believes in Him shall not perish but have eternal life. You will have eternal life once your body dies, but where will you spend eternity? Our human spirits, born again or still dead to God, cannot die. We are eternal beings. God will not destroy His creation of humankind, but there is a place for those not in His family to spend eternity, which is not with God and His family. To perish indicates going to hell, having eternal life (the word life means zoe), and after death is with God. You are a spirit, you have a soul, and you live in a body. Three-part being just like God, Father, Son, and Holy Ghost. Made in His image for fellowship on God's level of existence. Life and death are before you. Choose life with Jesus now! Whosoever believes in Him shall not perish.

# $\mathscr{M}ay$ 19

## WHO IS GOD TO YOU?

*Psalm 18:2*

*The Lord is my Rock, my Fortress, and my Deliverer; my God, my keen and firm Strength in Whom I will trust and take refuge, my Shield, and the Horn of my salvation, my High Tower.*

D avid speaks here on how he has discovered that God is basically seven things to him. He is a Rock. You can count on Him no matter what the circumstances. He won't bail on you. He's our fortress in times of life battles. We have someone to go to who keeps us from harm. He's our deliverer from evil, bad situations, bad people out to get us, etc. He is our strength when our energy has waned because God's strength is made perfect in our weakness (2 Corinthians 12:8-10). The Lord is our shield of protection in the heat of our confrontations and everyday challenges of demonic attacks. He is the horn of our salvation, calling every living soul to repentance and rightful entry into His Kingdom and family. And He is our high tower, the highest form of escape a battle-weary Christian can have. He is above the battles in our life, where we can look down and see our enemies' plans for us before they happen—positioning ourselves in the Lord before the fight is vital. To wait to be prepared for a battle is too late. Be a David; find out for yourself who God is to you. The deeper you seek Him, the more revelation will flow into knowing and trusting Him.

# *May 20*

# YOU AIN'T ALL THAT!
# AND NEITHER AM I

### Matthew 20:28

*Just as the Son of Man came not to be waited on but to serve, and to give His life as a ransom for many [the price paid to set them free].*

That strong sense of entitlement has run rampant in today's society. People expect you to cater to and do for them like their enabling parents have done all their lives. To come from that upbringing, you'd have some serious work to do to even think about helping someone else. We can be products of our environment, but we don't have to be. Living the Christian life requires a selflessness that most want nothing to do with. The benefits of serving will always come back to us. The best remedy for strong self-entitlement is to become a giver. We can humble ourselves under the mighty hand of God (1 Peter 5:6), or eventually, we will be humbled by life showing up. Tribulation is one of the tools used to get us out of our selfish heads. We think, react, and are motivated differently under life's pressure. Lose the silver spoon and get in the dirt.

# May 21

# A LOVE LESSON

*Matthew 22:39*

*And a second is like it: You shall love your neighbor as [you do]*
*yourself.*

Your neighbor is anyone you come into contact with anywhere and everywhere, not just the people living next to you on your street. Love covers a multitude of sins, according to the Bible. We can show love on many levels. Sometimes demonstrating love involves refraining from lashing out at someone who may deserve your wrath, avoiding individuals who consistently irritate you, and practicing patience by being slow to anger and quick to listen. To practice God's commandment of loving your neighbor as yourself, is to walk in His love. Sometimes tough love is necessary. Correcting someone who's dead wrong about something, and you know it's going to hurt their feelings, but you do it anyway; that kind of love can stop something worse from happening to the person. As we love each other God's way, it builds in us a maturity not otherwise obtained. Deny yourself and take up your cross because it's a sacrificial love (Matthew 16:24-26). There is no law that can come against you when you're living in the agape love of God.

# May 22

# COME BOLDLY WITH CONFIDENCE

*Hebrews 4:16*

*Let us then fearlessly and confidently and boldly draw near to the throne of grace (the throne of God's unmerited favor to us sinners), that we may receive mercy [for our failures] and find grace to help in good time for every need [appropriate help and well-timed help, coming just when we need it].*

Coming boldly to the throne of God speaks volumes about your fellowship with Him. If you're dealing with condemnation or feeling convicted about something, it's not as easy to seek God for help, yet alone boldly. Mercy awaits those who come no matter what you've done wrong. He knows we miss the mark from time to time so there's a way of escape always available to us when going to God (1 Corinthians 10:13). He's our Father in heaven ready to receive us at all times. We are more than conquerors in Christ (Romans 8:37) but we need a little help on occasion. Come to Him fearlessly, confidently, and boldly draw near to the throne of God in prayer.

# *May 23*

# THE LAW OF GOD

*Psalm 19:7*

*The law of the Lord is perfect, restoring the [whole] person; the testimony of the Lord is sure, making wise.*

The decrees of the Lord are trustworthy. We can always count on what God has decreed will come to pass. His utterances make the simple wise. Down to Earth, common folk of mild understanding become wise. The instructions of the Lord are perfect, totally in tune with the knowledge of the struggles of life. Jesus came down from heaven clothed in flesh to experience what we have experienced in this fallen state the world's in. He was giving God the Father a closer look and understanding of how sin has affected His creation, man, and woman. So now God's dispensation of grace has been upon us since Jesus died and was raised from the dead. Man will never reach His maximum potential without the input of God's instructions (the Bible, basic instructions before leaving Earth). Be all you can be in the army of the Lord.

# *May 24*

## STAY SALTY FOR JESUS MY FRIENDS

### 1 Peter 3:15

*But in your hearts set Christ apart as holy [and acknowledge Him] as Lord. Always be ready to give a logical defense to anyone who asks you to account for the hope that is in you, but do it courteously and respectfully.*

If someone asks about your hope as a Believer, always be ready to explain it. Shying away from your hope as a believer is like denying Jesus (Matthew 10:33). Our faith is built on the rock - Jesus. When we do not have a solid answer when asked about our hope as a Believer it speaks to our maturity in Christ, or lack of knowledge of who we're supposed to be. When we give a personal word to someone, by way of witnessing, it could be the word they need to prevent unnecessary trouble in their life or even their demise. The Christian Believer should have a ready word in their mouth, in season or out of season (2 Timothy 4:2). Always be ready and prayed up. We are the salt of the Earth (Matthew 5:13), but when we have lost our salt content we are useless in helping others or God's Kingdom. Stay salty for Jesus my friends.

# *May 25*

# THE BLESSING OF ANSWERED PRAYER

*1 John 5:14*

*And this is the confidence (the assurance, the privilege of boldness) which we have in Him: [we are sure] that if we ask anything (make any request) according to His will (in agreement with His own plan), He listens to and hears us.*

When we ask God for help, or anything, He hears us if we are asking according to His will. He will not answer a prayer asking to have another person's spouse. He will not answer your prayer if you ask Him to anoint you to rob a bank. Sounds funny, and ridiculous, but some folks ask outside of God's will with similar requests. You must know your Bible to get the results you desire. Angels listen to the voice of God. When we speak the Word of God with faith and true belief, the angels and demons can't tell it's not God speaking and they will react as such. Demons flee at the name of Jesus on the lips of a believing Christian. To wield the name of Jesus in power, you must have a knowledge of God's Word, the Bible. Ask God for anything according to His will, and you will have it in the season He has determined for you to have it. It is when we doubt and or don't wait in patience for it to manifest, that's when we miss God and the blessing of answered prayer.

# *May 26*

# WATCH YOUR MOUTH!

### *Luke 6:38*

*Give, and [gifts] will be given to you; good measure, pressed down, shaken together, and running over, will they pour into [the pouch formed by] the bosom [of your robe and used as a bag]. For with the measure you deal out [with the measure you use when you confer benefits on others], it will be measured*

The law of reciprocity has always been around. Seed, time, and harvest, the what goes around comes around idea, has always been a thing. As we give, it shall be given again unto us; good measure pressed down, shaken together, and running over shall men give to you. How and what you give out determines how and what you'll get back. You give out a lot of money, and a lot of money will come back. You give out a little love to others, and a little love comes back. You stir up trouble and sow discord amongst others, and that's coming back to you sooner or later. Many times, we're not mindful that we're sowing a dirty seed somewhere, and then we wonder, why is this bad thing happening to me. Infliction is a thing, too. We are accountable for every word coming out of our mouths, and will receive judgment for it as well. We will reap whatever we sow. So, sow words of light, not darkness; sow seeds of love and peace towards others as much as you can.

GIORON T. WILKINS, SR.

# May 27

# THE TEMPLE OF GOD

*1 Corinthians 3:16*

*Do you not discern and understand that you [the whole church at Corinth] are God's temple (His sanctuary), and that God's Spirit has His permanent dwelling in you [to be at home in you, collectively as a church and also individually]?*

We are the temple of God. In biblical days, after Jesus' death, burial, and ascension, it became possible for God to live in our newly, recreated human spirits. After the remission of our sin, He could take up His abode in us (Galatians 2:20). It's all spiritual, so don't try to figure it out with your natural mind; it's supernatural. We live, move, and have our being in Him and He in us. Once we've developed our relationship and close fellowship with God, we become more aware He's in us. Since our bodies are the temple of the living God (1 Corinthians 6:19-20), we should want to keep them in order by eating right, exercising, etc. He lives in us by His Spirit, and He's our Comforter, Helper, and Strengthener. Be that temple.

# *May 28*

# The Two We Need Everyday

*Psalm 23:6*

*Surely or only goodness, mercy, and unfailing love shall follow me all the days of my life, and through the length of my days the house of the Lord [and His presence] shall be my dwelling place.*

David speaks here on goodness and mercy. They (goodness and mercy) should be following you all the days of your life. God has promised it in His Word. As the Believer lines up with the words of God for their life, these two will follow them everyday. We can repel goodness and mercy by our actions and bad motives. Everything coming from God is based on our participation with His way of life. There is always His mercy that can scoop us up when we mess up. Our flesh has not been redeemed, only our human spirit. We are redeemed by the blood of the Lamb but our minds are not (Ephesians 1:7). It is vital we renew our minds, change our old way of thinking to how God thinks. It is obtainable through His Word, the Bible. As we follow our God-given purpose, goodness and mercy shall follow us all the days of our life, God will be more attentive to His plan being carried out by us, and protective of it being completed.

# *May 29*

# A SHOW OF HUMILITY

*James 3:13*

*Who is there among you who is wise and intelligent? Then let him by his noble living show forth his [good] works with the [unobtrusive] humility [which is the proper attribute] of true wisdom.*

Some of us are wise in the understanding of God's ways, and we should be demonstrating it with unobtrusive humility which is the proper attribute of true wisdom. For those of us who wear it proudly, you're not alone in this battle. The humility keeps us on track from the distractions that would lure us otherwise in the wrong direction. This world has so many distractions, temptations, and deceptions that it's almost impossible to follow the straight and narrow of your calling without humility's hand holding you in place (Matthew 7:13-14). Our good works are shown by living in a noble way before God. As we are closer than ever to Christ's return, the evil is ramping up in the world. We have to live smarter, wiser, cunning as wolves but harmless as a dove (Matthew 10:16). Evil has been an opposing force for a long time and can only be defeated the way Jesus did it - working God's Word (Matthew 4:4). He left His deity in heaven, so He won over evil using the word of God only. We can do the same, God expects that from us to win in life.

# May 30

# GET OFF YOUR HIGH HORSES

*Micah 6:8*

*He has showed you, O man, what is good. And what does the Lord require of you but to do justly, and to love kindness and mercy, and to humble yourself and walk humbly with your God?*

To act justly means to walk uprightly with the teachings and precepts of the Lord in mind. We always have a choice as to how we want to present ourselves. There's only one chance for a first impression. Your witness to others can make them or break them in some cases. Some people look up to you, and you'd want them to learn better about how you can be. Fake it, till you faith it. We always start dry in our unwanted tasks, but after some time, we get into it, knowing it's the Lord's will concerning us. There's always a deep-down desire to please God in our hearts. Life's struggles and issues are just always squashing it. To love mercy, we must be Christ inside-minded. The Lord was merciful towards us when we were His enemies. We can let some things go and not yield to the temptation of going off on somebody. Show mercy, and mercy will be shown back to you. Walking humbly is related to showing mercy. You can only have one with the other. It is the meek that shall inherit the kingdom of God. Today's encouragement is to get off our high horse of pride and get on the train of humility that leads to victorious living.

# *May 31*

# THE LOVE COMMAND

*John 13:34*

*I give you a new commandment: that you should love one another.*
*Just as I have loved you, so you too should love one another.*

Most people have heard of the ten commandments in the Bible. But Jesus said, "I give you a new commandment that you love one another as I have loved you." This new commandment fulfills the purpose of the ten commandments. If everyone loved one another, there would be no killing, lying, stealing, committing adultery, etc. This world would be a much better place if everyone would at least try to love each other. There is an evil in this world that would have everyone hate each other. As Christians, we're supposed to be the salt of the Earth and demonstrating the love of God, especially to that evil person we don't like. To walk in love can be a sacrifice, but the benefits you reap will outweigh the sacrifice of love you gave.

# *June 1*

# WHY ARE YOU AFRAID?

*Psalm 56:3*

*What time I am afraid, I will have confidence in and put my trust and reliance in You.*

Being afraid is common for us; getting rid of it isn't. Fear is a spirit to be dealt with by the blood of Jesus in the name of Jesus. It comes from Satan and his evil spirits. If the enemy can get and keep you afraid, you become useless to do anything of great value. Fear is a crippling force with a purpose to put people in bondage. When people are in bondage, they can't be effective in life. The answer to our deliverance is in trusting the Lord. God is love, and we are His children capable of removing fear out of our lives. Perfect, or mature love, drives out fear from the human heart, mind, and soul. We are equipped to fight and win over being afraid. The degree to which we walk in love with others will be to the degree of potency to come against fear in our lives. Love is the key that unlocks many doors of victory against the evil in this world because God is love, and we are His children with His love in us. When you are afraid, go to the scriptures and rightly divide the Word of truth for your situation and confess it out of your mouth with force. Fear will back down to the faith-believing, trusting child of God.

# *June 2*

# IS THE LORD YOUR SHEPHERD?

*Psalm 23:1-2*

*The Lord is my Shepherd [to feed, guide, and shield me], I shall not lack. He makes me lie down in [fresh, tender] green pastures; He leads me beside the still and restful waters.*

This verse is well-known by many. It is David declaring that God will take care of him and supply all his needs. The shepherds that watch over sheep are to feed, guide, and protect them. This is what the Lord does for His sheep, and sheep (Christians) know His voice and will respond to Him and Him only. The voice of a stranger they will not follow. We must learn to hear the Lord's voice to distinguish His guidance from all the other voices in this world. He leads us beside the still waters, which indicates peaceful surroundings.

The Lord is also our strength and our shield. When the wolves come (trials, crisis, trouble), He has already made a way of escape. As we live, move, and have our being in Christ Jesus, we find that place of refuge, comfort, and restful peace. We become confident in knowing we are under His umbrella of protection. When sheep go astray from the fold, we can more easily fall into diverse temptations. There is less guidance and protection once we go off the beaten path of the Lord's designated pasture we're supposed to be in. The Lord is our Shepherd; let Him lead the way.

# *June 3*

# THE LAW OF GOD

*Psalm 19:7*

*The law of the Lord is perfect, restoring the [whole] person; the testimony of the Lord is sure, making wise the simple.*

The decrees of the Lord are trustworthy. We can always count on what God has decreed coming to pass. His utterances make the simple wise. Down to Earth, common sense folk of mild understanding become wise, wisdom conscious from God's decrees. The instructions of the Lord are perfect, totally in tune with the knowledge of the struggles of life. Jesus came down from heaven clothed in the flesh to experience what we have experienced in this fallen state of existence the world's in. He showed us God the Father, allowing us to better understand how sin has affected His creation. So now God's dispensation of grace has been upon us since Jesus died and raised from the dead. Humans will never reach His maximum potential without the input of God's instructions (the Bible, basic instructions before leaving Earth). Be all you can be in the army of the Lord.

# June 4

# NO ORDINARY LOVE

*1 Corinthians 13:4*
*Love endures long and is patient and kind; love never is
envious nor boils over with jealousy, is not boastful or vainglorious,
does not display itself haughtily.*

When we say, "I love you," that doesn't mean we love like God. Many people love with a motive behind it. Some people say they love you, but don't love themselves at all, how can they love anybody correctly. The original love of God, agape, has been devilishly perverted, and so dumbed down to the flesh level of wanting to get and not give. The love of God is a sacrificial love, that does not look for something in return. It believes the best of every person, not easy. It trusts, hopes, and is patient and kind. The love of God is also intelligent, in that, God knows when you're not right, but will wait and still give you a chance to straighten out. Next time you say you love somebody, think about it, do you?

# June 5

# LOVE IS NOT ONE WORD FITS ALL

## 1 John 3:16

*By this we come to know (progressively to recognize, to perceive, to understand) the [essential] love: that He laid down His [own] life for us; and we ought to lay [our] lives down for [those who are our] brothers [in Him].*

The word *love* in the English language has different meanings. We love our spouses, but we may love ice cream. We love doing a certain task, or we love the summertime. It sounds more like we use this word love in place of anything we desire, crave, and even lust after. The *agape* love of God is a sacrificial love, showing a deep desire, and craving for walking in the commandments of the Lord. It is a giving love, not a selfish love (1 Corinthians 13:4-8). There are four descriptions of the word love in the Bible. *Storge*, which is an empathy bond. *Philia,* which is a friend bond. *Eros,* which is a romantic bond. Then, *Agape,* which is an unconditional "God" love. The love we, Christians, are to exemplify in our everyday lives is *agape* love. We are to show this love to our brothers and sisters in Christ especially (1 Peter 1:22). Jesus is the love God gave the world because He loved it so much.

# *June 6*

# THE SECRET PLACE

*Psalm 59:16*

*But I will sing of Your mighty strength and power; yes, I will sing aloud of Your mercy and loving-kindness in the morning; for You have been to me a defense (a fortress and a high tower) and a refuge in the day of my distress.*

Even though David was always getting into trouble, God saw him as the apple of His eye (Psalm 17:8). But David knew from experience that God is a Defender and a safe place when trouble came, even if self-inflicted. No matter what we get ourselves into, God has our backs. Don't let negative thoughts dominate you. God is always able, willing, and ready to help us with all of life's struggles, disappointments, and crises (Matthew 11:28-30). We have not because we ask not. It all depends on our relationship with God. How close are you to Him? Once we've obtained that close fellowship with Him, there's more favor and grace because then you're in the inner circle of His awareness, that secret place of the Most-High God where the darkness of this world cannot penetrate (Psalm 91:1-2).

# *June 7*

# YOUR WAY, OR GOD'S WAY?
# COME UP HIGHER

### Romans 15:13

*May the God of your hope so fill you with all joy and peace in believing [through the experience of your faith] that by the power of the Holy Spirit you may abound and be overflowing (bubbling over) with hope.*

Trusting Him is the answer to it all when it comes to the Lord. We can't see Him with our physical eyes, so it's a belief without seeing. We are in a world of tangible, visual, hands-on environment from birth till death. Faith, which is believing without seeing, seems too scary for some people. To trust someone you've never met in person physically isn't the norm unless God is in it. Joy and peace are two by-products of fellowship with God. Things go better with God in the mix. The problem is that most people don't know how to put Him in the mix. The only way is through the Lord Jesus Christ. He connects the dots between humankind and God. He's the Mediator, our Attorney who stands up for us when we get into trouble (1 Timothy 2:5). The way has been made for humankind, so there's no excuse not to do well in this life. Seek and you shall find, knock, and the door will be opened (Matthew 7:6). God will never force us to do anything; that's Satan's plot, to force you. Joy and peace are attainable if you really want them. Come up higher.

# *June 8*

# A HARD WORD

*1 John 2:6*

*Whoever says he abides in Him ought [as a personal debt] to walk and conduct himself in the same way in which He walked and conducted Himself.*

Those who live in God should live like Jesus. If we're saying we abide in Him, we ought (as a personal debt) to walk and conduct ourselves like Jesus did. Putting our money where our mouth is can be challenging. When it comes to walking in a manner pleasing to God, it takes self-discipline, long-suffering, and the ability to wield the Word of God. Having an understanding of God's Word gives an advantage to you in times of attack from the enemy. Knowing your authority in Christ Jesus is a must to advance to the abundant life God already promised (John 10:10), but it's not just going to fall into our lap. To live for Christ makes you a target of Satan. If you're a closet-type Christian (no one knows you are one), the devil doesn't pay you any mind. You are not a threat to him being a weak Christian. Those who want to be in the number of the marching saints of God's army are mature and crisis-tested, ready for a fight at any moment. To live like Jesus, is first to know Him. *"Meditate in this book of the law day and night, and you'll make your own way prosperous" (Joshua 1:8).* The Kingdom of God demands your allegiance for effective service to God and victorious living through all life battles.

# *June 9*

# CAN YOU DENY YOURSELF?

*Matthew 16:24-26, NIV*

*Then Jesus said to his disciples, "Whoever wants to be my disciple must deny themselves and take up their cross and follow me. For whoever wants to save their life will lose it, but whoever loses their life for me will find it. What good will it be for someone to gain the whole world, yet forfeit their soul? Or what can anyone give in exchange for their soul?"*

Jesus is laying down some very important guidelines for discipleship. Discipleship usually comes down to whether you want to do the work of keeping your flesh down or not. Having our own will isn't for doing anything we want to, or having anything we want all the time. Our will is to be invoked when our bodies don't feel like moving or doing what's right. Bringing into subjection every thought that comes into your mind, under the scrutiny of God's Word, is the beginning of discipleship (2 Corinthians 10:5). Renewing of our minds means using the Word of God, so we can begin to think and act like God (Romans 12:2). He's our Father and we are made in His image and likeness. Jesus said whoever (it's optional) wants to be His disciple. However, it is strongly recommended for victorious living, and service to the Lord. There are Christians who are saved, living however they want to, not following God's plan for their life, and living a mediocre life compared to what their full potential could bring them. Deny yourself and gain the Kingdom, not this world.

# *June 10*

# THE SCRIPTURES
# GIVE US HOPE

*Romans 15:4*

*For whatever was thus written in former days was written for our instruction, that by [our steadfast and patient] endurance and the encouragement [drawn] from the Scriptures we might hold fast to and cherish hope.*

There is a plan with full instructions on how to work God's Word (the Bible) in our everyday lives for victorious living. We are subject to our environment without the Word of God working in our lives, which will limit our potential. There is another lifestyle available for a better life. This lifestyle does not include negative people or people with ways that can lead you to your demise. Everything in this lifestyle is driven by love, peace, patience, kindness, self-control, and other God-like characteristics necessary for the abundant life God promises in the Bible, His Word. There will always be a cost for anything of great value and worth. With all the distractions, mayhem, confusion, fear, and evil in this world, we're starting from a downhill position in life to maneuver through these demonic forces that control the world's system. Even if you've learned how to survive in this world, God's way of living is so much more available.

# *June 11*

# PERFECT PEACE, DOES IT EXIST?

*Isaiah 26:3*

*You will guard him and keep him in perfect and constant peace whose mind [both its inclination and its character] is stayed on You, because he commits himself to You, leans on You, and hopes confidently in You.*

Our minds become steadfast because we trust in Him. He's the anchor of our souls and the stability of our minds. Trust is the key that opens the storehouse of God's provisions for His people. The inclinations and character of our minds must be glued to God and His ways (Romans 12:2). Every action starts with a thought first. Starve the negative thoughts by not yielding to them (2 Corinthians 10:5). Do not speak them out of your mouth because that is where the power of confession is released (Romans 10:17). Feed your faith by reading and hearing over and over the Word of God. The seed of peace has been planted in our newly recreated human spirits at the new birth, but being a seed means it must grow. It grows by being watered. It's watered by spending more and more time with the Prince of Peace, Jesus Christ our Lord. Peace cannot thrive without trust. Perfect peace is mature peace, the kind that passes all understanding. Give the Prince of Peace a place in your life, and you'll be glad you did.

# *June 12*

# SHOW YOUR LOVE, OBEY

*John 14:21*

*The person who has My commands and keeps them is the one who [really] loves Me; and whoever [really] loves Me will be loved by My Father, and I [too] will love him and will show (reveal, manifest) Myself to him. [I will let Myself be clearly seen by him and make Myself real to him.]*

Jesus speaks in today's text follow His commands. Our children obey our commands as parents for two basic reasons. One, they know you'll punish them for not obeying. Two, the child obeys out of genuine love for the parent. God's looking for the child who obeys His commandments. His commandments are for our own safety. There are laws in place, natural, and spiritual. Learning the laws and rules first and then obeying them is what God expects. We can't escape trouble or bad situations, so living above them is the way of the Lord, but we'll need to equip ourself for this journey we are all on together. Sometimes it's finding out what not to do in life that helps keep us safe.

# *June 13*

# THE LOST APPETITE

*Matthew 4:4*

*But He replied, It has been written, Man shall not live and be upheld and sustained by bread alone, but by every word that comes forth from the mouth of God.*

Jesus told the devil, in Jesus' time of trial and testing, that man shall not live by bread alone but on every word that comes from the mouth of God. We are natural and spiritual beings. We need physical food and spiritual food. The word of God is our spiritual food, which Jesus was referring to. We can't live by natural food alone. It would keep us on a lower level of existence in life. We get leadings and future insights into our path in life from our human spirits, which get downloads from God. When you're spiritually starving, you'll be led by your lower nature, animal-like, unleashed emotions. When you say, "I had a feeling I should have done that," that's the God-download trying to help you with the future. Spiritual food makes that download from God plainer to see and act on.

# *June 14*

# WITH ALL YOUR HEART

*Proverbs 3:5-6*

*Lean on, trust in, and be confident in the Lord with
all your heart and mind and do not rely on your own
insight or understanding. In all your ways know,
recognize, and acknowledge Him, and He will direct and make
straight and plain your paths.*

Once we put our hearts into trusting God, not just mentally assenting, but becoming a doer of the word of God (James 1:22-25), we leave this natural lower level of life's experiences. We can live a supernaturally motivated lifestyle designed by God for each of us according to our make-up. You have to let it all go. How you've always thought or acted must be changed to conform to a lifestyle of faith in God. The more we study to show ourselves approved (people who are not ashamed), rightly dividing the Word of truth in our everyday affairs, the more we will see this becoming a reality in our lives. Trust can be hard to come by, even with Almighty God. It's not easy to always trust people we can see, let alone the invisible. That's why we choose to trust the Bible as the truth, which is called faith. Believing without seeing comes from hearing something repeatedly (Romans 10:17). You will develop faith in a thing told to you relentlessly. Faith comes by hearing and hearing the Word of God. With all your heart is the key.

# June 15

# KINDNESS, DO YOU HAVE ANY?

*Ephesians 4:32*
*And become useful and helpful and kind to one another,*
*tenderhearted (compassionate, understanding, loving-hearted),*
*forgiving one another [readily and freely], as God in Christ forgave*
*you.*

To be compassionate, understanding, and loving-hearted is the kindness the Lord expects from us as Christians. It can be an uphill battle for some of us to do this. Since the Lord has said we can do all things through Christ (Philippians 4:19), it's simply invoking your will to follow God's plan. Forgiveness plays a big part in this. If you have unforgiveness in your heart, showing kindness will not be easy. Unforgiveness, being a dirty weed in your life, can block you from doing things God's way, out of love. Low love-levels in your life mean a low chance of being kind to others. Even though the person who hurt you was wrong, when you forgive them anyway, you become a magnet for God's blessings in your life because now you're acting like your Savior, Jesus Christ, who forgave you when you were His enemy. Because of sin, we were all His enemy before becoming Christian (Romans 5:10). Be kind and compassionate. Someone being kind and compassionate to you is an excellent seed to sow.

# *June 16*

# AGAPE LOVE 101

*Galatians 5:14*

*For the whole Law [concerning human relationships] is complied with in the one precept, You shall love your neighbor as [you do] yourself.*

If we all would love our neighbor as we love ourselves, this world would be unrecognizable from its present state. Love does no wrong and is the bed where the fruit of the newly recreated human spirit lies. You can't have full joy without love undergirding it. The Bible says the joy of the Lord is our strength. God is love, and we are children of a loving God. Love strengthens the foundation of joy so it can have the fullness of expression in a person. Loving yourself first is most important. You can't give what you don't have. The act of showing love can be expressed in many ways. Showing love can be not going off on someone who may deserve a good reprimanding. Showing love can be a kind word to someone really down in life. Sacrificial love could be going the extra mile in helping someone you don't know. Practicing walking in patience, kindness, humility, and self-control regularly gets you to loving your neighbor as yourself.

# *June 17*

# THE WAYMAKER HAS MADE A WAY

*Romans 6:23*

*For the wages which sin pays is death, but the [bountiful] free gift of God is eternal life through (in union with) Jesus Christ our Lord.*

When sin has matured in a person, eventually death is the outcome, according to the Bible (James 1:15). Since the fall of man, we have been dying because of sin, and the sinful nature in man's bloodline has been passed down throughout the ages. Jesus broke that sin bloodline at Calvary, but we have a part to play to not get caught up in the wrongdoings that are out there. Your body and mind have not changed at the new birth, only your human spirit. We must renew our minds with God's Word so we'll be able to live above the sin in the world (Romans 12:2). The free gift of God is eternal life; if you refuse it, that's on you.

# *June 18*

# WITHOUT JESUS WE ARE LOST, ETERNALLY DAMNED

*1 John 4:9*

*In this the love of God was made manifest (displayed) where we are concerned: in that God sent His Son, the only begotten or unique [Son], into the world so that we might live through Him.*

We live like Jesus by following His Earth walk. If you read the first four chapters of the New Testament, you'll have a very good idea of how Jesus lived. We are encouraged and even commanded to follow Jesus as Christians. He's the Alpha and Omega, the Author and Finisher of our faith. He walked by faith and used the Word of God in His everyday life to be victorious over evil (Matthew 4:3-4, NLT). God the Father sent Jesus into the world to collect data on how His creation (mankind) dealt with life's struggles. That's the light talk of His coming. Ultimately, Jesus came to destroy the works of the devil so men and women could be freed from the sinful nature holding us in bondage to habitual wrongdoings (1 John 3:8). God's love for us wouldn't allow mankind's mistake in the Garden, (whereas they were disobedient to God's guidelines, and command), without Him doing something about it. God so loved the world that He gave His only begotten Son to become a sacrifice to satisfy justice (John 3:16).

# June 19

# THE TESTING ROOM FOR BUILDING FAITH

*Romans 8:28*

*We are assured and know that [God being a partner in their labor]
all things work together and are [fitting into a plan] for good
to and for those who love God and are called according to [His]
design and purpose.*

Since we are called according to His purpose and answer God's call, He's there every step of the way to help. When we love the Lord, there's an obedience that goes with it to His commandments. We love the Lord by obeying His wishes. He only wants good for us and works through all the vicissitudes of life for our good. In prayer, all things work together for our good because God also answers our prayers. God is on the scene of our lives on two levels of existence to do good. So, when you're in the next crisis of your life, know that you are simply in the testing room of building faith. Without faith, it is impossible to please God (Hebrews 11:6). All answers to prayer come by faith. You trust things will work out even though everything looks like you're going down for the count. It's just the first round of the fight. Trust every word of God to be true and act on it like your life depends on it because, bottom line, it does.

# *June 20*

# MY GOODNESS!

*1 Chronicles 16:34*

*O give thanks to the Lord, for He is good; for His mercy and loving-kindness endure forever!*

O h, taste and see that the Lord is good. Some people must have issues with their taste buds because once you know the goodness of the Lord, it should be a lock on your faith and confidence. We should give thanks to Him because of His goodness. His goodness sent Jesus to die on the cross in your stead for your sins. His goodness isn't always recognized because some of us live a more privileged lifestyle. It's harder to see that which you always have as a blessing, you haven't known lack in that area of life. Then there are those of us who recognize God's goodness more so because we've seen God supply a dire need when there was no way out (1 Corinthians 10:13). That kind of faith in God pulls the goodness of God from Him at the right time, in the right way. Give Him a chance to show His goodness to you no matter what your lifestyle. Give Him thanks for it, and He'll keep blessing you, for He is good.

# June 21

# HOW TO BRING DAD BACK TO THE HOUSEHOLD

*Malachi 4:6*

*And he shall turn and reconcile the hearts of the [estranged] fathers to the [ungodly] children, and the hearts of the [rebellious] children to [the piety of] their fathers [a reconciliation produced by repentance of the ungodly], lest I come and smite the land with a curse and a ban of utter destruction.*

There is hope for that Father who has, for whatever reason, left his position as prophet and priest of his household. God will bring those dads home, but you have a diligent part to play. First, if you want him back home, much prayer is required. The father's will is involved, so God has to work through that. But your constant prayers to God give the Lord something to work with. So, time being the great equalizer, through faith and patience, we obtain the promises. Because of our will, God can't override it. Your children will come back to you with this same process of praying, believing, and waiting with a confident, favorable expectation, thanking God while you wait for the return of your loved ones. It is the Lord's pleasure to bring Dads and your children home, so do the work it takes and use your faith. Hang a sign on a wall in your house saying, welcome home Dad, before he arrives. That's your faith in action.

# *June 22*

# THE STRAIGHT AND NARROW

*Matthew 7:13-14*

*Enter through the narrow gate; for wide is the gate and spacious and broad is the way that leads away to destruction, and many are those who are entering through it.*

*But the gate is narrow (contracted by pressure) and the way is straitened and compressed that leads away to life, and few are those who find it.*

It is not easy to follow, the straight and narrow path of God. Being too far away from the straight and narrow path, you could end up somewhere you don't want to be after your body dies. Walking the straight and narrow path means you have invoked your will in making yourself follow God. No one enjoys the work of keeping our emotions out of the way to live the lifestyle of Jesus. But in the end you've proved to God and the devil you're with God. Being with the Lord is being in His family and a guaranteed spot in heaven. You have to show your love for God down here on Earth now, with all the distractions and the very present evil in this world designed to keep your thoughts and actions away from God. So you must invoke your will to choose God. Once you've made the choice for God, go after it like a bulldog on a bone, never giving up! Don't take the wide gate into destruction, the straight and narrow gate is possible for all.

# June 23

# DID YOU MESS UP THIS WEEK?

### John 1:29

*The next day John saw Jesus coming to him and said, Look! There is the Lamb of God, who takes away the sin of the world!*

Jesus was referred to as the Lamb of God in the Bible. He took away the sins of the world. But why are we still doing wrong? The sin nature is still in our bodies, so the appetite for sin is still there (Romans 7:19-25). Our human spirit, on the other hand, has been recreated into a brand-new man, or woman. Through the Lamb of God, our Lord Jesus Christ, our sins have been forgiven. Our souls, our mind, have not been touched through the new birth of our human spirit. Here's where the work begins, we are to renew our minds with the Word of God (Romans 12:2). Begin to put into action the knowledge we obtain by reading and meditating on the Bible. Once we are born again, there should no longer be habitual sin in our lives. We all miss the mark now and then, but the idea is to try to live a life of honor and integrity without yielding to the temptation of wanting to do wrong. God helps us stay clean if we want to be. When we miss the mark, we ask for forgiveness and keep it moving.

# *June 24*

# POWER OF RECONCILIATION

*2 Corinthians 5:18*

*But all things are from God, who through Jesus Christ reconciled us to Himself [received us into favor, brought us into harmony with Himself] and gave to us the ministry of reconciliation [that by word and deed we might aim to bring others into harmony with Him].*

We have the ministry of reconciliation. We are commissioned to go out and spread the Gospel's good news. We must aim to bring others into harmony with Him by word and deeds. We are part of the body of Christ. Jesus, being the head of the body, had completed His part when He walked the Earth. Now, it's our turn to implement the reconciliation plan. Winning souls for the Lord is the highest priority in the Kingdom of God. It is the "greater works" Jesus said we'd do after His departure back to heaven (John 14:12). People getting healed of sickness and disease is big, but bringing someone to the one that heals is bigger. The price has been paid for us to spend eternity with the family of God instead of burning in hell with Satan and his crew. Justice must be satisfied because of our wrongdoings. Jesus satisfied justice on the cross for anyone who reaches out for salvation. Jesus is the way, the truth, and the life. God has reconciled us back to Himself, but without asking Jesus to save you, your final destiny will be paying for your sins in hell forever. Now that you are saved, introduce the power of reconciliation to someone else today.

# June 25

# THE BIG THREE

*1 Corinthians 13:13*

*And so faith, hope, love abide [faith—conviction and belief respecting man's relation to God and divine things; hope—joyful and confident expectation of eternal salvation; love—true affection for God and man, growing out of God's love for and in us], these three; but the greatest of these is love.*

Faith, hope and love, but the greatest of these is love. These are attributes of the Christian character. What you do with them once you are saved will determine whether or not these three are evident in your life. Everything in life is supposed to be in a growing state. There's seed, time, and then harvest for the growth of living things. But our development in Christ should be as such. God is love, so it is the greatest of all three. Faith works by love, and faith is the title deed of things we hope for. It is the proof of things not yet seen (Hebrews 11:1). That is why faith is so important in the kingdom of God, and for us on Earth in order to prosper. Without faith, it is impossible to please God, and without hope there is nowhere for faith to go, and without love everything we do in life will be limited.

# *June 26*

# COULD THIS BE YOU?

*Colossians 3:12*

*Clothe yourselves therefore, as God's own chosen ones (His own picked representatives), [who are] purified and holy and well-beloved [by God Himself, by putting on behavior marked by] tenderhearted pity and mercy, kind feeling, a lowly opinion of yourselves, gentle ways, [and] patience [which is tireless and long-suffering, and has the power to endure whatever comes, with good temper].*

Some of us may look at this scripture and say, who is he talking about? We are purified and Holy and well-beloved by God Himself. Most people do not see themselves as such. As our behavior becomes marked by tender-hearted pity and mercy, kindness, and we have a lowly opinion of ourselves, gentle ways about us, and patience, we begin to line up with God's Words of this text today concerning us. It is how He sees us even when we're still growing in grace. These Godly qualities are transferred in us at the new birth when we become Christians. It's our job to allow the fruit of your newly recreated human spirit to develop (Galatians 5:22-23). God says in His Word, *"Be ye holy for I Am holy"* (Leviticus 11:44). Most of us don't want to do the work it takes to get there, and that's between us and God.

# *June 27*

# POWER HAS A PURPOSE, NOT FOR PERSONAL GLORY

## *Acts 1:8*

*But you shall receive power (ability, efficiency, and might) when the Holy Spirit has come upon you, and you shall be My witnesses in Jerusalem and all Judea and Samaria and to the ends (the very bounds) of the Earth.*

In the Old Testament, the Spirit of God would come upon His people, whereas today, His Spirit lives in born-again Christians. The finished work of Jesus at Calvary has made it possible for God to live in the heart of the newly recreated human spirit of humankind. This power of God emanates from within us as opposed to an outward leading and anointing from God. Each time the Lord needed to communicate with His people back in the Old Testament, He had to allow the Spirit of God to come upon them, but today, He speaks to us from our insides, our human spirit, where God lives in us by faith. This power in today's text is for ability, efficiency, and might in witnessing to people about the Gospel of the Lord Jesus Christ. Our job of reconciliation is ongoing and never-ending while still on planet Earth. We must cultivate hearing God's still, small voice from deep down in us. We must often block out the noise from around us to hear clearly. On-going quality time with the Lord is necessary to hear His voice in you. Be His witness and make Him proud.

# *June 28*

# THE LOVE MOTIVE

## *John 13:35*

*By this shall all [men] know that you are My disciples, if you love one another [if you keep on showing love among yourselves].*

The worst display Christians could exemplify in their walk with God is to lose it in front of non-Christians. People of this world are always looking for hope out of their mess. We are the hope of the world as we follow Christ and His way of life. It is vitally essential for the Lord's disciples to show the love of God at all times, if possible. We're not perfect and won't be until the return of Christ, but for now, our thoughts should at least line up with the idea of trying to live at peace with everyone (Romans 12:18). As we love one another, the love of God will mature in us. It's an invoking of the will of man (based on the Word of God) to ensure this coming to light. Maturing in Christ is maturing in love because God is love, and we are His children. Walking in the light of our inheritance in God and His attributes helps show the reality of God's existence without ocular proof. Others will think we are weird, slightly off the rocker, seeing the consistency of God's love operating in someone. The motive of love will always override the plan of evil against you.

# *June 29*

# TWO TYPES OF SORROW

*2 Corinthians 7:10*

*For godly grief and the pain God is permitted to direct, produce a repentance that leads and contributes to salvation and deliverance from evil, and it never brings regret; but worldly grief (the hopeless sorrow that is characteristic of the pagan world) is deadly [breeding and ending in death].*

Godly sorrow brings repentance that leads to salvation and leaves no regret, but worldly sorrow brings death. God's intentions are always for the good of mankind. Satan intends to kill, steal, and destroy. Jesus came that we might have life and have it more abundantly (John 10:10). Without salvation, we are eternally death-doomed people, only knowing Earth as our life experience. Still, the saved person will only know Earth as a hell experience. When sorrow comes, it needs to be looked at carefully. If the sorrow seems to never end, week after week, or even worse, month after month, it's a worldly sorrow that, if left unchecked, can morph into death. When God allows His children to be tested with sorrow, it's to make us better, stronger Christians, not kill us. To repent means to turn away from whatever we're doing that's causing a disconnect between us and the Lord; the disconnect is due to sin in our life. Repent and keep it moving.

# *June 30*

# WHY SHOULD GOD CARE ABOUT YOU?

*Psalm 8:3-4*

*When I view and consider Your heavens, the work of Your fingers, the moon and the stars, which You have ordained and established,*

*What is man that You are mindful of him, and the son of [Earthborn] man that You care for him?*

God cares for us because we are the creation that was created so He could have someone on His level to commune with, to fellowship with (Genesis 1:26-27). Since Adam and Eve disobeyed God in the Garden of Eden, the rulership of the Earth was handed over to the devil (John 14:30). The effect of man's sin has left him in a fallen, almost unrecognizable state from God's original creation. Fellowship with God, needless to say, has taken a serious turn south. We don't want to have fellowship with God because our nature has changed to be more like the devil. The remedy for this fallen state of man, to bring man back in line to God's way of life, is Jesus Christ (John 14:6). But God knew we couldn't change ourselves back, so He sent Jesus to destroy the works of Satan done against us, to restore our place of fellowship with God. But now our flesh is so strong in the fallen state if we don't exercise our will to want God, it won't happen. This is why God is mindful of and cares so much for us.

# July 1

# You Ain't Gettin' My Money

*2 Corinthians 9:7*

*Let each one [give] as he has made up his own mind and purposed in his heart, not reluctantly or sorrowfully or under compulsion, for God loves (He takes pleasure in, prizes above other things, and is unwilling to abandon or to do without) a cheerful (joyous, "prompt to do it") giver [whose heart is in his giving].*

This verse in the Bible is used before the offering is received in church. We are told here God loves a cheerful giver whose heart is in his giving. Giving our finances in church gives God the right of passage to bless us back more than we can receive. As we give, it shall be given again unto us, good measure, pressed down shaken together and running over shall men give into your bosom (Luke 6:38). The amount you give determines the amount you receive. So why give? Your participation in the law of reciprocity puts you in God's financial program with points like in credit card use. It helps us stay away from the temptation of "the love of money" (which is the root of all evil, 1 Timothy 6:10). Our finances are very connected to us; once God sees your liberation from it, He can trust giving you more than you have room to receive, and that's so you can give to others less fortunate. Boom!

# *July 2*

# CHANGE THE WAY
# YOU THINK

*Romans 12:2, NLT*

*Don't copy the behavior and customs of this world, but let God transform you into a new person by changing the way you think. Then you will learn to know God's will for you, which is good and pleasing and perfect.*

Renewing your way of thinking is vital to your mental health as well as your spiritual health. Learn how to respond to different situations, offenses, etc. Instead of being reactionary, letting our emotions rule the moment, we can respond based on what the Bible says concerning that issue. Being quick to hear and slow to speak should be practiced in our lives (James 1:19). We should give an opportunity for the entire thought of a person to be expressed before we cut them off. We must lose the defensive attitude. The world's system, rules and regulations can't stop the force of God's purpose in you from being completed (Philippians 4:13). When we start thinking in a way that resembles God we allow His grace, favor, and mercy to enter our lives. These qualities become crucial in navigating through difficult circumstances that may seem impossible. Once you've done all that you know to do, it's time just to stand your ground until the manifested desire has come. Change the way you think.

# *July 3*

# FEAR NOT, THE FATHER KNOWS

*Psalm 23:4*

*Yes, though I walk through the [deep, sunless] valley of the shadow of death, I will fear or dread no evil, for You are with me; Your rod [to protect] and Your staff [to guide], they comfort me.*

Even being close to death, King David didn't have concerns of dying. He knew God had his back at every turn. And how did David have such great trust and reliance on God, that even in the face of possible death he was not afraid. This, my friends, is the catapult to total freedom and peace in the midst of a storm. When we've walked with God for many years there's a deep down knowing that no matter what comes our way, we win! If I die, it is far better to be with Christ. But like Paul said *"...it is better for you that I remain here on Earth for your continued growth in Christ."* (Philippians 1:23-25) Faith in God is all you need. Trusting the Master to always be there is the greatest accomplishment any human can achieve. You'll live free of the restriction's mankind tries to put on you. Our faith can override, (not break) human laws and rules when it comes to you fulfilling your God given purpose and destiny. Things go better with God. Fear not, the Father knows.

# *July 4*

# KEEP IT MOVING, GOD'S GOT YOU

*Galatians 6:9*

*And let us not lose heart and grow weary and faint in acting nobly and doing right, for in due time and at the appointed season we shall reap, if we do not loosen and relax our courage and faint.*

We are encouraged to continue doing good when we start getting weary. The joy of the Lord is our strength, and when we are weak, then are we strong (2 Corinthians 12:10), because God's strength is made perfect in our weakness (2 Corinthians 12:9). It matures when we are too weak to get in God's way of strengthening us. Many times, we must encourage ourselves in the Lord. We must persevere in going forward knowing no matter what things feel like, look like, or seem to be, God has us in His hand. From time to time, it will feel like God's not there, maybe He went on vacation, but no, He's testing our faith to see if we're going to give up or start encouraging ourself in the Lord so His strength can come into us. To never give up is to never lose. Time is the great equalizer. Keep it moving, God's got you.

# July 5

# THE NEVER-ENDING BATTLE

*Galatians 5:25*

*If we live by the [Holy] Spirit, let us also walk by the Spirit. [If by the Holy Spirit we have our life in God, let us go forward walking in line, our conduct controlled by the Spirit.]*

Our flesh (or bodies), still have the godless human nature with its passions, appetites, and desires. When you become a Christian, the only part changed of our three-part makeup, is our human spirit. Our flesh or bodies were created to be able to survive here on Earth. Your soul (your mind) has not been changed by the new birth either, and we should renew our minds with the Word of God, (Romans 12:2) doing things and living life as He subscribes. To keep in step with the Spirit, we must be vigilant in our time spent with the Lord. We recharge when we pull away from it all, and get quality time with God, being still and knowing He is there (Psalm 46:10). Your life is your own, full of choices, and distractions, agitating spirits, and moral conflicts. We need a governor to watch over our lives, to regulate, and keep us during confusing times, and then we can keep it together more easily. That governor, that mediator, which goes between us and God, is Jesus (1 Timothy 2:5). He dealt with everything we as humans have to deal with and was victorious through it all so we can be as well.

# *July 6*

# A LIFE OF FAITH

*Roman 1:17*

*For in the Gospel a righteousness which God ascribes is revealed, both springing from faith and leading to faith [disclosed through the way of faith that arouses to more faith]. As it is written, The man who through faith is just and upright shall live and shall live by faith.*

The person who is in right standing with God shall live by faith. In other words, your five senses should no longer be your ultimate guide in living or making decisions. To live by faith means you have a sense of the supernatural connecting with this natural world. You become the connector to the spirit realm. God is in the spirit realm, along with Satan and his demons. To receive what's necessary to live a victorious life from God, we must believe He has set up this system of faith, trusting without seeing or knowing from natural knowledge. It's a gut feeling that instills a small voice giving input from the throne of God. He's very connected to every living thing, as He is in all things of creation. We are the righteousness of God in Christ Jesus. Our righteousness isn't of ourselves, but that which Jesus provided for us, by going through calvary (Philippians 3:9). We walk by faith, not by sight, we are to be led by our spirits, not by our flesh.

# *July 7*

# HE IS OUR REFUGE

*Nahum 1:7*

*The Lord is good, a Strength and Stronghold in the day of trouble;
He knows (recognizes, has knowledge of, and understands) those
who take refuge and trust in Him.*

The Lord is good, a strength and stronghold in the day of trouble. He is a refuge in times of trouble for those who trust Him. The key for God's help is to know He's got you before He manifests the help you need. He knows those who trust Him, and that fuels His response to get you what you need. If we want to be free from pursuit, danger or trouble, He is our refuge. Walking by faith, and not by sight (2 Corinthians 5:7) is the rule of thumb to enter the shelter that God has already supplied because He knew we would need it from time to time. Being led by our spirits (Romans 8:14), and not by our flesh (emotions) is the way of life we should aspire towards. What does that mean? Some call it intuition, or "I had a feeling," or "something told me I should have done this or that," ultimately that's God telling you something that can keep you from harm, or to avoid an unnecessary bad situation. He is our refuge.

# *July 8*

# THE FEAR FACTOR

*Proverbs 29:25*

*The fear of man brings a snare, but whoever leans on, trusts in, and puts his confidence in the Lord is safe and set on high.*

The fear of man will prove to be a snare, but whoever trusts in the Lord is kept safe. Fear can cripple us, and it can keep us from natural harm. When a big truck is coming down the street and you're in the way, your natural fear of death will motivate you to get out of the truck's way. There is the other side of the coin that says the thing you fear most will come upon you as you keep talking about it and yielding to its thoughts. The crazy thing is that we often worry about that thing that never happens. Perfect love drives out fear (1 John 4:18), so we should develop our love walk constantly. The perfect balance of fear is having the wisdom to yield to natural fears for safety and not yielding to the demonic fear Satan wants you to have, which is designed to ruin your life.

# July 9

# UNNATURAL LOVE

*Luke 6:35*

*But love your enemies and be kind and do good [doing favors so that someone derives benefit from them] and lend, expecting and hoping for nothing in return but considering nothing as lost and despairing of no one; and then your recompense (your reward) will be great (rich, strong, intense, and abundant), and you will be sons of the Most High, for He is kind and charitable and good to the ungrateful and the selfish and wicked.*

Love your enemies, be kind, and do good according to scripture. Can you do that without God? Probably not. God so loved the world that He gave His only begotten Son to die for our sins, and before Jesus went through the crucifixion, we were enemies of God. We were enemies because of our sinful nature (Romans 5:8). Once we are saved and become Christians, we take on God's nature. So, the ability is in us to love our enemies. The Lord set the example for us to love our enemies. It doesn't mean you must always hang around them. It could be simply avoiding them until you can forgive them, which is a very low level of agape love (the God kind), but it's a great start. Showing them kindness and being good to them would be the next step in showing God's kind of love. Once we're more mature, we can come very close to God's example; He loved us when we didn't deserve it.

# *July 10*

# WORD POWER

*Isaiah 55:11*

*So shall My word be that goes forth out of My mouth: it shall not return to Me void [without producing any effect, useless], but it shall accomplish that which I please and purpose, and it shall prosper in the thing for which I sent it.*

These are God's Words explaining to us that when He has spoken, things will line up with His words, and what He has declared and decreed will become. When the Lord's words are spoken out of our mouths mixed with faith (you believe your words will produce the desired outcome), those words will not return to you, void of results. So, as we pray God's Word (the Bible) back to Him, He cannot resist a response to help us. There are many words from many people in the atmosphere all the time, the spirit world where Satan and his crew are kept busy making men and women say things like, "I can't believe it," "You're killing me," "I don't know what I'm gonna do." These statements seem harmlessly true at the time, but their confession keeps us thinking naturally and excluding God's help by our negative confession. God's Words in your mouth are spirit and life. God hears and responds to His word, prayed back to Him, do it.

# July 11

# THE LORD TAKES PLEASURE

### Psalm 147:11

*The Lord takes pleasure in those who reverently and worshipfully fear Him, in those who hope in His mercy and loving-kindness.*

God gets pleasure from us when we reverence Him and hope in his love. He, like some of us, wants to be depended upon. God wants to help us, but since we do not see Him with our physical eyes, we don't think to involve Him. Out of sight, out of mind. He is a rewarder of those who diligently seek Him (Hebrews 11:6). *"Meditate in this book of the law, day and night and you'll make your way prosperous."* (Joshua 1:8) Throughout the Bible, God is found helping people with everything concerning their lives. When we fear God, it brings grace to us not otherwise received. The fear of the Lord is the beginning of wisdom (Proverbs 9:10). So, we can have wisdom in every area of our lives by reverencing God. Knowing what to do, and knowing what not to do in every situation is where wisdom plays a big part. To hope in God's steadfast love is an assurance to the Lord you are on board for blessings and a better life.

# *July 12*

# IS YOUR REPENTANCE OBVIOUS?

*Matthew 3:8*

*Bring forth fruit that is consistent with repentance [let your lives prove your change of heart]...*

The Bible says we should bring forth fruit (proof) of our repentance, manifestations of our behavior, and actions that show, when life hits hard we are still not going to turn to the dark side for answers. However, when we should keep our cool until God delivers us. If we belong to God, we have an advantage over this world's evil system of operation. Working on yourself to become a better you towards others, gets you in the circle of trust with God. In the circle of trust there's integrity, wisdom, and Godly knowledge of how to stay a step ahead of this world's distractions, pitfalls, deceptions, and evil plans against you and your faith in God. Repentance means to turn away from and do not go back to it. Christians have to acknowledge they were sinners, repent, and then Jesus came into their lives. Is your repentance obvious?

# *July 13*

# GIVING TO THE NEEDY

*Matthew 6:3, NLT*

*But when you give to someone in need, don't let your left hand
know what your right hand is doing.*

Giving to the needy, or the poor is very important to God (Proverbs 19:17). When we give it should be out of love, not to get praise from man because you did an honorable thing. Giving just because says a lot about a person. Then there are those who purpose to work the "give and it shall be given back to you law" (Luke 6:38) for selfish reasons. Pressure comes to us all, but if you can trust, God's timing is always perfect, even when it seems we've already failed, He won't leave you hanging. The key is to believe in God regardless of how bad things are, that's faith. A giving heart will never lack anything. The law of reciprocity works for saints and sinners alike. Give to the poor, and you'll be in God's good graces.

# July 14

## TWO FEAR TYPES

*Proverbs 29:25*

*The fear of man brings a snare, but whoever leans on, trusts in, and puts his confidence in the Lord is safe and set on high.*

We should be afraid of no one. However, reverential fear is different; that is, a respectful, honoring attitude toward men and women because of the office they have been appointed to, like the Presidency of the United States or a King or Queen. When you have a fear of others, they sense it and can use that fear against you to manipulate and control you. Fear is a crippling spirit motivated by Satan to keep you down. God has not given us a spirit of fear but of power, love, and a clear-thinking mind (2 Timothy 1:7). Putting our trust in God for everything we do will eliminate the fuzzy thoughts and the negative fear of people and free us to soar into our God-given purpose and destiny. Many unseen forces in this world negatively affect us, and they are designed to stop anything you do that's good, and that will help other people. Because the spirit of fear works for the devil, who is here to kill, steal, and destroy. Jesus came that you might have life and have it more abundantly (John 10:10).

# July 15

# WASH MY FEET?

*John 13: 14, NLT*

*And since I, your Lord and Teacher, have washed your feet, you
ought to wash each other's feet.*

Back in biblical times, it was a sign of humility to wash someone's feet. The roads were all dirt, and with only sandals for shoes, your feet were exposed to the elements. The act of Jesus washing the disciples' feet was done as an example for us. It's more of a mental adjustment to be humble toward others, preferring others before yourself (Romans 12:3). Some people think certain tasks are beneath them. A pride thing going on could block your thing with God. Pride is a faith killer, which must be kept in check. Think of yourself highly, but not more highly than you ought to. Growing in wisdom will be the key to control pride, and walking in love will kill pride to a greater degree. Jesus, being the only begotten Son of God, came from the highest level of royalty and priesthood prominence, and He still humbled Himself even to the point of dying a crucified death. A kind act toward others can make a world of difference, especially to a crushed heart that life's hardships have beaten down.

# July 16

# MASTERING THE DARKNESS

*Colossians 1:13*

*[The Father] has delivered and drawn us to Himself out of the control and the dominion of darkness and has transferred us into the kingdom of the Son of His love.*

We, Christians, are no longer under the dominion of darkness. That doesn't mean that we do not have to deal with it. God, the Father has delivered us from the darkness to have legal authority over us. Jesus broke that rulership of darkness when He went to hell for our sins. (1 Peter 2:9). After becoming a Christian only our human spirit has been changed, our minds and bodies have not been. So, the renewing of our minds to conform to God's way of thinking and acting during difficult situations, is vitally important for mastering the darkness. The darkness is always going to be on Earth, so God's plan is for us to live above the effects of the darkness. We are the light of the world for the Father to shine the glorious light of the Gospel to this dark world (Ephesians 5:8).

# July 17

## SEASONED SPEECH

*Colossians 4:6*

*Let your speech at all times be gracious (pleasant and winsome), seasoned [as it were] with salt, [so that you may never be at a loss] to know how you ought to answer anyone [who puts a question to you].*

Let your conversation be always full of grace, seasoned with salt, so that you may know how to answer everyone. These are the words written to the early church in the Bible and hold true for us today. Our words can de-escalate a bad situation or make things worse. How we speak to each other is important. A person with a message to give to another can be expressed differently than intended, depending on the words used. Our understanding of words spoken and comprehended can vary from person to person. Simple direct words of truth and honesty can never be misconstrued. You will know how to answer everyone as your words are seasoned with salt. Think before you release the words in your mind, so you deliver exactly what you intended for the other person to understand. Let's be slow to speak, and quick to hear.

# July 18

# THE POWER OF THE
# WORD OF GOD

*Hebrews 4:12*

*For the Word that God speaks is alive and full of power
[making it active, operative, energizing, and effective]; it is
sharper than any two-edged sword, penetrating to the dividing
line of the breath of life (soul) and [the immortal] spirit, and
of joints and marrow [of the deepest parts of our nature],
exposing and sifting and analyzing and judging the very thoughts
and purposes of the heart.*

When God said, 'let there be light,' there was light and the sun, and moon were created. In the Bible are God's Words of life, which are alive and active, and full of power. His words will change any situation or deliver you from any and every trouble. Once we as Christians, find the promises of God to us in the Bible, we can use those words, and speak things into existence. To the degree we believe His words will produce, is the same degree of our results. God requires that we trust Him even though we cannot see Him, that's faith. The Word of God, the Bible, is sharper than any two-edge sword, and penetrates to the dividing line of the very breath of life. Use the power of the Word of God in your words.

# July 19

# HOW ARE YOU LOVIN'?

*1 Peter 4:8*

*Above all things have intense and unfailing love for one another, for love covers a multitude of sins [forgives and disregards the offenses of others].*

Our normal way of having good character and integrity, should be based on, and motivated by God's love. We have in us the ability to love the unlovely and in our maturity this is possible. Being like our Father God is the idea for our existence here and now. Our love for others can cover a multitude of sins, according to the Bible. Not sharing the business of someone who confided in you to get comfort from your words, even though they missed the mark. Tough love holds its ground when a friend or loved one can only understand their waywardness when you separate yourself from them. Love has many facets and attributes of expression. We as Christians, on a regular basis, love each other deeply, as the Bible subscribes. Smiling in a person's face and then talking about them like a dog behind their back isn't love on any level, and it's straight-up wrong. Most of us live by selfish love, I'll do for you if you do for me - no sacrifice there. Only a committed lifestyle to God's teachings and precepts can begin to grasp the understanding of the agape love of God.

# *July 20*

# FOR THE DEEPER
# CHRISTIAN LIFE

*Ephesians 1:17*

*[For I always pray to] the God of our Lord Jesus Christ, the Father of glory, that He may grant you a spirit of wisdom and revelation [of insight into mysteries and secrets] in the [deep and intimate] knowledge of Him,*

The spirit of wisdom and revelation are essential for the deeper life in Christ Jesus. Knowledge is necessary, but the proper allocation should be filtered through wisdom. Much knowledge can invite unwarranted pride and will attract a buffer to your body and soul (1 Corinthians 8:1). The buffer is a thorn in your flesh to bring you down to a less puffed-up state of mind due to much revelation (2 Corinthians 12:7). Revelation knowledge can be obtained through reading and meditating in God's Word, the Bible. Godly wisdom is winsome, easy to entreat, pleasant to the soul, and yields understanding to its seekers. Revelation comes directly from the Spirit of God into our human spirits and is perceived, directed, and manifested in our thinking processes. Our understanding becomes enlightened from the spirit of wisdom and revelation, which gives us insight into mysteries and secrets. For the deep and intimate knowledge of God, this is the way.

# July 21

## ARE YOU SAFE?

*1 Peter 3:13*

*Now who is there to hurt you if you are zealous followers of that which is good?*

There's more than one way to "skin a cat," concerning staying safe, and feeling safe if you can have faith. Most people aren't using all their abilities in life. We are spirit beings whether you know it or not. We can say with our mouths and believe in our hearts a thing will come to pass (based on the Word of God) and in time it will, good or bad (Mark 11:22-23). There's another law at work in the land called reciprocity, or seed, time and harvest. Planting positive words of faith toward what you want, or need will cause the law to activate. Your belief and confession of being safe will cause you to, in time, actually be safe. Because your faith will compel God to watch over you and keep you.

# *July 22*

# THE POWER OF TWO

*Ecclesiastes 4:9*

*Two are better than one, because they have a good [more satisfying]
reward for their labor;*

Two are better than one when it comes to getting jobs done more efficiently. And in the multitude of counsel there is wisdom (Proverbs 15:22). One-sided opinions or perspectives limit the possibilities of greatness. In prayer, one person puts a thousand to flight, but two people can send ten thousand to flight. The power of agreement takes things to another level of excellence and desired outcome. When we pray about or for something, there's more power involved with two or more people on the same page when believing God for what's been petitioned (Matthew 18:19). Having a prayer partner is vital for getting things done of great importance.

# *July 23*

# WHO FEELS LIKE REJOICING?

*Philippians 4:4*

*Rejoice in the Lord always [delight, gladden yourselves in Him];
again I say, Rejoice!*

To always be full of joy in the Lord takes work. We are also natural human beings who don't always feel like being joyful about anything. We must invoke our will to make ourselves rejoice in the Lord. It's not when feelings are conducive to praising God, but by faith, we do it. We don't always feel like going to work, but if we don't, money becomes a problem. Rejoicing in the Lord is like putting on a garment of light that shines so brightly it affects you and the people around you. The joy of the Lord is your strength, according to the Bible (Nehemiah 8:10). Stirring ourselves up in the Lord is a thing. You can praise your way out of trouble. Praise lights the fire of our confident, favorable expectations, which is hope for success in God's way. Keeping Him in the mix through the good times and bad will help develop the seed of joy imparted to you at the new birth. Because if He's really in the mix of your day, after many days, there becomes an awareness of His input into your life, which turns into comfort, a great foundation for joy's entrance into your soul. Rejoice in the Lord always!

# July 24

# THE THIRST IS REAL

### Isaiah 55:1-2

*Wait and listen, everyone who is thirsty! Come to the waters; and he who has no money, come, buy and eat! Yes, come, buy [priceless, spiritual] wine and milk without money and without price [simply for the self-surrender that accepts the blessing].*

*Why do you spend your money for that which is not bread, and your earnings for what does not satisfy? Hearken diligently to Me, and eat what is good, and let your soul delight itself in fatness [the profuseness of spiritual joy].*

Many of us are thirsty, but not necessarily for just water. We get thirsty for other things, but we won't talk about that today. The thirst I'm referring to is a spiritual thirst for the supernatural. We can all have it occasionally, but we don't know what it is. That could lead to using drugs, alcohol, and anything that might quench it. We are spiritual beings created by a spiritual God. There are waters from above that can only satisfy the thirst. Jesus told the woman at the well that He had water for her so that she would never thirst again (John 4: 10, 15). The waters of life flow from heaven to any of God's children who want it. Rivers of living waters should spring up out of our spirits to help others know God. The Word of God is our food and drink for spiritual maturity in Christ. Quench the thirst. Seek the Lord while He may be found.

# July 25

## GET IN THE FLOW

*Proverbs 11:24, NLT*
*Give freely and become more wealthy; be stingy and lose everything.*

We should be like a river; water comes in and flows out. There must be a constant flow of running water in and out to prevent stagnation. We become clogged when we allow blessings to come into our lives, and then don't release to others, keeping the flow. When you give, it shall be given again unto you (Luke 6:38). This continuous flow is necessary for our needs to be met, as well as our desires fulfilled. The law of reciprocity is always in effect. In the body of Christ there is God's system of finance flow. Once we get hold of that system, financial freedom will come. He supplies our need according to His riches in glory which is more than enough (Philippians 4:19). Hold on tight, and you'll eventually lose it, let it go freely and it will find its way back to you, good measure, pressed down, shaken together and running over. Your cup will be running over. Get in the flow.

# *July 26*

## CHOOSE LIFE TODAY

*2 Corinthians 5:17*

*Therefore if any person is [ingrafted] in Christ (the Messiah) he is a new creation (a new creature altogether); the old [previous moral and spiritual condition] has passed away. Behold, the fresh and new has come!*

This new creature talked about in 2 Corinthians 5:17 has to do with the rebirth of our human spirits. Your human spirit is the real you. Your soul has your emotions and we live in this body designed for planet Earth. We are eternal beings first because you won't die after you leave your body (John 10:28-29), You'll transition into that spiritual world of existence where God and His angels live. The question is where you will spend eternity. There are two choices, one is made for you, and the other is a choice to be made before transitioning time happens. We all are death doomed eternally until we invoke our wills and accept Jesus as Lord and Savior of our life (Romans 10:9-10). This will grant you eternal life instead of eternal death with Satan and his crew. God won't destroy any of His creation including fallen angels or Lucifer himself. Therefore, there's a place originally created for the fallen angels that rebelled against God (Matthew 25:41). Any human going along with this world's ways without Jesus will join the fallen crew headed for hell. Choose life today!

# *July 27*

# THE PURPOSE IS REAL

*Proverbs 19:21*

*Many plans are in a man's mind, but it is the Lord's purpose for him that will stand.*

Once we understand God's purpose for us and we follow it, we will stand and prevail in our planning. It is the Lord's purpose that prevails. God will always see His agenda come to pass. As we get on board with His agenda for our lives, nothing on Earth can stop it. His Word will not return to Him void of results. He is the constant force that never sleeps or slumbers (Psalm 121:4-5). He's always ahead of the game in this life journey of ours. His purpose is the plan of reconciliation being carried out. He needs ambassadors of the Gospel to do the work. Every one of us has a God-given plan to be discovered. Once you know your calling, purpose, and God-given destiny and begin to walk in it, your pathway will be blessed for victorious living. And most importantly, you'll be fulfilling the Lord's purpose. The Lord's purpose prevails. It's time to get on board. He is a rewarder of those who diligently seek Him (Hebrews 11:6).

# *July 28*

# FAITH EXPLAINED

*Romans 10:17*

*So faith comes by hearing [what is told], and what is heard comes by the preaching [of the message that came from the lips] of Christ (the Messiah Himself).*

Faith in the things of God comes by hearing the message of the Lord Jesus Christ, the Gospel. Since it is impossible to please God without faith, it is the most vital thing to obtain as a Christian. You had faith to receive Jesus as Lord and Savior of your life; you believed without seeing. As we constantly meditate on God's Word day and night, we make our own way prosperous (Joshua 1:8). Then, at one point, our faith must be tested to grow more and more. It's like a muscle; the more you use it, the more it grows. There is weak faith, strong faith, ever-increasing faith, little faith, etc. It's up to you which level of faith you want. Trails in the life of Christians come for many reasons. Sometimes, there's a self-inflicted situation of trouble catching up with the bad seed you sowed against someone, and you never made things right with that person. Then there's the time when the Word of God in you demands to be tested. Growth in faith comes from hearing the word and then practicing it in your everyday life against trials and crises. God's Word covers all issues of this life. Every word of God backs the power of faith. The power of faith is released with your confession of God's Word concerning your specific challenge. Be careful what you hear and say because faith works both ways for your good or for bad.

# July 29

# IS YOUR ARMOR IN PLACE?

*Ephesians 6:11*

*Put on God's whole armor [the armor of a heavy-armed soldier which God supplies], that you may be able successfully to stand up against [all] the strategies and the deceits of the devil.*

When we have on the whole armor of God, there's no worrying necessary. There will be those times in life when we don't know what's going on. The armor is mostly for defense protection from the enemy. You are a Christian soldier first, whether you know it or not. The devil hates Christians, and has come to kill, steal from us (John 10:10), and destroy us when we don't have on the armor of God. The belt of truth is for keeping us honest. The breastplate of righteousness keeps us in right standing with God. The gospel of peace should be our conversation to all. The shield of faith protects us from the unseen attack coming (Ephesians 6:16). The sword of the Spirit (Ephesians 6:17), which is the Word of God is for offensive maneuvers against our enemy. Words out of our mouth are powerful, and Satan will use our words against us if we let him. He has no power other than that which we give him.

# *July 30*

## THE POWER OF FAITH

*1 Timothy 6:12*

*Fight the good fight of the faith; lay hold of the eternal life to which you were summoned and [for which] you confessed the good confession [of faith] before many witnesses.*

Fighting the good fight of faith is a good fight because we win. Without faith it is impossible to please God. We trust after working our 9 to 5 jobs at the end of the week we'll get a check. You trusted the word of your employer, and worked before receiving any money, and that is faith. Trusting the Word of God is a surer thing. Every word of promise from Him is valid, and full of power. If we could just believe without seeing, we'd have that which is unattainable any other way. Businessmen, and women are people of faith. Putting money up front without any natural guarantee of return. Use the inheritance given you by God and get what's yours.

# July 31

# ARE YOU THERE YET?

*Luke 16:10*

*He who is faithful in a very little [thing] is faithful also in much,
and he who is dishonest and unjust in a very little [thing] is
dishonest and unjust also in much.*

Why haven't you been exalted yet like the Bible says. It says
when you are faithful over little and God will make you
ruler over much (Matthew 25:23). If you haven't humbled yourself
in general, you won't be exalted by God (1 Peter 5:6). The devil can
exalt you in this world because he's the ruler over this world's system
(John 12:31, NLT). And he will exalt you eventually to a place of
destruction because that's his "MO." Without humility you cannot
be exalted by God. You may think you're walking in humility, and
be deceived, but in God's book you're just as ornery, arrogant, full of
yourself in a laid-back way, just like any other sinner in the world.
God's humility lays on the bed of agape love. In other words, you
should be willing to suffer at any given moment, to prefer the other
person, or to always take an offense to keep the peace, are you there yet?

# *August 1*

# DOWNLOADS FROM HEAVEN

*Psalm 143:8*

*Cause me to hear Your loving-kindness in the morning, for on You do I lean and in You do I trust. Cause me to know the way wherein I should walk, for I lift up my inner self to You.*

In Psalm 143:8, David was talking to God, asking Him to cause David to know the way wherein he should walk, by lifting up his inner self to God. The real you (your inner self), is your spirit, your heart. Your heart must be in it to get God's attention. The Lord can by His Holy Spirit speak to your newly recreated human spirit, and download direction, safety stops, and even how to go about your everyday business. Acknowledge Him in all your ways and He will direct your path (Proverbs 3:6). David had already put his trust in God from past experiences of victory in battle and now had experience with the Lord He trusted the fact that God always comes through on your behalf. God's unfailing love for us is always active, and in the morning, God would give David downloads for his assignments as king. As you slow yourself down from this fast-paced world, you'll begin to see things in a different light. If you don't make time, and space for God's direction you will not have it. Trust your gut, that still small voice of your conscience, the "knower" in you (1 Kings 19:11-13, AMPC). Most times, that's God speaking to you. As you study God's Word, clarity of the voice of God will be yours.

# *August 2*

# THANK GOD FOR TROUBLE

*Philippians 1:3*
*I thank my God in all my remembrance of you.*

The apostle Paul was thanking God for the saints at Philippi. We should have someone in our lives for whom we can thank God. Thanking Him for trouble is another side of the coin most of us do not want. We are blessed by the people in our lives who encourage and build us up, and that really help take care of that which concerns us. Thank God for them. Thanking the Lord for the trouble that comes to us from a natural standpoint seems crazy. As we mature in the ways of God, (His teachings and precepts) we learn to appreciate the fact that our faith must be exercised and tested from time-to-time. Giving God praise and thanksgiving during a crisis opens the door for the Lord to move more swiftly on your behalf to bring you through the trouble. Sense is sense, and faith is faith. We need our five senses for this natural world, but we need faith to activate and receive from God in the spiritual world. The spiritual realm affects the natural where we live. Thanking the Lord through your problems in faith, trusting and believing Him for deliverance based on His word is all that matters for successful victory.

# *August 3*

# SPRINGS OF LIFE
# OR DRIED CREEK?

*Proverbs 4:23*

*"Keep and guard your heart with all vigilance and above all that you guard, for out of it flow the springs of life."*

Which are you? Watching over our hearts is important because that's where life starts. As we become more knowledgeable of God's Word (the Bible), we can release the waters of life through our speech. Speaking God's Word with true conviction brings deliverance, healing, correction, and a life-giving source of God's manifested help for others. God's Words are spirit and life (John 6:63), so once the believing Christian knows this, he or she will become a dispensary enabling God's intervention to help people. Watching over your heart is vital. What we hear or are listening to regularly is essential. We are programmable individuals in that once something is repeated over and over in our ears, it will drop down into our hearts from our brains. Then, we begin to believe whatever we've heard, good or bad, and this will affect our spring of life. Meditating on God's Word day and night will keep us on the straight and narrow of guarding our hearts. We must live here amongst all the negativity and still find a way to live above the mess in this world. Program yourself for a higher life that has less trouble. Become the Lord's spring of life, for out of it flows the issues of life that people are starving to understand.

# *August 4*

# WILL YOUR
# FOUNDATION HOLD?

*Matthew 7:24*

*So everyone who hears these words of Mine and acts upon them
[obeying them] will be like a sensible (prudent, practical, wise)
man who built his house upon the rock.*

The Word of God, or words of Jesus, more specifically in this case, are spirit and life (John 6:63). They have the power to change things. The words of life can impact the person who trusts in, relies on, and acts on God's spoken word from their lips. God shall not be mocked, whatsoever a man sows, that shall he reap. Sowing seeds of God's Word can produce the most desired harvest. The storms of life come to us all. When you build your life on truth and allow life's words to dominate you, the storm will not overtake you unto disaster. Building our foundation for abundant life on God's Word will cause us to stand the trials and tests of life in total victory. It is wise to build a foundation of life using the words of the one who created life. As always, the choice is yours. Jesus said, *"Whoever hears these words of mine and puts them into practice is like a wise man who built his house on the rock."* Life can shake you; make your foundation sure.

# *August 5*

# TIMEOUT DOESN'T WORK FOR EVERYONE

*Hebrews 12:11*

*For the time being no discipline brings joy, but seems grievous and painful; but afterwards it yields a peaceable fruit of righteousness to those who have been trained by it [a harvest of fruit which consists in righteousness—in conformity to God's will in purpose, thought, and action, resulting in right living and right standing with God].*

Without any discipline, we'd be running amok in riotous behavior 24/7. We all need a governor on our human nature. Human nature has been in a fallen state (spiritually, and it has affected us physically) since Adam and Eve's disobedience in the Garden of Eden. God has offered a plan to rid human nature of its fallen state by eradicating our sinful nature into the sea of forgetfulness. Discipline is necessary to acquire deliverance from the fallen state of man. Don't be fooled because you're used to being a certain way all your life; it doesn't make you blameless in character or put you in right standing with God. Discipline is never pleasant during execution, but it opens a place for divine input to show us the right way to go without unnecessary repercussions. Most people are in prison, on drugs or alcohol, unruly, etc., due to a lack of correction or discipline.

# August 6

## GET SAVED NOW!

*1 John 4:15*

*Anyone who confesses (acknowledges, owns) that Jesus is the Son of God, God abides (lives, makes His home) in him and he [abides, lives, makes his home] in God.*

Here's the invitation to enter God's family. We must be born again to enter the Kingdom of God (John 3:1-6). Jesus is the mediator and door to Father God. You can call on the name of the Lord to save you. Believing in your heart that God raised Jesus from the dead, and confessing with your mouth that Jesus is Lord is how we became Christians (Romans 10:9-10). Then there's the growth process starting with the renewing of your mind. Your thinking must change to conform to the teachings and precepts of the Lord (Romans 12:2). We learn to walk by faith, not by sight and be led by our spirits, not by our flesh or our emotions (2 Corinthians 5:7). Those who are led by the Spirit of God, are the true sons, and daughters of God (Romans 8:14). Become God-minded, acknowledge Him in all your ways, and He'll direct your path straight into the abundant life He promised all His children. Become a light in this dark world, and get saved now before it's too late because the clock is ticking for the return of the king. Once He comes, you're either in or out.

# *August 7*

# LIP LOVE SERVICE
# DOESN'T CUT IT

*1 John 3:18*

*Little children, let us not love [merely] in theory or in speech but in
deed and in truth (in practice and in sincerity).*

Most of us can tell when love doesn't feel true. Ordinary love is a
dime a dozen. True love, agape love is real, without pretense or
falsity, it is full of wisdom that is winsome and easy to be entreated. The
love every human on the planet wants is the God kind of love, which
is more caring about others, if necessary, than self. Lip-service love
should be banned from every mouth. If you don't really love someone,
and you're telling them you do for personal gain, you are in trouble and
it leaves you open to the law of reciprocity (Galatians 6:7). That bad
seed that you have sown will come back on you. Actions will always
speak louder than words. Would you prefer someone only telling you
they love you, or showing you? The giver of this kind of love must have
a sacrificial mentality, and not expect a return on their love deposits to
others. That's God's love in action.

# *August 8*

# SEEK HIM AND
# GET WHAT'S YOURS

### *Psalm 34:4-5*

*I sought (inquired of) the Lord and required Him [of necessity and on the authority of His Word], and He heard me, and delivered me from all my fears. They looked to Him and were radiant; their faces shall never blush for shame or be confused.*

Our fears are released from us when we seek God. Nothing of great value comes to us for free. There is a discipline involved in seeking the Lord, and it requires invoking our will. We must purpose to do it regardless of how we feel. Most of us allow our feelings to dictate our behavior. When you are led by your spirit (Romans 8:1) and not by your flesh (feelings), you have crossed into the realm of faith's endless possibilities. We make ourselves get up to go to work, and it's the same mentality and work ethic. Perfect (mature love) drives out fear (1 John 4:18). Since God is love, the Lord is in you, repelling the fear away from you. The more of God in your life, the less fear you'll experience. He will answer you, and believing He will answer you is over half the battle in receiving from God. He will answer, but in His time, not ours. Let patience have its perfect work in you (James 1:4-8). It is through faith and patience we obtain the promises of God. Most of us have faith to believe but little patience to wait for the answer to manifest in our lives. Seek Him and get what's yours.

# *August 9*

# THE WISE WILL SHINE

*Daniel 12:3*

*And the teachers and those who are wise shall shine like the brightness of the firmament, and those who turn many to righteousness (to uprightness and right standing with God) [shall give forth light] like the stars forever and ever.*

Teachers and those who are wise shall shine like the brightness of the firmament. The sharing of knowledge is truly the ultimate gift to give. Our gifts to others are niceties we enjoy occasionally, but giving someone a gift that will never get old, go out of style, or lose its value is on another level. Survival is the first instinct we have innately. Without knowledge, enhancing that survival instinct for smooth sailing is impossible. Things must be done under rules and regulations. We can't just go and take what's not ours to survive. In today's world, we must be as wise as serpents but harmless as a dove in attitude (Matthew 10:16). The wise person has this method down to a science. They know to wait patiently for the right moment before they act. Impatience can be an unwanted side journey you can't afford. We are, by nature, attracted to the light of knowledge and the wisdom to rule that knowledge. You will shine brightly for others who need this gift to be passed on to them. Maneuvering around all the minutiae, the drama, crisis, calamities, relationships gone bad, and nasty people will take knowledge governed by wisdom to shine away the darkness of this world.

# *August 10*

# TRAINING GROUND
# FOR CHILDREN

*Proverbs 22:6*

*Train up a child in the way he should go [and in keeping with his individual gift or bent], and when he is old he will not depart from it.*

Training our children in the way they should go is essential when they are young. It'll stick better, and the words of the Bible in their hearts will not depart from them even when they are older. The power behind God's Word operating in the heart of a believer is the nightmare of Satan and his crew, who have come to steal, kill, and destroy. The foundations of our life are supposed to be built by the family unit (good morals, discipline, behavior, etc.,) preferably with dad in the picture. However, things are not hopeless without Dad. I was a single parent for three years, and I did Bible study with my two and four-year-old children every night, just the three of us. To this day, as adults now, they are flourishing in life with children of their own, learning about God's Word at a young age. The importance of training children in the way they should go is realized after they've gone through the hard places of life. The way we all should go is based on the living Word of God. It's alive and sharper than any two-edged sword. As children get older, they begin to assert themselves. As their will is involved, parents are to keep them in prayer simply. Trust God!

# *August 11*

# WHAT'S UP WITH YOUR THOUGHTS?

*Psalm 94:19*

*In the multitude of my [anxious] thoughts within me, Your comforts cheer and delight my soul!*

What do you do when there's a multitude of anxious thoughts in your head? I'm glad you asked. The thought-life of some of us can be very scary. We cannot control the thoughts that come into our minds, but we can decide what to do with them before we act on them. If you're a reactionary type, you'll need to focus and concentrate more when the anxious thoughts come and slow yourself down to digest what's being said and how the thought was intended. Bringing every thought into captivity and making it subject to the obedience of Christ (2 Corinthians 10:5). The thought-life is another realm of life that shouldn't be left to run amok. When left unattended, our thoughts have the power over time to control our lives, good or bad. The Lord is aware of our makeup and the struggle going on down here and has made a way of escape. His Word says, think on whatsoever things are trustworthy, pure, lovely, of a good report (Philippians 4:8), change channels in your mind, and put on anointed music until you can stand your ground with total mastery over your thoughts. Thoughts come, but they don't have to rule you.

# August 12

# HELP FOR A BROKEN HEART

*Psalm 34:18*

*The Lord is close to those who are of a broken heart and saves such as are crushed with sorrow for sin and are humbly and thoroughly penitent.*

If your heart is broken, the Lord is close. He saves those who are crushed in spirit. A broken heart of emotions is bad enough, but to have a crushed spirit hurts from the core of your life. Since God is our manufacturer, seeking Him for help makes perfect sense. He's higher than all creation but low enough to live in and fix you. He is a gentleman, so we must approach Him first for help. He won't go against our will because He gave man dominion on the Earth, God needs our permission (Genesis 1:26). He'd go against all He stands for by overriding our will. Faith is approaching a God we cannot see with our physical eyes, but we believe He's there to help anyway. Once we have a strong relationship with Him, the hard times aren't as bad as we thought. If your heart is broken, go to the manufacturer for repairs.

# *August 13*

## Father's Day

*Psalm 103:13, NIV*

*As a father has compassion on his children, so the Lord has compassion on those who fear him…*

The word fear in Psalm 103:13 means reverence Him. Our heavenly Father has set the example for Earthly fathers to follow. So, we must learn of Him to know what that is. Everything we need to live a godly, holy, and enjoyable life is in the Word of God (2 Peter 1:3). Fathers must take their rightful position in the family unit. The rest of the family members will line up when Dad has control over himself first, and then able to lead his family. This happens when the father is a praying man who spends quality time with God in his everyday life. Fathers have the greatest responsibility in the family, and when he walks in it, the rest of the family follows. In other words, fathers set the tone for either success or failure based on their interactions with the family. The right mix of discipline and love must be in order. Never let your emotions rule, but your knowledge of God's Word will be the final authority. So, fathers we must know the Word of God and what God says about family is all that matters.

# *August 14*

# THESE BODIES OF OURS

*Romans 12:1, NLT*

*And so, dear brothers and sisters, I plead with you to give your bodies to God because of all he has done for you. Let them be a living and holy sacrifice—the kind he will find acceptable. This is truly the way to worship him.*

We are spirits, we have a soul, and we live in a body. Our bodies are the temple of the Holy Ghost (1 Corinthians 6:19-20). We should do our best to keep it running in optimal condition, eating right, exercising regularly, etc. The captain of your ship should be your spirit because all marching orders from God are delivered there first. Then, our mind or soul interprets the message into our way of thinking, and our bodies physically carry out the assignment. We become a living sacrifice for the Master's use. But the benefits are supernatural grace and favor (things just happen to work out in many areas of our life). After all that has been done for us to have a great life, we still must decide to live this way. Time is short as things are getting worse in this world. It is a sure sign; according to the Bible, we're close to the end of this age (Matthew 24:6-13). Choose to live clean now or continue to wallow in the dirty lifestyle you've had. The appetites of your body should not be ruling you.

# *August 15*

## WHO CARES?

*Psalms 55:22*

*Cast your burden on the Lord [releasing the weight of it] and He will sustain you; He will never allow the [consistently] righteous to be moved (made to slip, fall, or fail).*

Cast your care, anxiety, and worries on the Lord because He cares for you. How you do that is important. Before we can accept the idea of receiving help, there must first be trust that that person is capable. God is able. God requires a relationship and then close fellowship for that ever-ready help in times of trouble (Psalm 46:1). You must know Him. To the degree you know the Lord is to the degree you can relax in knowing He takes care of that which concerns you (Psalm 138:8). The temptation to worry haunts us all. It's what you do with it when it comes that counts. Your relationship with God must be bigger than the cares of this world.

# *August 16*

# NEVER GIVE UP!

*Hebrews 11:6*

*But without faith it is impossible to please and be satisfactory to Him. For whoever would come near to God must [necessarily] believe that God exists and that He is the rewarder of those who earnestly and diligently seek Him [out].*

We have no physical or ocular (visible) proof of God's existence, so it is a belief that each person must come to on their own. We choose to believe God exists without seeing Him or touching Him. It invokes your will to believe in spite of your five natural senses. There's another part of life existing in another realm of reality. The spiritual realm is where the Lord lives along with His angels. That world existed before Earth was created. The invisible realm created the visible realm, Earth (Hebrews 11:3). That world will never pass away, but Earth the way we know it today, has begun its deterioration toward the end (Revelation 21:1). Faith is believing without seeing, touching, hearing, smelling, or tasting. Faith is simply believing the Bible is true. The good fight of faith is, winning over the thoughts that say God isn't there. It's the quiet times when our prayer hasn't been answered for a long time. That's a test of your faith. He's a rewarder of those who diligently seek Him, especially during those more challenging times. Keep on believing that God's got you. Never give up!

# *August 17*

# THE GREATEST AMONG US

*Matthew 23:11*

*He who is greatest among you shall be your servant.*

The proper order or way of the greatest among us is to serve the less fortunate around us. The greatest among us in this present world is quite the opposite. We obtain wealth and prosperity to bless those who don't even have the basics to survive this life. As God blesses us, we become the pipeline of God to bless others. The channel gets what's flowing through it in abundance. The more we allow the blessings to flow through us to others, the more significant in value we become to the Lord. To become valuable to God is an excellent place to be in life. Greed, the love of money, and the pride of life will surely bring you down.

# August 18

# FIGHT THE GOOD FIGHT

*1 Timothy 6:12*

*Fight the good fight of the faith; lay hold of the eternal life to which you were summoned and [for which] you confessed the good confession [of faith] before many witnesses.*

Fighting the good fight of faith should be a way of life. We come into all sorts of trails, crises, hurts and pains. Trusting the Lord through them until victory over them is achieved, is the position we must take in general. Faith is simply trusting and then acting on it. When we do this, no power can come against that. Confessing with your mouth and believing in your heart is how you release your faith (Romans 10:9-10). It's a good fight because you always win. We are called to eternal life when we make that great confession of our belief in the finished work at Calvary. Many are called, but few are chosen (Matthew 22:14). Eternal life with God is for everyone who will accept it. It isn't forced on you, because God wants willing souls to come to Him. We come by faith, trusting it's real. You were chosen when you received Jesus Christ as Lord and Savior of your life. We walk by faith, and not by sight (2 Corinthians 5:7). Trust God's Word over facts, because facts can be superseded by God's truth. Use your faith to change the things around you that affect you. Truth is faith's forerunner, so run with it and fight the good fight.

# *August 19*

# GOD MADE IT ALL

*Psalm 19:1*

*The heavens declare the glory of God; and the firmament shows and proclaims His handiwork.*

God's creation of the heavens tells of the wonders of God, and the skies declare what He has done. Just look around you, everything in existence didn't just show up itself, and there was no big bang theory of how creation came into being. Too many strategic detailed realities prove there was an intelligent entity full of wisdom shaping and forming everything in life to be conducive to man's life on planet Earth. The Bible says humankind will be without excuse not realizing there's a God behind creation. Deception is always around us. Jesus is the way, the truth, and the life, no man comes to the Father but by Him. Scientists have their theory on creation, but the way I see it, a theory is nothing more than a supposition established upon ignorance of the subject under discussion. In God, we trust. He made it all!

# *August 20*

# THE NAME THAT COUNTS

*Acts 4:12*

*And there is salvation in and through no one else, for there is no other name under heaven given among men by and in which we must be saved.*

Calling on the name of Jesus gets you saved, saved from what? Saved from a burning hell and unnecessary trouble while still on planet Earth. After all, Jesus went through hell on Earth when He was here, ultimately dying on the cross and then literally going to hell for three days to be punished for our sins, and He never committed any sin Himself. There is and never will be any other name by which we can be saved. In that name resides the fullness of the power of the Godhead when we use it in faith. In all you do, do it in the name of Jesus. There is no other way to the Father but by Him. (John 14:6)

# *August 21*

# AREN'T WE SAVED?

*1 John 1:9*

*If we [freely] admit that we have sinned and confess our sins, He is
faithful and just (true to His own nature and promises) and will
forgive our sins [dismiss our lawlessness] and [continuously] cleanse
us from all unrighteousness [everything not in conformity to His
will in purpose, thought, and action].*

Why do Christians Sin? Being a Christian doesn't mean we're
capable of not sinning anymore. Until Christians have
renewed their way of thinking (renewed their mind with the Word of
God (Ephesians 6:11-12), wrongdoings are inevitable. Unfortunately,
some Christians in the body of Christ are immature in God. Most
want to do something other than the work of growing up in Christ.
The only thing that changes when we become Christians is our human
spirit. Our mind and body have not been touched. All temptations and
moral conflicts are first dealt with in our minds. If we don't deal with
those thoughts and defeat them there, we will eventually act them out
physically, leading to trouble and being out of the Lord's good graces.
You'll still be saved, but trouble will be your buddy occasionally. The
way out is no different than the way into becoming a Christian. Confess
with your mouth the sin you committed and ask God to forgive you,
then believe in your heart God forgave you. Do not allow your mind
to persuade you to think God didn't forgive you. It's written, and it's
your job to believe. The work has been done at Calvary. You are saved!

# *August 22*

# THIS YEAR, BELIEVE GOD!

*Philippians 4:6*

*Don't worry about anything; instead, pray about everything.*
*Tell God what you need, and thank him for all*

The command from the Bible says, don't worry about anything. Now for most of us that's not possible without God's help. To not have any anxiety about anything means, you're totally trusting, and believing God's got you covered no matter what's on your plate. Even when it looks like you've already failed, the Lord can even change an outcome, and turn it around into your victory. Many times we don't totally trust God until things turn around for the good because we give up waiting. Through Faith and patience we obtain the promises of God. Worry is a mild symptom of insanity. You've worried yourself sick, and the thing you worried about never happened. This year, believe God!

# *August 23*

# ASK, SEEK, AND KNOCK UNTIL YOU GET IT

*Matthew 7:8*

*And this is the confidence (the assurance, the privilege of boldness) which we have in Him: [we are sure] that if we ask anything (make any request) according to His will (in agreement with His own plan), He listens to and hears us.*

For everyone who asks receives, everyone who seeks finds, to everyone who knocks, the door will be open (Matthew 7:7). You must try in life, to give your best effort. We have not because we ask not. We don't find because we're lazy in our pursuit. The doors aren't opened to you because you're not knocking. We are laborers together with God, He won't do the work for you (1 Corinthians 3:9). He needs our best effort of faith accompanied by our actions, to move His hand on our behalf. Persistence is a necessary component in receiving from God. It's not a, "I tried it and it doesn't work" thing, it's a lifestyle of being a doer of the Word of God (James 1:22-25), and not a hearer only. Many people mentally assent to God's Word, but they're not believing in their heart which completes the faith circuit to move God. You're agreeing in your mind with the Bible, which is powerless without heartfelt faith. In the future when you've got solid direction from God, go after it like a bull dog on a bone, and don't give up until you have what you've gone after. Ask, seek, and knock until you get it.

# *August 24*

# GOD BREATHED SCRIPTURES

*2 Timothy 3:16*

*Every Scripture is God-breathed (given by His inspiration) and profitable for instruction, for reproof and conviction of sin, for correction of error and discipline in obedience, [and] for training in righteousness (in holy living, in conformity to God's will in thought, purpose, and action),*

Scripture is God-breathed, given by inspiration, and is profitable for instruction, reproof and conviction of sin, correction of sin, correction of error, and discipline in obedience, training in righteousness in holy living, in conformity to God's will in thought, purpose and action. That's a mouth full but straight from the scriptures. The Bible, which could stand for; *basic instructions before leaving Earth,* has all we need in it to live a righteous, holy before God kind of life, which He intended for us to live when He created us (Leviticus 11:44). Many demonically motivated people have taken the laws and understanding of how life works according to the Bible and have used it in a deceptive way to get ahead. Once we understand the teachings and precepts of how to live right, life becomes easier to deal with on every level.

# *August 25*

# THE ROAD TO PEACE

*John 14:27*

*Peace I leave with you; My [own] peace I now give and bequeath to you. Not as the world gives do I give to you. Do not let your hearts be troubled, neither let them be afraid. [Stop allowing yourselves to be agitated and disturbed; and do not permit yourselves to be fearful and intimidated and cowardly and unsettled.]*

The Lord is speaking here with the intent of you following His teachings and precepts. Without them, it won't be easy to keep your peace. First of all, Jesus is the Prince of Peace, and to have the peace that passes all understanding, you must have Jesus in your life (Isaiah 9:6). When you have more of Jesus in your life, more of His peace can be experienced. When we allow drama-filled people and situations that create drama into our lives, we won't have any peace of mind. We can control the natural things that can take away our peace. Then, there's the other side of life, the spiritual side that needs your attention. Our life is either controlled by us or a spiritual entity behind the scenes we're unaware of (Ephesians 6:12). The spirit of fear is very real. You can't see it, but it's around and attracted to the area you're oblivious to. Fear can rob your peace; mature, perfect love will drive it away (1 John 4:18). Walk in love and lose the drama in your life. Peace will be right there waiting.

# *August 26*

# CHRISTIANITY: THE GOSPEL EXPLAINED

### John 1:14

*And the Word (Christ) became flesh (human, incarnate) and tabernacled (fixed His tent of flesh, lived awhile) among us; and we [actually] saw His glory (His honor, His majesty), such glory as an only begotten son receives from his father, full of grace (favor, loving-kindness) and truth.*

The word flesh used in the Bible refers to our bodies and sometimes its unruly appetites. Jesus came down from heaven in physical form to do the work God sent Him here to do (1 Timothy 3:16). It was necessary for Jesus to become flesh, to experience the evil humankind has been dealing with since the fall of Adam and Eve in the garden. He became the mediator between God and humanity. (1 Timothy 2:5-6) Justice must be satisfied, so a plan was put in place (the Gospel) for the redemption of all humankind. The living sacrifice was born and grew in grace and knowledge unto the only one having never sinned (Hebrews 4:15). So, here's a sinless man ripe in the eyes of Almighty God for the perfect offering to satisfy justice. And Father God had to go through turning His back on His only begotten Son (while He was on the cross) for us, His enemies at the time, to set things straight between God and humankind. We have seen His glory and now it is our duty to share the Gospel.

# *August 27*

# READING OF THE RIOT ACT

*1 Corinthians 12:25-27, NLT*

*This makes for harmony among the members, so that all the members care for each other. If one part suffers, all the parts suffer with it, and if one part is honored, all the parts are glad. All of you together are Christ's body, and each of you is a part of it.*

We are all a part of the body of Christ. Each member has its own function and purpose. Some of us are pillars for the local body (local church), and some are more boots-on-the-ground soldiers for God's army in the field. All members are essential regardless of the fame and glitter of the position. Some are sent to the mission field in the worst parts of the world. Some local missionaries evangelize outside the local church walls. Regardless of your position in Christ, you are important (Ephesians 4:15-16). If one part of the body of Christ is suffering, we take part in the suffering. If another part of the body is rejoicing, we should all take part in that. Once you've received your assignment from God, no matter how different it may be to others, follow God's command no matter what. Everyone may not agree with your assignment from God, but they don't have to for you to carry it out. We're on the same team and don't need friendly fire because of another's ignorance of your God-given assignment. So, I'd like to ask all the gossipers, naysayers, itching ears, simple, one perspective type understanding person to stand down and let us do our job.

# *August 28*

# AN INFAMOUS THOUGHT LIFE

*Philippians 4:8*

*For the rest, brethren, whatever is true, whatever is worthy
of reverence and is honorable and seemly, whatever is
just, whatever is pure, whatever is lovely and lovable,
whatever is kind and winsome and gracious, if there is any
virtue and excellence, if there is anything worthy of praise, think
on and weigh and take account of these things [fix your minds on
them].*

Our thought life can take us on journeys we don't want. We can't
control the thoughts that come into our minds, but we can
decide what to do with them when they do and not let them control
us. I speak out this verse repeatedly when constant evil thoughts come.
Speaking God's Word out of your mouth with true belief gets the
job done. The spirit of those bad thoughts cannot stand the constant
confession of God's Word without eventually leaving you alone. Think
on whatsoever is true, worthy of reverence, honorable, just, pure, lovely,
and whatever is kind, winsome, and gracious, think on these things.
Change the channel in your head. This is going toe to toe with mind-
bending spirits and bad thoughts at their highest intensity. Please get
rid of bad thoughts; work the Word until they go.

## *August 29*

# THE LORD OF ALL AND CHILD OF PROMISE

### Isaiah 9:6

*For to us a Child is born, to us a Son is given; and the government shall be upon His shoulder, and His name shall be called Wonderful Counselor, Mighty God, Everlasting Father [of Eternity], Prince of Peace.*

For a child is born to us... That child was Jesus, the Son of the living God. Immanuel means, God is with us, and He'll never leave us or forsake us. He is the same yesterday, today, and forever. He's the Wonderful Counselor, Mighty God, Creator of the Universe, the lily of the valley, Prince of Peace, God of comfort, Lord of all, the only begotten Son of God. He is the Light of humanity, the Way, the Truth, and Life. He is the Mediator between God and man - the door. Throughout history, the world has often attempted to undermine the role and significance of God in individuals and hinder the spread of the Gospel across the land. Jesus is and always will be the highest supreme being to have lived the human experience on planet Earth (as a man) and to overcome all our worst nightmares. He has won passage through the evil one's demonic plans against us to make us right with God again. He deserves all the praise and worship due to His name. Jesus is Lord.

# *August 30*

# WHEN TROUBLE COMES

*1 Peter 5:10*

*And after you have suffered a little while, the God of all grace [Who imparts all blessing and favor], Who has called you to His [own] eternal glory in Christ Jesus, will Himself complete and make you what you ought to be, establish and ground you securely, and strengthen, and settle you.*

art of the human experience on Earth is to suffer a little while. After you have suffered a little while, the Lord will restore you. You can't be the ultimate best you until you have successfully gone through some stuff, bad stuff (Hebrews 5:8). The trials, and yes, especially a crisis in your life, come because of certain circumstances. Still, in God's eyes and purpose for your life, they come to strengthen you. Every storm, or the storms of life we all go through will always pass, and that's when God will restore you. The storm must be allowed to do its job for you to grow up.

# *August 31*

## GET HIM INVOLVED

*Proverbs 16:3*

*Roll your works upon the Lord [commit and trust them wholly to Him; He will cause your thoughts to become agreeable to His will, and] so shall your plans be established and succeed.*

As we commit whatever we do to the Lord, He will establish our plans. He will cause our plans to come to pass as we are committed and submitted to Him. Plans of evil, confusion, or wrong motive, He will not establish. Acknowledge Him in all your ways, and He will direct your path (Proverbs 3:5-6). The reason for the creation of man was for the fellowship of God with someone on His level of existence. You are made in His image and likeness, is that so hard to believe? The Lord wants to be involved in our everyday lives (1 Corinthians 3:9). Commit everything you do to Him, and with Him involved, and He'll take your plans further than you ever could alone.

# *September 1*

# THE TRIPLETS PLUS FAITH, STIR UP SUCCESS

*Matthew 7:7, NLT*

*Keep on asking, and you will receive what you ask for. Keep on seeking, and you will find. Keep on knocking, and the door will be opened to you.*

The scripture here is exemplifying the consistency of not giving up or giving in to your circumstances. If we never ask, we'll never know, or have, if we never seek, we'll never have knowledge, or obtain the thing we want most. If we never knock the door will not be opened to our success. By nature I'm the guy that won't instinctively go after this method of having God's best in my life, but I have to use my faith, and now in life, I can discern the voice of God well enough to get the instructions I need to achieve the same desired goal for successful, victorious living. By continuing to NOT give up, God sees your determination, and that is a clear sign of faith, because you wouldn't continue like that if you didn't believe it was possible. Hope is the forerunner to faith's journey. Ask by faith, seek by faith, knock in faith believing, and the hardest part is done. Now, patience must have its perfect work in you to allow the promises of God to manifest. Premature harvest isn't God's best, wait on the Lord, your strength will be renewed like the eagles, while the promise is delivered in season.

# *September 2*

# HEAD FAITH VERSUS HEART FAITH

*James 1:22-24*

*But be doers of the Word [obey the message], and not merely listeners to it, betraying yourselves [into deception by reasoning contrary to the Truth]. For if anyone only listens to the Word without obeying it and being a doer of it, he is like a man who looks carefully at his [own] natural face in a mirror; For he thoughtfully observes himself, and then goes off and promptly forgets what he was like.*

When we only listen to the Word of God, and do not do what it says, we deceive ourselves. It's attributed to someone who looks in the mirror, goes away, and immediately forgets what he looks like. We must be doers of the Word not hearers only. Many Christians mentally assent to the Word, like a seed planted in very shallow ground not having deep roots. In that case, trouble comes and there's no root of stability to keep you anchored. The Word of God must be lived, not just understood mentally. Get it in your heart, not just your head. Meditate in the Word day and night, and you will make your way prosperous.

# *September 3*

# IS IT POSSIBLE TO HAVE PEACE THESE DAYS?

*John 14:27, NLT*

*"I am leaving you with a gift—peace of mind and heart. And the peace I give is a gift the world cannot give. So don't be troubled or afraid.*

Before Jesus left the Earth to go to the Father in heaven, He told His disciples He was leaving them His peace, being that He is the Prince of Peace who had just conquered the evil in this world. The peace that passes all understanding is ours for the asking. It passes all understanding because when Jesus defeated Satan in hell, He took the keys of death and hell (peace robbers). Jesus has become the answer to all life's negativity and unanswered questions. We tend to lose peace over things we don't understand or fear. The knowledge of God is our basis and foundation for peace. Jesus left His peace behind when He ascended on high. It must be discovered like any other treasure on Earth. Lay your foundation for peace by studying God's Word so that you can receive it by faith. Get away from people who are not peaceful by nature. We must deal with anti-peacemakers occasionally, but most of our lives should be spent with people and situations that lend themselves to a more peaceful outcome. Otherwise, more time with the Prince of Peace brings you closer to a more peaceful life.

# *September 4*

# THE COMMAND FOR STRENGTH

*Joshua 1:9*

*Have not I commanded you? Be strong, vigorous, and very courageous. Be not afraid, neither be dismayed, for the Lord your God is with you wherever you go.*

It is a command from God to be strong. The message to be strong is based on you being connected to God, otherwise it's in your own strength. While doing things in your own strength, you are limited to it. Having supernatural strength is linked to God and God alone. There's a real enemy out there who specializes in attacking Christians, and he's known to use some Christians for his purposes. If you're a closet Christian, (you don't know who you are in Christ, lacking the power) in that case the enemy isn't as concerned about you because you're not a threat to Him. He knows the Christians who have tapped into God's power and who hasn't. We're in God's army now, and we must do things God's way for total victory. There's more available for you to tap into, but no one's going to make you. So, if you're feeling down and out, dismayed, or afraid, it's time for a new method of living because yours isn't working. Hook up with the King and obtain your strength.

# *September 5*

# WHAT MATTERS MOST

### *Joshua 1:8*

*This Book of the Law shall not depart out of your mouth, but you shall meditate on it day and night, that you may observe and do according to all that is written in it. For then you shall make your way prosperous, and then you shall deal wisely and have good success.*

The B.I.B.L.E. is an acronym for "Basic Instructions Before Leaving Earth," study this book of instructions continually. Meditate on it day and night so you will be sure to obey everything written in it. Only then will you prosper and succeed in all you do. We have to reprogram our way of thinking to conform to God's way of thinking so everything we do lines up with the prearranged blessings already positioned in our lives by God (Romans 12:2). Many times, we move ahead of God and miss the prearranged help provided before our birth. Oh, how we must think outside the box concerning God's ways, and even then, we'll find His ways are above ours, but we can relax in faith when we don't understand because things will work out. Fellowship with God is no different than with people on Earth. The more time you spend with someone, the more you understand and know them. How much time have you spent with the Lord today?

## *September 6*

# YOUR HEART OF HEARTS

*Psalms 73:26*
*My flesh and my heart may fail, but God is the Rock and firm*
*Strength of my heart and my Portion forever.*

When your heart isn't in something, that's the time you wait or don't take on that task at all. We have physical hearts that pump blood through our bodies, and on the spiritual side of our makeup, we have the inner man's heart where God speaks to our re-created human spirit. Our gut feeling, our intuition, when you get that strong feeling about something, that's your inner man, your other heart speaking to you. Your flesh and heart may fail, but God is the strength of our hearts; He has both under His control.

# September 7

# THE WINDOW IS CLOSING

### Isaiah 55:6-7

*Seek, inquire for, and require the Lord while He may be found [claiming Him by necessity and by right]; call upon Him while He is near. Let the wicked forsake his way and the unrighteous man his thoughts; and let him return to the Lord, and He will have love, pity, and mercy for him, and to our God, for He will multiply to him His abundant pardon.*

Seek the Lord while He may be found, is what the Bible says. There's coming a time, sooner than we think, that it will be too late to find God. Once the rapture happens, it's too late. Call on Him while He is near. The way this world is structured and operates, there's no inclusion of God, and it will become increasingly harder to get to heaven as sin continues to grow in this world. God's grace will increase as sin increases (Romans 5:20), but you must decide to follow God, and following Him right into heaven is the idea. Don't be left behind on the last day, because it's coming very soon now. For one to keep telling themselves, I'll do that later (get with God), I have time. Seek Him while He may be found. The window is closing.

# September 8

# NO CONDEMNATION IN CHRIST

*Romans 8:1*

*Therefore, [there is] now no condemnation (no adjudging guilty of wrong) for those who are in Christ Jesus, who live [and] walk not after the dictates of the flesh, but after the dictates of the Spirit.*

In the new birth of our salvation, our spirit man, which was spiritually dead to God, has become alive to the Lord unto being in right standing with Him. Justice has been satisfied on our behalf. We must act on the work Jesus accomplished at Calvary, or we are still on our way to hell after death. Being in Christ Jesus now and walking or living your life according to the Gospel, there's no condemnation. The Holy Spirit may convict us of sin, but Satan will attempt to condemn us. However, God will forgive us. If we are still yielding to the temptation of sin after getting saved, it's evident we need growth in God. We can only behave in a particular manner if we know the power necessary to do it. Acknowledge today that we need to walk after the spirit, not the flesh, in the Word of God, His Bible. When you know you haven't done anything against God's Word, but the thoughts of condemnation are coming, the devil and his crew are trying to get you off your game. There is now no condemnation to those who are in Christ Jesus. Believe the Lord, not Satan.

# September 9

# Fierce Belief

*Romans 10:17*

*So faith comes by hearing [what is told], and what is heard comes by the preaching [of the message that came from the lips] of Christ (the Messiah Himself).*

Everything you hear has the ability to stick in your mind. Faith comes by hearing and hearing by the Word of God. In a way, we are blank pages ready to be imprinted upon. Like a computer, we can be programmed and be controlled by programming. Faith comes by hearing, hearing, and hearing. Whatever you hear over and over, sticks in your mind after a while, then it drops down into your spirit and you begin to speak it out of your mouth (Luke 6:45). When we totally believe a thing, we could become that thing, good or bad. We are faith beings by nature, but when we go on the offensive with our faith, miracles can happen. Investors go by faith in their business dealings all the time. They invest large amounts of money with no guarantee the investment will succeed. But their trust, hope, and fierce belief it will happen overrides their fear of losing the money. If you trust God that way, the possibilities in life are without limits. God already promised an abundant prosperous life to us (John 10:10), but we must go after it with a fierce belief.

# *September 10*

# THE ROUTE TO GREATNESS

*Romans 5:3-5*

*Moreover [let us also be full of joy now!] let us exult and triumph in our troubles and rejoice in our sufferings, knowing that pressure and affliction and hardship produce patient and unswerving endurance. And endurance (fortitude) develops maturity of character (approved faith and tried integrity). And character [of this sort] produces [the habit of] joyful and confident hope of eternal salvation. Such hope never disappoints or deludes or shames us, for God's love has been poured out in our hearts through the Holy Spirit Who has been given to us.*

If we can successfully go through pressure, affliction, and hardship, it will produce patience and unswerving endurance. Now, you may be thinking you don't want to deal with the suffering part, but those seemingly bad things no one wants to go through in life will help produce in us qualities leading up to, and including, approved faith in God's helping us through it and tried integrity. Integrity comes with a cost to our natural way of doing things, as we always have. Integrity becomes a built-in governor, keeping us on the righteous path even though the pressures of life give us desperate thoughts. When we yield to those negative thoughts, there's a break in our character and integrity, because in those thoughts, God's nowhere to be found in the decisions we make out of being pressured by a crisis. Steadfastness and endurance during trials is the only route to greatness.

# *September 11*

# ANOTHER PERSPECTIVE
# OF LIFE

*Revelation 4:11*

*Worthy are You, our Lord and God, to receive the glory and the honor and dominion, for You created all things; by Your will they were [brought into being] and were created.*

You may have asked yourself, why is there life on Earth? What was the original purpose for the creation of life? God said in the beginning, let Us make man in Our own image and likeness. Father, Son, and Holy Spirit were having a corporate meeting before any creation began (Genesis 1:26-27). God wanted someone to fellowship with on His level of existence. It may be hard to accept this, but man, and woman are little god's or little christs. We were created for God's pleasure. The angels and different creatures in heaven aren't made in God's image and likeness, we are. (Revelation 5:6-14) This world, run by the devil, has been programed to keep that reality away from our understanding so we won't know our true potential. Knowing who you are in Christ Jesus and the authority that goes along with it, is priceless once obtained and acted upon.

# *September 12*

# KEEP HIM IN THE MIX

*Isaiah 53:6*

*All we like sheep have gone astray, we have turned every one to his own way; and the Lord has made to light upon Him the guilt and iniquity of us all.*

All of us like sheep have strayed away. We have left God's path to follow our own. We are laborers together with God, we are not supposed to be a solo act. Simply because we don't see God with physical eyes, we tend to think He's not there, and thereby don't include Him in our plans. Having someone who knows what's coming next in our life is vitally important for the abundant life God has promised. It's a lifestyle to have God continually in the mix for successful, and victorious living. The Creator of life and all things has the perfect plan for our life, but in order to know the plan, we must know God through quality fellowship. According to the Word of God, all things work together for our good, and we can do all things through Christ who strengthens us. Keep Him in the mix!

# *September 13*

# THE NAME ABOVE EVERY NAME

*Colossians 3:17*

*And whatever you do [no matter what it is] in word or deed, do everything in the name of the Lord Jesus and in [dependence upon] His Person, giving praise to God the Father through Him.*

We are representatives of the kingdom of God when we use the name of Jesus. The fullness of the Godhead resides in that name (Colossians 2:9). Once a Christian knows his or her authority in Christ, the power will be in their hands to fight the enemy, and to help change bad circumstances. We have the power of the Holy Spirit with measure, not like Jesus who had the power without measure when He walked the Earth. As we become married to that name, with intense intimacy, we grow in power, and grace. Demons tremble at the mention of that name, knowing the power that is behind that name, (James 2:19) and they're counting on us not knowing it, so they can come hug a little tighter. As we do our due diligence in seeking God and exercising His teachings and precepts, we can only become more powerful with the use of the name of Jesus, the name above every name.

# *September 14*

# HEAVENLY MINDED

*Colossians 3:2*

*And set your minds and keep them set on what is above (the higher things), not on the things that are on the Earth.*

We as Christians are sojourners here on planet Earth. We are passing through, and along the way we must bring as many unsaved people with us as possible. That would be setting our minds on things above not on Earthly things. Since we are ambassadors for Christ, it is imperative that we are more concerned about God's business than our Earthly day-to-day business. Yes, we must function in this world being in it, but we're not to be of this world. God said in His word, we shall eat the good of the land, and He promises us abundant life here and now. But if we get caught up with the things of this world, it will take us off our God-given purpose and destiny. If so, then, *'Houston we have a problem!'* We should be showing the world Jesus in our everyday lives, boldly declaring the Gospel to any and everyone. If you're still a closet Christian it's time to come out. If your acquaintances and friends can't tell you're about that Christian-life, then you're still in the closet. The renewal of our minds (with God's Word, the Bible) is vital to keeping our thoughts on things above.

# *September 15*

# LIFE BEATERS: WORRY AND ANXIETY

### Matthew 6:34

*So do not worry or be anxious about tomorrow, for tomorrow will have worries and anxieties of its own. Sufficient for each day is its own trouble.*

Worry is the thief of tomorrow's strength, joy, peace, comfort, and more. It's almost crazy worrying about something that may not ever happen. The remedy for that is, always being ready to fight the good fight of faith for anything you are going through using God's Word and the name of Jesus. You must know your authority in Christ, or you could stay in the worry zone (Luke 10:19). Being concerned is different than worrying. Being concerned isn't overreacting to a moment of despair, but beginning to calculate your plan of attack against the issue. Worry is designed to keep us worn out so we cannot function normally. Since worry and fear are buddies, we can use love to drive them out. "Perfect love drives out fear" (1 John 4:18), and we are commanded not to be anxious or worried about tomorrow. Why would God tell us not to participate with these two life-beaters if the ability was not in us. We have these treasures in our Earthen vessels (our bodies). Learn how to draw from the Lord that which is necessary for victorious living and stop worrying now! It will be alright.

# September 16

# THE FREE GIFT

*Acts 1:8*

*But you shall receive power (ability, efficiency, and might) when the Holy Spirit has come upon you, and you shall be My witnesses in Jerusalem and all Judea and Samaria and to the ends (the very bounds) of the Earth.*

But you shall receive power when the Holy Spirit comes upon you. What power? Dunamis power, it's like spiritual dynamite. We can wield this power to drive off the enemy. This power is not physical or natural but very effective in pulling down strongholds, principalities, and powers of the air, the unseen forces influencing humankind since the beginning. There's a fight going on that we cannot see, but affects us in this natural world. There's more to life than our eyes can see, and with this power, we become more aware of it. The power is the gift of the Holy Spirit's impartation of a deeper dimension of God through speaking in tongues, which is still active today. We get spooked about this area of the Christian life because of our ignorance of the subject. This is a necessary impartation for power to witness the Gospel more effectively. And praying in tongues builds up our newly recreated human spirits, which can infuse our faith to act. Ask God, and He will freely give it to you.

# September 17

# WHO IS THIS KING OF GLORY?

*Psalm 24:10*

*Who is [He then] this King of glory? The Lord of hosts, He is the King of glory. Selah [pause, and think of that]!*

The King of Glory is the Lord of Hosts, the God of battles. God has been coming against the evil in this world since the fall of man. God has enemies just like us. It is better to be on the Lord's side in battle than the evil side. How do you know which side you're on? Good question; if you have zero relationship with God, then you can guess the right answer. You may have a relationship with God because you're a Christian, but without fellowship, we live as those who don't. The King of Glory has set us free through the blood of the Lamb. We don't have to be on the wrong side of life if we follow the teachings and precepts of the Bible. Just existing without Godly purpose behind us brings zero fruit of fellowship with God. It also leaves us more susceptible to Satan's attacks. The Lord of Hosts fights our battles when we put Him first in everything we do.

# *September 18*

# ONCE YOU DIE, IT STILL AIN'T OVER

*Zechariah 14:9*

*And the Lord shall be King over all the Earth; in that day the Lord shall be one [in the recognition and worship of men] and His name one.*

There's coming a time when the Lord will be King over the whole Earth. After the rapture and when the new Jerusalem sets down on Earth (Revelation 21:2), there will be no devil in play. There will be no more sun in the sky because the Lord will be the light that shines (Isaiah 60:19). There will be one Lord, one God, and a theocracy-ruled world. He will rule with the perfect balance of love, correction, justice, and with honest labor for everyone. The element of secret unjust motives will no longer exist. No more hurt, or pain of any kind will be our portion once the Lord is King over all the Earth. No one will be a part of this new world coming that hasn't been saved or born again. Making Jesus Lord and Savior of your life before your death, gets you in.

# *September 19*

# THE VINE CONNECTION
# IS VITAL!

### John 15:4

*Dwell in Me, and I will dwell in you. [Live in Me, and I will live in you.] Just as no branch can bear fruit of itself without abiding in (being vitally united to) the vine, neither can you bear fruit unless you abide in Me.*

It is essential to live our lives based on the Word of God. The closer we get to lining up with His Word in our thought-life, which will control our actions, the closer we get to His favor and grace. We can bear much fruit on His behalf as we stay connected to the vine, which is Jesus. He is the vine, we are the branches, and we are to produce fruit. Fruit is witnessing to others about the Gospel. It's leading someone to Christ or praying for others to get healed, and they do. We are little Christ's in the Earth, about our Father's business. Jesus is the Head of the body of Christ, and we Christians are His body in the Earth. We get instructions from the Head that we, His body, still being on Earth, must carry out. Our Head is now in Heaven (Mark 16:19), so we must be sensitive to His Spirit to receive our marching orders of bearing fruit.

# *September 20*

# CRY ON MY FRIEND

*Psalm 126:5*

*They who sow in tears shall reap in joy and singing.*

The Bible says that God collects our tears (Psalm 56:8). It is for a purpose later, I'm assuming after the rapture, and possibly around the judgement seat of Christ when we're examined for the works we've done down here on Earth. The Lord is aware of our tears, but that alone won't get God moving to help us. He's looking for those that have relationship with Him, and knows His Word, which means you know God, not you know of Him. The hand of faith is what moves the hand of God. Our tears are sometimes necessary to release the internal clutter of disbelief. When we've messed up and get reprimanded for our actions, in our heart of hearts we feel remorse, maybe guilt, and shame. Our tears help release the pressure of these feelings. And when a person can admit they've missed it, true repentance is at the door of their soul, and at that point, joy comes in the morning. Cry on my friend, your tears are being collected by God, and He is the God of comfort and will help get you through what you're going through (2 Corinthians 1:3-5).

# *September 21*

# HIS MIGHTY WORKS

*Psalm 77:11-12*

*I will [earnestly] recall the deeds of the Lord; yes, I will [earnestly] remember the wonders [You performed for our fathers] of old.*

With the parting of the Red Sea, turning water to wine, healing the sick, and all the miracles performed in the Bible, none come close to the new birth. The new birth is when your old death-doomed human spirit becomes born again, recreating without the sin nature. Jesus told His disciples, *"...Greater works than these shall you do..."* (John 14:12). I believe the greater works He spoke of were getting more people saved and witnessing to people about the Gospel. Turning someone's fate from being hell-bound, to life everlasting with the family of God in heaven, which is most definitely a greater thing for humankind. Most of us are not thinking about life after death because we're so caught up in trying to survive today's life struggles. The Lord's life insurance is the best, fire protection included. Your human spirit, the real you, never dies (John 3:16), only this Earthly-suit (your body) you've worn all your life will perish. God's mighty works are innumerable, and the Earth could not contain all the books necessary to write about them (John 21:25).

# *September 22*

# THE HEAD FIGHT

*2 Corinthians 10:5, NLT*

*We destroy every proud obstacle that keeps people from knowing God. We capture their rebellious thoughts and teach them to obey Christ.*

By bringing every thought into captivity under the scrutiny of the knowledge of Christ, we protect the truth. Many people have theories of God and how He is from a perspective totally out of line with His truth. A theory is a supposition established upon ignorance of the subject under discussion. They don't know God from a personal relationship with Him, which is a big difference. We have no control over the thoughts that come into our minds, but they should be dealt with immediately before we act on them. Every thought should be brought into subjection of the knowledge of God's Word first. Some thoughts are strong thoughts of temptation which aren't easy to resist but can be done. The Bible says, *"Resist the devil, and he will flee"* (James 4:7). The words before that verse say first to be submitted to God, and then Satan will leave. Without God's help, the devil is hugging you a little tighter. The battleground of our thought-life occurs in the mind, where we are instructed to renew our minds to conform to God's will. The fight is in your mind first, and you demonstrate you are more than a conqueror there.

# *September 23*

# PEACE BE STILL, DRAMA BE GONE!

### *John 16:33*

*I have told you these things, so that in Me you may have [perfect] peace and confidence. In the world you have tribulation and trials and distress and frustration; but be of good cheer [take courage; be confident, certain, undaunted]! For I have overcome the world. [I have deprived it of power to harm you and have conquered it for.]*

In this world we have tribulation, trials and distress and frustration, but the good news is Jesus deprived this world of its power to harm us. We give this world power over us by our association with it, and agreeing with things of this world that we shouldn't. Our peace in this world is in our own hands. The peace that passes all understanding is ours as Christians (Philippians 4:6-7). Everything around us can be in disarray and out of control, but once God's peace is ruling your inner self, or your mind, you won't freak out like most people under pressure. The key to peace is invoking your will to seek after it first (Romans 14:19). This could mean eliminating certain people out of your life because they love drama. If you're into the hype and gymnastics of drama, then the peace of God isn't for you. Even separating yourself from drama folk, that alone won't get you the peace that passes all understanding, but spending time with the Peacemaker is vital (Isaiah 9:6). Ask Him for this peace, and then, diligently go after it.

# *September 24*

# THE DIRTIEST WEED OF ALL

*Colossians 3:13*

*Be gentle and forbearing with one another and, if one has a difference (a grievance or complaint) against another, readily pardoning each other; even as the Lord has [freely] forgiven you, so must you also [forgive].*

Unforgiveness is a dirty weed that needs to be plucked out of our lives. Everyone has or will experience hurt. It is a part of being human. What you do with hurt is what matters most. How have you been handling offense and hurt? The person that holds it all in or suppresses it, is a walking time bomb for internal and external disasters. Unforgiveness is a slow poison to your heart, mind, and eventually sickness in your body. The person that will not forgive is the one being punished, because unforgiveness will not let you rest and the thoughts are relentless. Holding on to offense is an open door for other detriments working on you like oppression, and depression, because you are not allowing the offense or unforgiveness to leave you, so you feel trapped internally. Unforgiveness keeps you blinded to your own health going to the gutter, because you will not let what that person did to you go. It is not always easy to forgive but look at what it is doing to you. Let go of unforgiveness today.

# *September 25*

# CONFESSION HAS A PURPOSE

*James 5:16*

*Confess to one another therefore your faults (your slips, your false steps, your offenses, your sins) and pray [also] for one another, that you may be healed and restored [to a spiritual tone of mind and heart]. The earnest (heartfelt, continued) prayer of a righteous man makes tremendous power available [dynamic in its working].*

Confessing to others your faults and slip-ups in your life takes humility. When you cannot talk about or simply admit that you messed up, that's a sign of your pride meter being in the red. A person that always wants to be right no matter the cost to others, doesn't have a humble bone in their body (1 Peter 5:6). This frame of mind is detrimental to their life. If you mess up, ask for forgiveness from the other person or God if it were a private sin, and keep it moving (1 John 1:9). Don't get hung up on condemnation after you've repented. If people can't forgive you when you mess up, then you're around the wrong people. No one can live sin free other than Jesus when He walked the Earth. When we confess our sins, God is faithful and just to forgive us, that's His own words. Healing from God is hindered from getting to you because of the sin in your life. Get rid of it, confess your way out of sin, and into healing.

# *September 26*

# REJOICE WHEN
# TROUBLE HITS!

### Habakkuk 3:17-18

*Though the fig tree does not blossom and there is no fruit on the vines, [though] the product of the olive fails, and the fields yield no food, though the flock is cut off from the fold and there are no cattle in the stalls, Yet I will rejoice in the Lord; I will exult in the [victorious] God of my salvation!*

When things look grim concerning living provisions, and you have no idea where your next meal is coming from, can you, at that point, praise God anyway? And why should you, right? Because when we offer up praise to God during trouble, that shows God we trust Him no matter what comes. It has been said praising and thanking God before the manifested answer clears the way for God to get it to you sooner. Regardless, like a bulldog on a bone, we should never loosen our stronghold of faith in God. He cares for us faithfully and watches over us eagerly (1 Peter 5:7), especially when He knows we trust Him to come through on our behalf. He'll climb over a million people to reach the faith-filled heart of expectancy. Our faith will soar by keeping negative faith-killer words out of our ears, along with people who are so Earthly and fleshly-minded.

# September 27

# YOU ARE NOT ALONE

### Isaiah 43:2

*When you pass through the waters, I will be with you, and through the rivers, they will not overwhelm you. When you walk through the fire, you will not be burned or scorched, nor will the flame kindle upon you.*

When the Bible talks about passing through the waters or the fire, it indicates big trouble or troubles. It's saying as we walk through the fire we will not be burned. It is not saying we will be kept from the fire itself, but the intervention of God takes place here, so we pass through unscathed. Trouble and storms of life come to us all, there's no escaping it. Learning how to pass through victoriously is key. The weapons of our warfare are not carnal first of all. We are wrestling against the principalities and powers of the air which are evil spirits behind the scenes working against Christians especially. We carry the light of the world, and evil represents darkness. Light has to do with exposure and truth which they can't deal with, and it reminds them of the Holy beat-down Jesus gave Satan in hell. God will be with us through struggles, crises, or anything else. Walking through the valley of the shadow of death has no hold on the trusting, believing Christian who knows their authority in Christ. We should be on the offensive while God has our backs at every turn.

# *September 28*

# THE WISDOM FROM ABOVE

*James 1:5*

*If any of you is deficient in wisdom, let him ask of the giving God [Who gives] to everyone liberally and ungrudgingly, without reproaching or faultfinding, and it will be given him.*

G od gives wisdom to all who ask Him. Wisdom is the proper allocation of knowledge at any given time in any situation. Sometimes, it's best to keep your mouth shut instead of getting into a heated discussion with an ignorant person; that's wisdom. God's generous gift of wisdom is received by those who realize something is going on behind the scenes of our lives that's bigger than our normal thinking alone. Even a fool is considered wise when he holds his peace (Proverbs 17:28). Wisdom also regulates our faith. God's Word is directly connected to His wisdom, and it's best not to believe for something that could potentially hurt you after you get it, wisdom understands that. God's wisdom is winsome, easy to approach, and gentle. This world's wisdom is all about self, devilish in its motivations.

# September 29

## GOD'S NOT SLOW, HE'S MERCIFUL

*2 Peter 3:9*

*The Lord does not delay and is not tardy or slow about what He promises, according to some people's conception of slowness, but He is long-suffering (extraordinarily patient) toward you, not desiring that any should perish, but that all should turn to repentance.*

God is patient with us. When we pray to the Lord for help or anything, He answers that prayer right away. There's no visible evidence of answered prayer while you are praying. So that's where faith and patience should be holding hands very tightly until the answer is a reality in this realm. *"...Through faith and patience, we obtain the promises of God" (Hebrews 6:12).* God's timeline is different from ours. We are of the microwave generation because we want it now and don't want to wait longer than we have to. We have to understand how God moves on our behalf. He's aligning things behind the scenes to have a domino effect of blessings. Many times, our answered prayer comes as a multi-fold blessing to not only help you but someone else who may have been hurting. He's patient because, first of all, he wants everyone to be a part of His family, and many people need time to decide if they want God. He knows when we need more time to figure stuff out. Sometimes we need more time to hit bottom, so we know what we've been doing all along doesn't work. God's not slow, He's merciful.

# *September 30*

# SPIRITUAL HELP IS NECESSARY
# IN THIS NATURAL WORLD

*Romans 8:26*

*So too the [Holy] Spirit comes to our aid and bears us up in our weakness; for we do not know what prayer to offer nor how to offer it worthily as we ought, but the Spirit Himself goes to meet our supplication and pleads in our behalf with unspeakable yearnings and groanings too deep for utterance.*

Sometimes, we don't know what or how to pray as we ought during trouble. The smokescreen of trouble has our attention. It's a smokescreen because the devil tries blocking your understanding of working God's Word, which can bring you out of it. The Spirit of God helps us in our weakness. We often won't have the proper words when attacked, and our faith-filled words are the key to confessing our way to victory. We can have what we say as long as God's Word comes out of our mouths (Mark 11:23-24), nothing negative. There's a deeper dimension of God that most people and Christians are afraid of, thanks to Satan. Praying in tongues has not passed away. Praying in tongues is praying the perfect will of God back to Him, which will correct your situation. It is the gift of God for Christians. It also gives us greater power to witness to others the Gospel. Use all the help God has provided. You'll need it just to level the playing field of life.

# October 1

# THIS IS TOO DEEP FOR YOU

*Colossians 3:1, NLT*

*Since you have been raised to new life with Christ, set your sights on the realities of heaven, where Christ sits in the place of honor at God's right hand.*

If you have been raised from the dead with Christ, then go after those things which are above, eternal, that you can't see with your natural eyes. We live in a world that was created by a place that existed before Earth was. The heavens where God, and His angels live is the real world. When Jesus came down He brought the plan of redemption, we can now draw our needs from that other realm of existence. But everything must go through Jesus to receive down here. It's our faith in Christ that connects us to the other realm where God lives. Setting your hearts on things above, puts you in position for heavenly help.

# *October 2*

# WHO'S YOUR FRIEND?

*Proverbs 17:17*
*A friend loves at all times, and is born, as is a brother, for adversity.*

Friends always show their love, but that will be tested sooner or later. Sometimes, we think someone has our back because "we're friends," but when trouble hits the fan, your "friend" shows their true colors and leaves you hanging out to dry by yourself. The one true friend we can count on when no one else is available is Jesus (Proverbs 18:24). "What a friend we have in Jesus" is how the song goes. With all the vicissitudes of life we deal with in this world, there must be a stabilizing force to hold us down. When you have that one friend that sticks close to you no matter what, your ride-or-die partner, that's a gift in this world that is not easy to find. Life hits us all, but having someone to stand with you in prayer, in battle, and just to tell you it will be alright is priceless. A good friend will correct you when you're wrong, even though it's gonna hurt. If your friend can't accept the correction, then you were never friends in the first place, and it's best to leave them alone.

# *October 3*

# ONWARD CHRISTIAN SOLDIERS

*1 John 4:4*

*Little children, you are of God [you belong to Him] and have [already] defeated and overcome them [the agents of the antichrist], because He Who lives in you is greater (mightier) than he who is in the world.*

Although greater is He that is in you than he that is in the world, we must allow the greater one in us to have the ascendancy of our choices, and major decisions in life. The greater one in us can keep us one step ahead of the evil one, if we give Him the forefront of our thoughts and actions. No matter what this world throws at us we are more than conquerors through Christ Jesus who has already defeated our enemies on our behalf (Romans 8:37). We must tap into what has already been provided by God. It is, and always will be our choice of how we fight. The weapons of our warfare are not carnal, but mighty through God to the pulling down of strongholds of any kind (2 Corinthians 10:4). We fight with the tools the Greater One gave us. Confession of God's Word and prayer are the key factors for victory on every front of the battles we face.

# *October 4*

# TRUST ISSUES LEAD TO WORRY

*1 Peter 5:7*

*Casting the whole of your care [all your anxieties, all your worries, all your concerns, once and for all] on Him, for He cares for you affectionately and cares about you watchfully.*

One of the hardest things for people is not to worry. Being concerned should be the beginning of planning defensive or offensive maneuvers to resolve an issue. Worrying is a no-plan, hopeless, crippling attitude that puts us in bondage. Worry has no place in our lives because of its negative effects on us. It takes the life out of our expectations and dreams for today and leaves us high and dry for tomorrow's regularly scheduled program. Hope is a confident, favorable expectation for a desired outcome. Worry will take hope out of the picture. God gave us a command not to worry, so it's possible. He expects us to include Him in resisting worry since it can be a spirit. The spirit of fear carries the symptom of worry. Since perfect love (mature love) drives out fear, it will take worry with it. Simply because God cares for us, He has made a way to escape worry. It is up to us to take God's way out so the temptation of worry won't overtake us. All cases concerning the temptation to worry can be avoided by trusting God's Word of promise to you concerning it. Jesus Christ has defeated worry, so stop giving it a second round. Fight's over. Boom!

# *October 5*

# MY STRENGTH AND MY SHIELD

*Psalm 28:7, NLT*

*The Lord is my strength and shield. I trust him with all my heart. He helps me, and my heart is filled with joy. I burst out in songs of thanksgiving.*

The Lord is our strength and our shield. As we trust in Him more and more, that shield becomes even more fortified, and our strength is made perfect (mature) through our weakness (2 Corinthians 12:8-10). Once physical strength is depleted, the supernatural kicks in. Now if you don't believe it, it won't be happening for you. We must believe with our hearts (no ocular or physical proof, not with your understanding). The key words in the text today are, "I trust Him with my whole heart..." When we lose ourselves in believing for God's promised provisions for our lives, and having cast all our care on Him, because He cares for us (1 Peter 5:7), then we reap the benefits of our confessed faith in Him, and His Word. Faith is, and always will be the hand that receives from God. Without faith it is impossible to please God, and when we please God, blessings begin to overflow in our lives (Hebrews 11:6). So, when you get weak, strength is available, and when you need protection, He is your strong tower.

# *October 6*

# STAND FIRM IN YOUR WAY, THE DECEIVER IS COMING

*1 Corinthians 15:58*

*Therefore, my beloved brethren, be firm (steadfast), immovable, always abounding in the work of the Lord [always being superior, excelling, doing more than enough in the service of the Lord], knowing and being continually aware that your labor in the Lord is not futile [it is never wasted or to no purpose].*

We are to be firm, steadfast, and immovable, always abounding in the works of the Lord. Our labor is not in vain. People or circumstances often try to take you off your path. That is when we are to stand firm and steadfast. Anything or anyone that tries to remove you from your God-given purpose and destiny has been sent to see if you are grounded in your plans and secure in your thoughts and actions. Many of us have our God-given plans in motion, and we're about our own business, and here comes someone who thinks they have a better plan or way of accomplishing yours. That is because they haven't found their God-given plan yet and want to run yours. Be careful with people without a purpose in life, that act like they know yours better than you. Stay on course, stay firm, and remain steadfast on your pathway. God may have you take a left instead of the planned right turn down the road (Isaiah 30:21). Be sensitive to that still small voice in you, your gut feeling. That's where God speaks to you.

# *October 7*

# TIME TO READ THE METER

*James 1:19*

*Understand [this], my beloved brethren. Let every man be quick to hear [a ready listener], slow to speak, slow to take offense and to get angry.*

Where do your integrity and character-meter point to? "Be quick to listen, slow to speak, and slow to anger." If you are good at this, you're in the ballpark. With understanding, it's much easier to be slow to anger. When we understand another person's hardship or the fact they're incapable of comprehending or digesting different perspectives, a person of integrity and character will walk away from an accelerated overheated moment. When we are reactionary to offenses, we leave the area of being slow to speak behind; you've just come down a few digits on the integrity and character meter. This isn't for new converts or novices but for those who've decided to grow up in this area. Smart people are drawn to others of like-mind. It may be time to change your circle of influence and get free and in a position to live above a lot of nonsense in this world. There is a place in the kingdom of God for you to flourish.

# October 8

## WHEN SICKNESS CALLS, AND PROBLEMS DOMINATE

*Isaiah 53:5*

*But He was wounded for our transgressions, He was bruised for our guilt and iniquities; the chastisement [needful to obtain] peace and well-being for us was upon Him, and with the stripes [that wounded] Him we are healed and made whole.*

By the stripes laid on Jesus' back (He was severely whipped), we are healed from every sickness or disease that was, that is, and ever will be. He took our infirmities and weaknesses and was nailed to the cross with them so we could live above them. That may sound a bit spooky or super spiritual, but as we learn about the things of God, we realize there's a belief system already in place for our use. Our proof of victory is simply to take God at His Word concerning our situation. There's a scripture for every area of life, for the troubles and problems that go along with it. Our job is to study and show ourselves approved by rightly dividing the Word of God for our individual needs in life (2 Timothy 2:15). Jesus prayed to God not to take us out of the world but that we might live above the evil in the world. If you need healing in your body, mind, or soul, it's been covered by Jesus long ago. Our part is to find God's Word concerning our issue, confess that scripture like taking medicine every day, and believe Him that things will work out for our good, and if we're patient, they will.

# October 9

# ENCOURAGE, EXHORT, AND BUILD OTHERS UP

*1 Thessalonians 5:11*

*Therefore encourage (admonish, exhort) one another and edify (strengthen and build up) one another, just as you are doing.*

Part of the Christian lifestyle is to help admonish, strengthen, and build each other up, not tear each other down. We have allowed the world's attitude into the church. Encouraging one another in the Lord is iron sharpening iron, talked about in the Bible (Proverbs 27:17). When we come together and share testimonies and revelations from God we may have experienced, that's iron sharpening iron. We were born into a world dominated by satanic rule. It's an uphill battle to shake off the world's way of doing things. The world's way is not hurting people's feelings or being overly concerned about what people think about us. What people think about us is out of our control. Their thoughts will be guided by what they perceive, although their discernment is false. How can anyone help us with encouragement or build us up when they have worldly unfounded negative thoughts about us? We can only help others when we have the right information concerning that person and God's way of life has been our portion for many years, or we have at least matured in the things of God long enough. If you've been helping people God's way, keep it going because the Lord really needs you to.

# *October 10*

# THE BILL COMES DUE

*Revelation 7:9-10*

*After this I looked and a vast host appeared which no one could count, [gathered out] of every nation, from all tribes and peoples and languages. These stood before the throne and before the Lamb; they were attired in white robes, with palm branches in their hands. In loud voice they cried, saying, [Our] salvation is due to our God, Who is seated on the throne, and to the Lamb [to Them we owe our deliverance]!*

Deliverance from habitual wrongdoing has been made available to the entire world. The challenge today is that we live in a world not interested in eternity. It wants our attention to be constantly in the moment to distract and keep our minds off the fact we are all going to one day leave this Earth. Where you stay after death is dependent on your decision-making today. Salvation is from the Lord. He desires our deliverance and freedom from the constant struggles that sin brings into our lives. When we accept Jesus as Lord and Savior, we gain a place in Heaven. According to Jesus, He said, *'I go away now (to heaven) to prepare a place for you after you die on Earth' (John 14:3).* If you do not accept the work Jesus completed at Calvary - being beaten, whipped until His skin was ripped off of him, nailed to the cross naked, then you don't accept what He did for the wrong doings (sin) you committed. You will have to pay the price of it yourself by spending eternity in hell. The bill will come due, and no one can afford it, but Christ.

# October 11

# GRACE, AN UNREALIZED HELP FROM GOD

### 2 Corinthians 9:8

*And God is able to make all grace (every favor and Earthly blessing) come to you in abundance, so that you may always and under all circumstances and whatever the need be self-sufficient [possessing enough to require no aid or support and furnished in abundance for every good work and charitable donation].*

Through God's grace, we become self-sufficient and need no aid or support because the Lord has us covered for walking in abundance for every good work and charitable donation. He gives us grace and favor to fulfill our God-given purpose. Grace takes the friction out of an uphill task of vital importance. Grace gives confidence to our thought processes to help us deal with our everyday struggles. We become like well-oiled machines doing the work of the kingdom of God, and our often emotional battles can cool the flame of adversity in general. Yielding to the grace of God when it arises in you makes all the difference. The grace of God comes by way of trusting God for everything. It takes time to trust like that, but it's doable for the steadfast believer. His mercies are new every morning (Lamentations 3:22-23), but His grace is effective night and day.

# October 12

# AGAPE COMES IN SEED FORM

## John 13:34

*I give you a new commandment: that you should love one another.*
*Just as I have loved you, so you too should love one another.*

We are commanded to love one another. A command from the Master Himself to love. You can love from a distance if necessary. I don't have to like you to love you. Walking in love with someone has very specific differences than liking someone. I may not like you, but if I see you're hurting, or in dire need of help, out of the love in my heart I can meet you at the point of your lack. For example, let's consider the attitude of dealing with an unruly family member or one with a difficult personality, we're still family. There's always a way to deal with most people, and the way of God's love is the only way. The love of God, agape love, has been shed abroad in our hearts by God's Spirit at the new birth when you become a Christian (Romans 5:5). It comes in seed form which needs development and growth. To cultivate the love of God in you, we practice showing love through random acts of kindness and compassion, even to people who don't deserve it. This establishes a system within you that no matter what or who you're dealing with, you'll stay rooted in love and its attributes and qualities. It's sacrificial work, so roll up your sleeves.

# October 13

# THE POWER WE MUST REALIZE WE HAVE

*Proverbs 18:21*

*Death and life are in the power of the tongue, and they who indulge in it shall eat the fruit of it [for death or life].*

The tongue has the power of life and death. When you speak with faith, it releases creative power. Confessing with your mouth and believing in your heart is the basis for becoming a Christian. We use the Holy Spirit with measure, which means individually, we can and will have what we say over time. We can speak ourselves into victory or defeat. Satan will bring temptation to you, and if you take the bait, you will begin to speak that thing and as you believe it, the power is released against you. For example, we say something like, *"You're killing me"* when someone makes you laugh hard. Or, *"You'll never amount to anything in life."* These negative expressions release demonic influences in the world. The devil has been using the power of the tongue against humankind for thousands of years. He knows our make-up and understands how spiritual things work. He hates us because of God kicking him out of heaven. Lucifer was his name then (he was God's worship leader in heaven). The meaning of his name from the old English Latin is light bringing, morning star. In Isaiah 14:12, he is called "son of the morning." The dark side knows the power of the tongue. Now you know, so run with it straight into victorious living.

# *October 14*

# JUST WAIT, YOU
# WILL NOT FAIL!

*Psalm 130:5*
*I wait for the Lord, I expectantly wait, and in His word do I hope.*

Waiting on the Lord is an action. We are waiting with the expectancy of His promises to manifest in our life. Hoping in His Word is where our heads should be, pondering what His Word says about our situation. Those who wait on the Lord shall renew their strength (Isaiah 40:31). It is expected of the Lord that we wait on Him, and as we do, the prayer of thanksgiving should be offered to Him. Thanking God for something that you haven't received yet is faith in action. Believing that you have received *before* you have the manifestation is the lifestyle necessary to walking with God in total victory in every area of your life (Mark 11:24). But it's not going to just fall in your lap. We must study His Word to show ourselves approved, rightly dividing the Word in truth. (You can't believe God to help you get another person's spouse, or to help you rob a bank.) Knowing God's Word for yourself puts you in agreement with His way of doing things for your life. Wait on God, it won't be too late when He answers you. Earthly deadlines mean nothing to God, He'll change that too if necessary. Trust Him until the end, and then keep trusting Him. You will not fail!

# October 15

# MAKE DISCIPLES

*Matthew 28:19*

*Go then and make disciples of all the nations, baptizing them into the name of the Father and of the Son and of the Holy Spirit.*

When the Disciples were told to go make disciples of all nations, they didn't have worldwide technology like we do today. They walked or rode animals back in their day to spread the Gospel. Today, we have the Internet, so we can go into all the world and make disciples of all nations. It was a direct command from God to not only spread the Gospel of Christ, but to make disciples which means giving them the Gospel, and then walking them through how to be a disciple. If every Christian would share one verse from the Bible every day on social media, the command of discipling all the nations could be a faster process.

# *October 16*

# THE PROGRAM TO SEE GOD

*Hebrews 12:14*

*Strive to live in peace with everybody and pursue that consecration and holiness without which no one will [ever] see the Lord.*

As much as lies within us we should thrive to live at peace with everybody, and to be holy, because without holiness no one will see the Lord. To be holy is obtained by walking in the fruit of our newly recreated human spirit, (which happens at the new birth). Love, joy, peace, patience, kindness, goodness, faithfulness, gentleness, and self-control. Nine fruits that rest on the bed of love. All these fruits must be developed to the best of our God-given ability. Peace will be our portion regularly as we exercise these fruits of the spirit in our everyday lives. Practicing being mindful of these God-given attributes will position us for the holy living the Lord has prescribed. Self-control is one of the most necessary fruits during development. Because people will test you to pull you out of the program. Patience must have its perfect work in you as well (James 1:4). Try not to overreact over the little things. Choose your battles, keep your peace, and be holy as your Father God is holy.

# *October 17*

# WHAT IS THE GLORY OF GOD?

*Habakkuk 2:14*

*But [the time is coming when] the Earth shall be filled with the knowledge of the glory of the Lord as the waters cover the sea.*

The glory of God is one of the most foundational questions to answer in all Christianity. It is so central to the Gospel, God's Word. The glory of God can be known as the manifested presence of God, which can happen during a church service or conference. It is when God, through the praise and worship of His people, shows up in this natural physical realm to heal or deliver those in need. When a miracle occurs, that's the ocular proof of the glory of God. The parting of the Red Sea, Jesus healing people when He walked the Earth, and anything that breaks through the natural laws that govern this world. It is a move of God that always brings comfort. In the Bible, it's talked about as the glory cloud, which, when you're in it, you become overwhelmed with such peace, comfort, and warmth in your soul you can't explain, and sometimes you can't even stand in it (2 Chronicles 5:14), but you love it when it happens. The text today is saying how the Earth shall be filled with His glory. A move of God is coming that the entire world will be aware of. This move of God will manifest His glory in different ways. However it comes, it will be in agreement with God's plans for these last days on Earth as we know it (Matthew 24:35).

# October 18

# A HUMBLING THOUGHT

*1 Peter 5:6*

*Therefore humble yourselves [demote, lower yourselves in your own estimation] under the mighty hand of God, that in due time He may exalt you.*

A s we humble ourselves under God's mighty hand, He will exalt us in the right season. Normally we get humbled because of our inflated pride. Pride goes before a fall. It is inevitable (Proverbs 16:8). It is a dirty weed that needs to be plucked out of your life. The meek shall inherit the Earth according to the Bible (Matthew 5:5). Being under God's mighty hand requires faith in Him, to deliver, strengthen, and take care of what concerns us. We sometimes build up a pride wall around ourselves, it is a false sense of protection, or comfort. It is encouraged by Satan himself. Pride is the sin that got Lucifer, who is now Satan, kicked out of heaven (Luke 10:18). He was God's right-hand man, or angel, and that must have hurt God, at least to a certain point. We can either humble ourselves before God or be humbled through a crisis or an extenuating circumstance that could break us into the person we should be before God. Humble yourself!

# October 19

# FOR THE MATURE ONLY

*Galatians 5:22-23, NKJV*

*But the fruit of the Spirit is love, joy, peace, longsuffering, kindness, goodness, faithfulness, gentleness, self-control. Against such there is no law.*

The fruit of our newly recreated human spirit can produce love, joy, peace, patience, kindness, goodness, faithfulness, gentleness, and self-control. When the Holy Spirit is allowed to work through our newly recreated human spirits, He helps develop the seeds of the fruit of the spirit in us. As we allow this process to have full latitude and longitude, it takes us from living below our potential to a destination of abundant life, and victorious living in general. All the fruit rests on the bed of love. God is love and we are children of a loving God (1 John 4:8). To the degree we allow God in our lives is to the degree we'll have good success in life. If you're not totally satisfied with who you are and where you are in life financially, socially, materially, mentally, spiritually, or any other way, then develop the fruit within you. Do the work and you'll reap the benefits.

# October 20

# THE SLEEP WE NEED

*Psalm 4:8*

*In peace I will both lie down and sleep, for You, Lord, alone make me dwell in safety and confident trust.*

Because God alone makes us dwell in safety we can lie down and sleep in peace. He has said, when you lie down your sleep shall be sweet (Proverbs 3:24). These are promises from God, so we can latch on to these truths and expect to experience them. The spirit of fear lurks around for unsure Christians. When we believe the scripture to be true and act on it, the results are inevitable. When our foundation in Him is anchored to our souls, nothing will be impossible or withheld from us. Love drives out fear so your faith can work because faith works by love. When your faith is strong you are ready for anything. Sleep is important in the scheme of things because when we are overly tired everything seems harder to accomplish, it is like an unnecessary uphill battle that could be avoided by getting proper sleep.

# October 21

# WITH ALL THE HEART

*Psalm 119:2*

*Blessed (happy, fortunate, to be envied) are they who keep His testimonies, and who seek, inquire for and of Him and crave Him with the whole heart.*

The Lord is a rewarder of those who diligently seek Him (Hebrews 11:6). Searching for Him with all your heart and not with mental assent. When we really mean something, when our entire focus is on a thing or person, our hearts will be involved. And when our heart is the runner of our actions (not our emotions), that can trigger the Supernatural's involvement. We cannot tap into the spirit realm with our minds or bodies. Our spirits are the real us; we have a soul, and we (our human spirits) live in a body. To search for God, the Bible is where we start. Going to the right church is important as well. According to the scripture verse today, obeying His laws once we know them will bring us joy. The motivation of the heart is where the search begins inside us. There's a longing for God and the supernatural in every person, whether realized or not. Some people mess around with Ouija boards or have seances seeking the supernatural. This world has developed the best distractions, counterfeits, and deception to keep the truth at bay of God's original plan for us. Obeying His laws will bring joy to the diligent soul whose heart's desire is the Lord.

# *October 22*

# IS GOD WITH YOU?

*Isaiah 7:14*

*Therefore the Lord Himself shall give you a sign: Behold, the young woman who is unmarried and a virgin shall conceive and bear a son, and shall call his name Immanuel [God with us].*

God gives us more of a personal sign of His plans these days. Back in the days of Mary and the virgin birth, we didn't have the Spirit of God in us. God would visit the men and women of God, which was more of an external contact with humankind. Today, in this new dispensation of God's plan, the Spirit of God dwells within us (1 Corinthians 3:16). Now we can cultivate relationship through God's Word and the study of it, hearing God's voice within us. The teachings and precepts in the Bible, and God's voice in our spirit, should agree in what's being said to us. He lives in His people by His Spirit which communicates with our human spirit. No more fleeces or sending Prophets (as in the past) to tell us what God says about us or the direction for us. It comes now by hearing that still small voice in our hearts - our human spirit. (Romans 8:14) After the finished work Jesus did at Calvary, humankind can truly say, *Immanuel*, God is with us.

# October 23

# THE WAY TO ETERNAL LIFE

*Matthew 1:21*

*She will bear a Son, and you shall call His name Jesus [the Greek form of the Hebrew Joshua, which means Savior], for He will save His people from their sins [that is, prevent them from failing and missing the true end and scope of life, which is God].*

The Greek form of the name Jesus, or more specifically Joshua, means Savior. He literally saved the world from having to go to hell to pay for their sins. But when Jesus is received (by faith) as Lord and Savior of our lives, He literally went to hell and dropped off our sins so we don't have to. Otherwise, you pay the price of sin by going to hell yourself after you die. It takes forever to pay the price of sinning on Earth without getting forgiveness in advance. Jesus is the way, the truth, and the life; no one goes to Heaven without Him, and the contract with Him must be signed before leaving planet Earth (John 14:6). God won't be the one to blame once you stand before Him and try to explain why you didn't accept His Son before you died. Life after death can be wonderful or horrible; the scary part is that it's your choice. Take up stock in Heaven for the next life; you'd want prime real estate instead of the heated option below.

# *October 24*

# BE SMARTER THAN YOUR PROBLEMS

*Colossians 3:16*

*Let the word [spoken by] Christ (the Messiah) have its home [in your hearts and minds] and dwell in you in [all its] richness, as you teach and admonish and train one another in all insight and intelligence and wisdom [in spiritual things, and as you sing] psalms and hymns and spiritual songs, making melody to God with [His] grace in your hearts.*

Jesus is the vine and we are the branches to bear fruit. The only way to bear fruit is to know the words of Jesus. Jesus is the living Word of God who was manifested in the flesh (given a human body) on Earth (1 Timothy 3:16). God's Word should be on our lips on a regular basis. Our words are important, they should be life-giving and not death, doomed-filled words. As His words dwell in us richly, we will become more attractive to God, and His grace and favor start to show up in our lives. Everything that we do should be motivated by God's Word. God made this statement to His people long ago, *"My people are destroyed for lack of knowledge."* Knowledge is vital to a successful life, and wisdom is the proper allocation of knowledge. Once you've been turned on to this, you will out-smart your problems and troubles.

# October 25

# LET HIM IN

*Revelation 3:20*

*Behold, I stand at the door and knock; if anyone hears and listens to and heeds My voice and opens the door, I will come in to him and will eat with him, and he [will eat] with Me.*

God will never force Himself and His way of living on anyone, He is a gentleman. The devil, however, has been forcing, tempting, overwhelming people into doing his will from the beginning of time. Without God in your life, how much choice do you have but to submit to the evil system we live in of this world? We live here but shouldn't conform to this world's way of life. God respects our free will, but our will can be swayed when the right temptation comes our way. We should be equipped, working the Word of God, to help us maintain the godly position in life the Lord intends for us to have. He stands at the door of your heart, and knocks, so let Him in.

# *October 26*

# THE POWER OF WORDS

*Proverbs 18:21*
*Death and life are in the power of the tongue, and they who indulge in it shall eat the fruit of it [for death or life].*

A well disguised lie is from the pit of hell. The Bible says you can, and will have what you say, good or bad (Mark 11:22-25). The words of God are like a two-edge sword, whatever He speaks will produce what He has said. "Let there be light" for example in the beginning, words formed and created everything we see in nature. As we use harsh words against another person, after a while those words will produce whatever is being said. When we confess with our mouths and believe in our hearts, the unseen force of faith is at work to create. Not on God's level but over time you will have what you have been saying, good or bad. The power of words can cut deeper and take much longer to heal than a knife wound. Speaking life-filled words is the goal. The tongue can bring life or death, the power is in your possession, use it wisely.

# October 27

# WHEN YOU ARE TIRED OF BEING TIRED

*Jeremiah 31:25*

*For I will [fully] satisfy the weary soul, and I will replenish every languishing and sorrowful person.*

G od will fully satisfy the weary soul and replenish every languishing and sorrowful person. It has already been done for you and everyone who needs this. The hands-on way of receiving this from the Lord is no different than receiving anything from God. All you need is faith. Anything and everything promised to us in the Bible, which is God's Word, has been given to the entire world. His Word is most definitely conditional, though. There are certain requirements to have God on the scene helping in your everyday life. It requires us to deal with our flesh, the part of us that wants to enjoy the pleasures of sin. That temptation of sin doesn't totally go away until we die, but it can be kept under submission, working the Word of God in our lives (2 Corinthians 10:5). Sometimes you're just tired of being tired.

# *October 28*

# OLD THINGS HAVE PASSED AWAY

### 2 Corinthians 5:17

*Therefore, if any person is [ingrafted] in Christ (the Messiah) he is a new creation (a new creature altogether); the old [previous moral and spiritual condition] has passed away. Behold, the fresh and new has come!*

Once a person is saved, or born again, and becomes a Christian, the old moral and spiritual condition of that person changes. You become a new creation in Christ Jesus. The old, spiritually dead person you were, becomes alive to God. You were once hell bound, in position to burn forever with no hope of getting out of it. Therefore, the fact of not paying for your sins, which would take forever, should be enough reason for a person to want Jesus. Justice will be satisfied in the end. God wants people willingly to come to Him, not grudgingly. Become something that has never been before, get saved, and live for God now!

# October 29

# THE ULTIMATE TRAINING PROGRAM

*Ephesians 5:1*

*Therefore be imitators of God [copy Him and follow His example], as well-beloved children [imitate their father].*

Taking on God's example means walking in love. Following Jesus all the way (to the best of our ability and God's combined) will bring you through whatever comes your way victoriously. There's no law against love; love overrules man's morals, and man's negative thoughts and shortcomings can become long-term victories. God loved humankind while we were His enemies, and He acted on it by sending His only begotten Son to die for something He was never guilty of. Mature love gets over offenses a lot faster than natural, human love (1 Corinthians 13:5). Most of the world and Christians operate under the lower level of love, not agape, the God kind of love. Our feelings are very real with raging emotions and having been trained all our lives to react with that eye for an eye and tooth for a tooth response without considering the bigger picture. This is an imperfect world with imperfect people in it. There will always be another bad situation coming. This isn't a negative statement but a reality of God's training program for your life.

# *October 30*

# RARE LOVE, WE NEED IT

*Matthew 5:44*

*But I tell you, Love your enemies and pray for those who persecute you,*

L ove your enemies, is that possible? Not outside of God's help. Sometimes, it's best to love them from a distance. Loving them doesn't have to mean spending time with them regularly. But helping them when they're down and out, even though they did something to you that seems unforgivable. Can you still be a good humanitarian despite an offensive act done to you (Romans 12:20)? Can you remain the same no matter what's been done to hurt or harm you? Can you be a loving person regardless of your circumstances? For this consistency of love in your life, you'll need a strong presence of God's agape love working in you (Romans 5:8). The kind that put Jesus on the cross, and He was blameless. He shouldn't have had to take punishment rightfully due to us, but out of His love for us, He did (we were His enemies, sinful). He decided to do that for us; He willed it, and it wasn't easy for Him, as He asked God to remove the cup of a crucified death on the cross (Matthew 26:39). And we get offended by someone's nasty words toward us. The wisdom of God in you is the governor of our battles. Choose wisely when to confront and when to love instead.

# October 31

# WORRY, THE THIEF OF TOMORROW

*Matthew 6:25*

*Therefore I tell you, stop being perpetually uneasy (anxious and worried) about your life, what you shall eat or what you shall drink; or about your body, what you shall put on. Is not life greater [in quality] than food, and the body [far above and more excellent] than clothing?*

D o not be anxious about your life. God has a plan for you. Can you take a punch? If not, you may have some growing in the Lord to do. Not being anxious or worry is knowing God's got you covered for anything bad coming your way. This is basic training is for every new Christian. We are in the army of the Lord, and there will be battles. Learning how to fight the good fight of faith takes time (1 Timothy 6:12). Many tests, trials, and crises must pass through our midst to help us grow into the soldiers God intended us to be. Every area of your life must be tested for surety and confidence in the Lord. Once properly trained, we can now take no thought for tomorrow, what it may bring, because we know God's got us no matter how bad things look. Worrying about what might happen tomorrow keeps us in bondage today. In most cases, you worried for no reason, and that makes you get old faster. Live for today, tomorrow will have enough worry of its own (Matthew 6:34).

# *November 1*

# THIS IS THE WAY

*Isaiah 25:1*

*O Lord, You are my God; I will exalt You, I will praise Your name, for You have done wonderful things, even purposes planned of old [and fulfilled] in faithfulness and truth.*

When we purpose to do a thing in faithfulness and truth, we invite the hand of God to endorse it. Our God-given plans, when followed, lead to success at every turn. God's purposes were planned long ago. He had things figured out even before the fall of humanity in the Garden of Eden. As we include faithfulness and truth in our motives, that's a whole other level of existence for many people. Most people are not totally honest with you or themselves. In many cases, they assume you're as dishonest as they are and will treat you that way. Bad morals create bad behavior which lacks faithfulness and truthfulness. Having a plan in advance could mean the difference between success and failure. The human mind plans his way, but the Lord directs his steps (Proverbs 16:9). The common denominator here is acknowledging the Lord in all our ways, and He will direct our path (Proverbs 3:6).

# *November 2*

# HOW TO HANDLE TROUBLE

*1 Corinthians 16:13*

*Be alert and on your guard; stand firm in your faith (your conviction respecting man's relationship to God and divine things, keeping the trust and holy fervor born of faith and a part of it). Act like men and be courageous; grow in strength!*

W̶e must invoke our will to be strong in the Lord and the power of His might (Ephesians 6:10). Help is available for all, but sometimes we just must 'man-up' to live the faith-life God has prescribed. It is a life of adventure, with difficulties, but through it all your faith is being developed which is your most valuable asset for a supernatural victorious lifestyle. Your enemy searches throughout the world seeking to devour weak-minded, simple people who don't know who they are in Christ (1 Peter 5:8). Once you have learned how to wield the power of God to push back your enemy, your troubles won't be over, but you'll know how to fight every battle and win. You are in the army of the Lord. Learn how to fight the good fight of faith (1 Timothy 6:12), because you are a victor in Christ, you are more than a conqueror in Christ, you are strong in the Lord and in the power of His might. This is what God has said about us, as we follow His life plan. Trouble is coming, learn how to manage it once and for all.

# *November 3*

# SOMETIMES YOU GOTTA GET LOUD

*Psalm 47:1*

*O clap your hands, all you peoples! Shout to God with the voice of triumph and songs of joy!*

Shouting to God with the voice of triumph is a confession of praise for victory before it happens. Once we have prayed to the Lord for something, especially of great importance, that's when we must fight the good fight of faith. We can use our praise to God as proof of ownership of the blessing before the manifestation of it. Cries of joy to the Lord get His attention. We would not do that if we didn't believe He was there. Believing in someone or something without oracular proof is straight up faith. We do it all the time on a natural level. We go to work for a company, and we trust their word that we will get paid. You work first, and then you wait for the check. We shout because it stirs up the spiritual realm. We must declare and decree a thing with a vehement attitude to pierce the spiritual realm (James 5:16). When God's Word and the name of Jesus is used, all things natural and spiritual must give way because God comes on the scene for us. Shout to God with the voice of triumph and get what's yours. Get loud!

# *November 4*

# THE POWER OF AGREEMENT

*Matthew 18:20*

*For wherever two or three are gathered (drawn together as My followers) in (into) My name, there I Am in the midst of them.*

You may know about the tower of Babel in the Bible, where all the people were in agreement to build a tower that could reach heaven, to where God is. God said, *"I must go down and confuse their language, so they won't be able to understand each other"* (Genesis 11:7). The people are of one mind and purpose, anything they image to do will happen. Thus, we have had different languages since that day. When two or three people come into agreement in prayer, Jesus is in the mist of it to ensure it happens. Two in agreement must have the same motives, same confession after praying, they should be a symphony, in perfect union. The power we have together when we are truly on one accord (Genesis 11:6).

# *November 5*

# WE ARE MORE THAN FLESH AND BONES

*Mark 8:35*

*For whoever wants to save his [higher, spiritual, eternal] life, will lose it [the lower, natural, temporal life which is lived only on Earth]; and whoever gives up his life [which is lived only on Earth] for My sake and the Gospel's will save it [his higher, spiritual life in the eternal kingdom of God].*

There are two parallel realms of life in existence: the higher spiritual eternal life and the lower natural temporal life, which is lived only on Earth. Whoever gives up his life (which is lived only on Earth) for Jesus's sake and the Gospel will save his higher, spiritual life in the eternal kingdom of God (Matthew 16:25). Most of us don't have a clue about these things because we're not exposed to the knowledge of it. We do what everyone else does and has been doing concerning living. The message here isn't to die physically for Jesus but to change our way of living to conform to Almighty God's reconciliation plan. Each of us has a life plan from the Lord, from birth to death, but we must tap into it. We all have a part to play in the plan of reconciliation, so as we get too busy for God and ourselves, we don't connect to our God-given destiny and purpose. Once we've tapped into our purpose here and now, we will secure our spiritual life after death. Whosoever shall call on the name of the Lord will be saved. (Romans 10:13)

# *November 6*

# HEART TRUST VERSUS MIND TRUST

*Proverbs 3:5-6*

*Lean on, trust in, and be confident in the Lord with all your heart and mind and do not rely on your own insight or understanding. In all your ways know, recognize, and acknowledge Him, and He will direct and make straight and plain your paths.*

The Bible says, trust in the Lord with all your heart, and lean not to your own understanding. In other words, letting your heart lead the way for you, and not your mind. Our thoughts can be subject to change because of our emotions. Our heart properly connected to God is not ruled by emotions, but by the Holy Spirit who does not change. In everything we do in life, we should acknowledge Him. He wants to be involved in our everyday lives, and then He will direct our paths. We are laborers together with God (1 Corinthians 3:9), so we should be on a dialogue basis with Him, not a one-way conversation. To the degree we renew our minds with God's Word (Romans 12:2), the Bible, will be to the degree we can hear God's voice more clearly. There's no fear when you trust God with your heart.

# *November 7*

# THANK GOD FOR HIS MERCY

*Psalm 107:1*

*O give thanks to the Lord, for He is good; for His mercy and loving-kindness endure forever!*

The mercy of God is everlasting and new every morning. Without His mercy and loving-kindness, we would all be on our way to hell, which is one of the most important, acts of mercy shown to humankind. Sending Jesus to be crucified on the cross and He never did anything wrong, is a complete act of God's mercy and love for us (John 3:16). Most of humanity does not have this understanding of God's mercy because it does not affect us now, in our everyday life. But once your body dies, you will know His mercy and love if you are a Christian. The Lord's mercy reaches out to our everyday life as well. His mercy is behind the scenes of our life. Mercy means you deserved punishment for the wrongdoing you committed, but God's sovereignty intervened on your behalf. Thank God for His mercy.

# *November 8*

# HOW'S LIFE TREATING YOU?

*James 5:13*

*Is anyone among you afflicted (ill-treated, suffering evil)? He should pray. Is anyone glad at heart? He should sing praise [to God].*

In whatever state of being you find yourself in, there's always an answer to why you're there. Sometimes it's self-inflicted and sometimes it's just life showing up when things go south. We can write our own ticket concerning most of our circumstances and life experiences, by keeping God in the mix (Proverbs 3:6). When we are in a time of jubilee, everything's going really well on every side of life, that's when we can sing praises to God because we are loving life. Then the other side of life comes in like a bat out of hell to mess you up. And this is when we force ourselves to sing praises to God. After a time of praising and worshiping God, His presence comes in and takes over, that's when we feel the Lord's comfort and peace caressing us. Yes, sing praises to God when all is well, but more so when you are going through your 'wilderness' experience of trouble. No matter what state of mind or being you are in, there is a way out (1 Corinthians 10:13). Storms and fiery trials eventually pass, it's how you handle yourself while you're in the smoke that counts. Let the true piety of your experience be known.

# *November 9*

# WHAT'S IN YOUR HEART?

*Psalm 19:14*

*Let the words of my mouth and the meditation of my heart be acceptable in Your sight, O Lord, my [firm, impenetrable] Rock and my Redeemer.*

Are the meditations of your heart pleasing to God? It depends on what you've been hearing over and over. Faith comes by hearing and hearing by the Word of God (Romans 10:17). If you're always listening to negativity and speaking out loud that negativity, guess what the meditations of your heart are. We are like computers; we program ourselves with good or bad. We become what we always say about ourselves. Think of yourself highly, but not more highly than you ought. Keeping a watch on the ear-gate of your programming is vital. If you say something enough, it'll eventually drop down in your heart and become a reality. We control the meditations of our hearts by not putting in the poison available from this world.

# November 10

# THE WAY OF WORSHIP

*Psalm 100:2*

*Serve the Lord with gladness! Come before His presence with singing!*

Not only should we do as the Lord prescribes with singing and praising Him, but in our everyday lives we can worship Him with our lifestyle before others. As we live a holy consecrated life before the Lord, it brings attention to others that He may be trying to draw to His family. God uses us who are steady and rooted in the things of God to grow His family. *"...I wish that all men would be saved and come into a saving knowledge of the truth" (1 Timothy 2:4).* Our lifestyle of worship will do the job in assisting God's plan of reconciliation. No hypocrites allowed in the unadulterated lifestyle of God's elite forces out to harvest His called ones into the fold. Our attitude is very important while doing whatever we're called to do. Two people with the same abilities for a job, same education, same potential, etc. But one of them has a not so desirable demeanor, and the other person is upbeat, delightful, and pleasant in attitude. Which one would you hire? Worship the Lord with gladness, come before Him with singing, and you'll have His undivided attention.

# *November 11*

# ARE YOU RIGHT WITH GOD?

*Proverbs 21:21*

*He who earnestly seeks after and craves righteousness,
mercy, and loving-kindness will find life in addition to
righteousness (uprightness and right standing with God) and honor.*

Anyone earnestly seeking right standing with God, finds life, prosperity, and honor. When we want to be right with God, not feeling condemnation, or guilt, and we diligently seek that like gold, we'll get that and much more. He is a rewarder of those who diligently seek Him (Hebrews 11:6). He is aware we have our busy day-to-day duties, but when we make the effort to put the Lord in the mix of our day as a priority, He will honor us back in ways that count for victorious living. Press in toward rich fellowship with God, make it happen, you'll be glad you did afterwards.

# *November 12*

# HOW MUCH CAN YOU TAKE?

*Proverbs 12:25*
*Anxiety in a man's heart weighs it down, but an encouraging word*
*makes it glad.*

We must always protect our hearts. What we hear and see are gateways into the heart. What we watch on TV, or on the Internet can profoundly affect our hearts. When we hear or see something all the time, we become attached to it, and it to us, good or bad. Hearing, "you're no good" all the time will begin to make you feel like you're no good. Seeing horrible imagery all the time will affect us negatively. To worry is to be overly concerned about something that may never happen. You're throwing today's happiness away because you're using unwarranted energy which belongs to tomorrow, it's exhausting. The importance of being surrounded by positive, happy people is vital to help keep anxiety and worry at bay. But ultimately, God has not given us the spirit of fear, but of power, love, and a clear-thinking mind (2 Timothy 1:7). There's no room for worry when a clear-thinking mind is in charge. We are human and from time-to-time an encouraging word can lighten the load and bring gladness.

# *November 13*

# THE KINGDOM CALL TO ADVANCE

*Romans 8:14*

*For all who are led by the Spirit of God are sons of God.*

The true sons of God are those who are led by their human spirits not by their flesh (emotions). When you are being led by God, His Holy Spirit speaks to your human spirit, and then your mind has to make a decision to obey. To the degree you renew your mind with the Word of God, the Bible, is to the degree you will be led by God Himself into all victory of every area of your life. With the same mentality we must be merciful just as our Father God is merciful to others. That takes patience and practice in our everyday tasks. We get mercy when we give mercy. The law of reciprocity is in effect. What goes around comes around. Good or bad whatever is sowed will be reaped by the sower. God will not be mocked (Galatians 6:7). To be led by our spirits, and to show mercy when necessary is a major step forward for the kingdom of God, and a big slap in Satan's face concerning him messing with us.

# *November 14*

# PRAYING IN THE SPIRIT

*Ephesians 6:18*

*Pray at all times (on every occasion, in every season) in the Spirit, with all [manner of] prayer and entreaty. To that end keep alert and watch with strong purpose and perseverance, interceding in behalf of all the saints (God's consecrated people).*

When today's church people hear about praying in the spirit, for many, it goes right over their heads as far as what that means. The uncut answer is, it's a way to pray the perfect will of God back to Him concerning any and every life issue we experience. It's a deeper dimension of God. It also builds up your newly recreated human spirit to accentuate and boost your faith in God. It is praying in tongues. The only thing that passed away from the upper room experience in the book of Acts is the Apostles (Acts 2:4). The unbelievers of "talking in tongues" are Satan's vehicles to keep you from the ultimate experience of God living and working through you. To be saved is the first level of the Christian experience, but the next vital level in your fellowship with the Lord is the baptism of the Holy Spirit through evidence of speaking in tongues. It's a gift for all Christians. It's that missing ingredient that you wonder about other people who have that something about them and why they are so blessed and used for such mighty exploits for God. Pray in the spirit on all occasions, clear your path of unnecessary obstacles.

# *November 15*

# THE STRONG TOWER AND SECRET PLACE

*Proverbs 18:10*

*The name of the Lord is a strong tower; the [consistently] righteous man [upright and in right standing with God] runs into it and is safe, high [above evil] and strong.*

The person in right standing with God can run into that safe place of refuge. There are special places of safety; the Lord has provided for the righteous to go when under attack. There is the secret place of the Lord Most High (Psalm 91:1-2). Those in close fellowship with God usually find it. It's a place under the shadow of the all-mighty where no evil can exist; all evil would burn up if it got too close to the secret place. We Christian soldiers are the army of the Lord. God has enemies on earth. Anything or anyone that's so heart-fixed in coming against God's plan of reconciliation of humanity is an enemy. Trying to block the gospel from going forth is a big no-no with God. His plan will prevail, and in the end, God will have His way. The name of the Lord is a strong tower. Use it to fight. Once we believe, everything bows and is subjected to that name, which is above every name, equipped with the full power of the Godhead backing it.

# *November 16*

# TAKE THE WAY OUT!

*2 Corinthians 3:17*

*Now the Lord is the Spirit, and where the Spirit of the Lord is, there is liberty (emancipation from bondage, freedom).*

There is a form of bondage that goes along with the way this world system has been set up by the evil behind it. This world has been given over to be ruled by Satan because of the fall of mankind in the garden of Eden long ago. Adam and Eve sinned before God by obeying the devil when they ate the forbidden fruit (Genesis 2:17). That sin caused the rulership of humankind to be turned over to Satan through disobedience to God. Once the fruit was eaten, the knowledge of good and evil entered the world. Men and women through this experience have learned how to be bad and have taken on the sin nature. Evil influence comes from the Devil, whom to this day has a hold on all unsaved, spiritually dead people. To become free from this control of the world system and Satan, a person would have to accept the completed work at Calvary done by our Lord and Savior Jesus Christ. We are all limited without this transformation, from being spiritually dead to God, to becoming the righteousness of God in Christ Jesus (2 Corinthians 5:21). Take the way out!

# *November 17*

# WE SHINE BRIGHTER FROM GOOD MORALS

*Matthew 5:16*

*Let your light so shine before men that they may see your moral excellence and your praiseworthy, noble, and good deeds and recognize and honor and praise and glorify your Father who is in heaven.*

Moral excellence, does that still exist? Today's world questions and wants to re-evaluate morals. Good morals are an internal governor that can control bad behavior. God put the moral system into place when He created us. Over time, the deteriorating idea of good morals has been grossly attacked and brought to its knees by the sinful nature of mankind. The light of your life is affected by bad morals (1 Corinthians 15:33). We are the light of the world (Christians). We bring the uncomfortable feeling of conviction to people's hearts that wash out in wrongdoings. This world and the Lord see your works on the Earth, good and bad. We shine brighter from good morals.

# *November 18*

## SEEK THE ONE

*Matthew 6:33, NLT*
*Seek the Kingdom of God above all else, and live righteously, and*
*he will give you everything you need.*

Seeking to live in the house of the Lord can be compared to seeking the kingdom of God and His righteousness. Knowing He is a rewarder of those who diligently seek Him ties it all together. By our spiritual nature (of being Christians), we are not creatures of time. We should avoid being caught up with this world's restraints and boundaries. As we seek to dwell in the house of the Lord, we will reap the benefits of the kingdom's blessings. Just understanding that I'm not of this world gives hope that this everyday struggle of life on Earth is temporary. But seek the kingdom of God and His righteousness first, and all these things (needs to be met) will be added unto you. When we are so focused on seeking the Lord, the concerns, pitfalls, trials, crises, and heartbreaks we deal with in life become subservient to God's Word. God can more easily deliver, restore, or mend us back to an acceptable outcome when we act on His word. When we are always in His face through prayer and reading His Word, we supersede this world's limitations on us. Seek Him now and stay with it.

# *November 19*

# TROUBLE ALONG THE WAY

*Psalm 34:19*

*Many evils confront the [consistently] righteous, but the Lord delivers him out of them all.*

The righteous person may have many troubles, but the Lord delivers him from them all. The enemy of Christ does not take a liking to us at all. He wants to kill, steal, and destroy. That's been his "M.O." from the day he hit the Earth to get back at God by coming against the children of God. The Lord has equipped us for battle in this world by giving us His all-powerful Word to use against Satan. The text reads, "the (consistently) righteous person..." The enemy is always looking for a way into that unprotected part of our lives that has yet to quite be developed. God can and will deliver us from all evil. Jesus prayed, Father, don't take them out of the world, but help them live above the evil in the world (John 17:15). The troubles have a purpose in our lives, but only that which God allows to come our way. Without the troubles or storms, we can't grow in faith. Faith is everything when it comes to God, so He allows the crises or troubles of life to drive us straight to Him.

# *November 20*

# ONCE YOU DIE, IT AIN'T OVER

*Zechariah 14:9*

*And the Lord shall be King over all the Earth; in that day the Lord shall be one [in the recognition and worship of men] and His name one.*

There's coming a time when the Lord will be King over the whole Earth. No devil will be in play after the rapture and when the new Jerusalem sets down on Earth. There will be no more sun in the sky because the Lord will be the light that shines. There will be one Lord, one God, and a theocracy-ruled world. He will rule with the perfect balance of love, correction, justice, and honest labor for everyone. The element of secret unjust motives will no longer exist. No more hurt or pain of any kind will be our portion once the Lord is King over all the Earth. No one will be a part of this new world coming that hasn't been saved, born again. Making Jesus the Lord and the Savior of your life before your death gets you in.

# *November 21*

# DIE TO SELF, LIVE FOR CHRIST

*Galatians 2:20*

*I have been crucified with Christ [in Him I have shared His crucifixion]; it is no longer I who live, but Christ (the Messiah) lives in me; and the life I now live in the body I live by faith in (by adherence to and reliance on and complete trust in) the Son of God, Who loved me and gave Himself up for me.*

I have been crucified with Christ and I no longer live, but Christ lives in me. The life we should now be living as Christians should be by the faith of our Lord Jesus Christ. The true sons of God are those led by the Spirit of God in their everyday life (Romans 8:14). Obtaining that sensitivity of hearing God's voice in your spirit is the most vital part of the Christian walk. If this is too far out there for you, you are not alone. Most of the body of Christ has not acquired this sensitivity to God's Spirit, or their just not obeying Him. It is work most people want nothing to do with it. How is your life going? Because that is the bottom line, but then there's our God given purpose to fulfill, which helps others. Most of us are just trying to make ends meet and that is exactly why we should do the work of cultivating a close fellowship with the Lord. You will understand so much about life and yourself. It will be worth the effort, and it will bring peace to your life that you never thought existed. No one can make you do anything, not even God. Die to self and live for Christ.

# *November 22*

# PURE RELIGION IS NOT WHAT YOU THINK

*James 1:27*

*External religious worship [religion as it is expressed in outward acts] that is pure and unblemished in the sight of God the Father is this: to visit and help and care for the orphans and widows in their affliction and need, and to keep oneself unspotted and uncontaminated from the world.*

To be in this world but not of it has been one of the most significant challenges for Christians. We are ambassadors for the Kingdom of God. Our temporary existence here on Earth may seem like the final destination, but it isn't. There is life after death. Without experience in working God's Word for your troubles regularly, you won't stand without being influenced by undesirable people and circumstances. The Word of God is our sword and shield against anything coming to kill, steal, and or destroy what God has developed in us. Once Christians have lost their salt-saving preservative qualities against evil, the world will have our undivided attention, and temptations will be harder to resist. God is always about helping people. He'd rather we go into the hardest, toughest, most undesirable places to share His Gospel than He cares about how many members the church congregation has grown. Pure religion is not what most church folk think it is.

# *November 23*

# THE STRUGGLE IS REAL

*Galatians 5:16*

*But I say, walk and live [habitually] in the [Holy] Spirit [responsive to and controlled and guided by the Spirit]; then you will certainly not gratify the cravings and desires of the flesh (of human nature without God).*

Human nature without God is a time bomb ready to happen at any point. There's no governing the person maxed out in their flesh. When our newly recreated human spirits lead us, we won't allow our emotions to dominate a bad situation. Instead, reacting with the truth at that moment, not emotions, will result in an easier ride in the long run of our troubles. Walking in the Spirit is not a hard thing once you've made up your mind to do it. How does walking in the Spirit get broken down in a way we know we're doing it? The fruit of the newly recreated human spirit has seeds of peace, patience, kindness, self-control, and other God-like characteristics which lay on the bed of love (Galatians 5:22-23). Pursue these attributes of God, and His precepts, and teachings. Then, you'll begin the process of walking in the Spirit. It's a daily management of your emotions. With God's help and invoking your will, it's attainable, and your life will be changed for the better.

# *November 24*

# WISDOM, THE RULER OF KNOWLEDGE

*Proverbs 9:10*

*The reverent and worshipful fear of the Lord is the beginning (the chief and choice part) of Wisdom, and the knowledge of the Holy One is insight and understanding.*

The reverent and worshipful fear of the Lord is the foundation of wisdom. Using obtained knowledge on any subject should flow through wisdom's hands first. Knowledge, running amok, is a doorway for pride, and pride goes before a fall (Proverbs 16:18). Wisdom from heaven is first winsome and easy to be entreated, but natural Earthly wisdom is demonically motivated, prone to failure in the long run. As we honor and revere the Lord, His wisdom will rise in us. Properly allocating knowledge in a way unique to the listener is true ministry in helping others. The Bible says, and God is speaking, *"My people are destroyed from lack of knowledge" (Hosea 4:6)*, so knowledge is essential and vitally important to humanities' survival. Knowledge of God is vital for a successful, abundantly prosperous lifestyle. Wisdom from above will help keep us steady and on the right track in life.

# *November 25*

# LIVE YOUR BEST LIFE NOW!

*Ephesians 2:10*

*For we are God's [own] handiwork (His workmanship), recreated in Christ Jesus, [born anew] that we may do those good works which God predestined (planned beforehand) for us [taking paths which He prepared ahead of time], that we should walk in them [living the good life which He prearranged and made ready for us to live].*

We are God's workmanship, created in Christ Jesus for good works. God has prepared paths for us to take that lead to the good life He pre-arranged and made ready for us to live. Each person has a purpose and a destiny to fulfill. Many of us don't have a clue what that is. Life comes from Almighty God who has given us a life worth living but many don't ever find it. The world's distractions are many and can keep us away from the original God-given plan for our lives. Many find their life through hardships or calamities which can drive any soul back to its Creator. Life and death experiences can turn our heads, and hearts to God, but the easier way to find your best life is to purposely seek the Lord for direction in general (Proverbs 3:5-6). He made mankind, we didn't just show up one day. Our life manual, the Bible, has all we need to live a godly, righteous life before Him. When we seek good, bad has less of a chance to overtake us.

# November 26

# The Ultimate Woman

*Proverbs 31:20*

*She opens her hand to the poor, yes, she reaches out her filled hands to the needy [whether in body, mind, or spirit].*

The Proverbs 31 woman is God's idea of a woman with purpose and to be admired. On top of taking care of her family, she's up early, starting her day with prayer, handling the everyday chores, going to the marketplace to buy what's needed, etc. She extends a helping hand to the poor and opens her arms to those in need. She is not a lazy woman, but she goes beyond tending to her family's needs and helps others. She is a noble wife, clothed with strength and dignity; she speaks with wisdom, and faithful instruction is on her tongue. The bottom line is, with all a woman has to deal with in her everyday life, the Proverbs 31 woman retains her integrity, character, faithfulness, and purpose through it all.

# *November 27*

# LET THE DEAD SAY AMEN

*John 11:25-26*

*Jesus said to her, I am [Myself] the Resurrection and the Life.*
*Whoever believes in (adheres to, trusts in, and relies on) Me,*
*although he may die, yet he shall live...*

Jesus is the resurrection of people and things like finances, or the dead relationship that you still want. He can resurrect any part of our lives that is vital to our calling and purpose. Ultimately, He has resurrected our dead human spirit into the righteousness of God when you received Him as Lord and Savior of your life (2 Corinthians 5:21). When Jesus was raised from the dead for our justification (Romans 4:25), we were raised with Him in all dead areas of life that this sin driven world killed from the beginning. But it doesn't come freely, as far as keeping the emotions in our flesh, under control. It's a day-to-day fight of faith to walk in the spirit of our resurrection from the dead. We must show God, His angels, and the devil we mean business. We mean business by following the teachings and precepts of the Bible, it's the only way to maintain a resurrected lifestyle of victory. Jesus rose from the dead and by doing so, destroyed everything that could stop us from having the life we all desire, let that sink in.

# *November 28*

# GUARD YOUR HEARTS, KEEP CLEAR OF NEGATIVE PEOPLE

*Proverbs 4:23*

*Keep and guard your heart with all vigilance and above all that you guard, for out of it flow the springs of life.*

Our hearts are the central point of our being. It pumps the blood throughout the human body, which sustains us for proper function and mobility. We take supplements to help the human heart beat and function properly. We take in God's Word to strengthen the spirit of man. We are three-part beings: spirit, soul, and body. Our hearts must be guarded from negativity, which comes from negative talk from people. When we hear something repeatedly, it drops into our spiritual hearts, eventually coming out of our mouths, and it will control us. Once we've believed what we've heard repeatedly, we become that, good or bad. Guard your heart, for out of it should flow the springs of life, the unadulterated Word of God to help others.

# *November 29*

# THE WAY OF COMFORT

*2 Corinthians 1:3-4, NLT*

*All praise to God, the Father of our Lord Jesus Christ. God is our merciful Father and the source of all comfort. He comforts us in all our troubles so that we can comfort others. When they are troubled, we will be able to give them the same comfort God has given us.*

Comfort comes from the God and Father of all comfort. He uses people who have gone through hell and high water successfully. They understand your frustration and can relate and respond with experienced comfort. When a person goes through a storm in life and is still standing, that's the one you want comforting you; it's real. A teacher teaching from book knowledge is good, but a teacher teaching from book knowledge and personal experience is better. The sympathy of God leads to life; the sympathy of this world, which is sorrow, leads to depression and eventually death. Godly sympathy and comfort leave you uplifted and give you hope to carry on. You want comfort, go to God; He'll either do it Himself supernaturally, or He'll send the perfect laborer.

# *November 30*

# WAIT A LITTLE BIT LONGER

*Psalm 40:1, NLT*

*I waited patiently for the Lord to help me, and he turned to me and heard my cry.*

Wait patiently for the Lord, and He'll turn to you and hear your cry. As we wait patiently and expectantly, it triggers the faith receptor in God. Our tears don't move God to action, although he collects them for later use, but it's our faith that moves God to act on our behalf. Through faith and patience, we obtain the promises of God (Hebrews 6:12). Many times, we run ahead of Him and miss Him because we left the position He was about to show up in. Everything must have the time to line up before He can manifest help, and He's never too late. He can push back the "too late" into tomorrow if necessary. As we wait on the Lord, He renews our strength (Isaiah 40:31), and then He downloads direction, encouragement, and clarity of purpose from Heaven, which are given in that quiet time with Him. When you prepare to wait forever, it won't take that long at all.

# *December 1*

# GUIDELINES WHEN YOU PRAY

*Matthew 6:6*

*But when you pray, go into your [most] private room, and, closing the door, pray to your Father, Who is in secret; and your Father, Who sees in secret, will reward you in the open.*

When a person has made their lifestyle one of discipline and structured it to suit God's ways and not their own, that person knows about not praying to impress the listener. When you pray to impress others, that's the beginning and end of your return blessing, those few minutes of showing off with big words or with that Elizabethan tone in your voice. God wants us to simply talk to Him no differently than we talk to other people, that's prayer. But when you have grown beyond trying to impress others with the way you pray, that's a sign of maturity. Now when you pray in your private time with the Lord behind closed doors, that's when you're getting things done in the spirit realm for success in the natural realm. When God sees us praying like that in secret, He will then reward us openly in front of others. The Bible says, let your profit show, but not as if it were by your own doings, in a prideful way. Nothing great in this world has been accomplished without the prayer of a man or woman of God working behind the scenes.

# *December 2*

# THE WISE WILL SHINE

*Daniel 12:3*

*And the teachers and those who are wise shall shine like the brightness of the firmament, and those who turn many to righteousness (to uprightness and right standing with God) [shall give forth light] like the stars forever and ever.*

Teachers and those who are wise shall shine like the brightness of the firmament. The sharing of knowledge is truly the ultimate gift to give. Our gifts to others are niceties we enjoy occasionally, but giving someone a gift that will never get old, go out of style, or lose its value is on another level. Survival is the first instinct we have innately. Without knowledge, enhancing that survival instinct for smooth sailing is impossible. Things must be done under rules and regulations. We can't just go and take what's not ours to survive. In today's world, we must be as wise as serpents but harmless as a dove in attitude (Matthew 10:16). The wise person has this method down to a science. They know to wait patiently for the right moment before they act. Impatience can be an unwanted side journey you can't afford. We are, by nature, attracted to the light of knowledge and the wisdom to rule that knowledge. You will shine brightly for others who need this gift to be passed on to them. Maneuvering around all the minutiae, the drama, crisis, calamities, relationships gone bad, and nasty people will take knowledge governed by wisdom to shine away the darkness of this world.

# *December 3*

# ARE YOU ON BOARD YET?

*1 Peter 4:10*

*As each of you has received a gift (a particular spiritual talent, a gracious divine endowment), employ it for one another as [befits] good trustees of God's many-sided grace [faithful stewards of the extremely diverse powers and gifts granted to Christians by unmerited favor].*

Each of us should use whatever gift we have received to serve others. Our gifts aren't to show off how great we are, but to use our gifts and talents to be of assistance to others (1 Corinthians 12:4-6). And in return when others use their gifts and talents to help you and others, there's an edification, a support system that would be unstoppable in fulfilling our purpose and God's great commission. Being faithful to our calling and service to the Lord, is what matters most. We all have been given a gracious divine endowment from God, (special giftings designed for our specific personality and makeup), using it for the Lord opens up a whole new world of blessings and opportunities that would otherwise not be available. Getting on the straight and narrow of our purpose and destiny rids us of unnecessary drama and undesirable baggage. The agape love of God in us, wants to get on board in helping and serving others. Are you on board yet?

# *December 4*

# LAY DOWN YOUR LIFE LOVE

## *John 15:13*

*No one has greater love [no one has shown stronger affection] than to lay down (give up) his own life for his friends.*

You would think if a person today would lay down their life for a friend's sake, that person could be a bit mentally off their rocker according to this world order. Most of us would be skeptical about dying for a family member. All this Jesus has done for us is to make us right with God. God's love sent His Son Jesus to die as a living sacrifice for our screw-ups and wrongdoings. Justice had to be satisfied before the eyes of God, so love in action was given to the entire world. The Love of God goes against all we've learned as people in this life on Earth. To be in this world but not of it takes God's love working in you. It's a sacrificial love when it needs to be. It's an understanding of love always. It's a comforting love when needed, and we won't let anything separate us from the Lord loving us. No greater love is exemplified in any way by anyone other than God. We are His children, and He has commanded us to love one another. Can we at least try? It's an act of our will. Let's make it happen for Jesus because we'd be lost without Him.

# *December 5*

# THE SHOCKING REALITY

*Romans 10:9*

*Because if you acknowledge and confess with your lips that Jesus is Lord and in your heart believe (adhere to, trust in, and rely on the truth) that God raised Him from the dead, you will be saved.*

It is not difficult to become a Christian, get saved, be born again, and know once your body dies that you will go to heaven and not the other place. It would be an eternal mistake to discover that heaven and hell are real after you die when it's too late. If you do not choose Jesus here and now, with all the distractions of this life, there is no other chance. We have free will. We can choose what we want or do not want in this life. The Lord grants us to be free agents of choice. "If you declare with your mouth, "Jesus is Lord," and believe in your heart that God raised Him from the dead, you will be saved." Because you go to church, that does not mean you're automatically a Christian. It is a personal relationship you must have for yourself. We can't get in on momma's good merits or grandma's hallelujahs. This time on Earth is not all there is. Choose life, my friend.

# December 6

## WAKE UP AND STAY WOKE

*Romans 10:13, NLT*
*For "Everyone who calls on the name of the Lord will be saved."*

Everyone who calls on the name of the Lord will be saved. To become saved is to become a Christian. And everyone must be saved to be with God in the end. A way to bypass the justice against us has been available for years since Jesus paid the price. If we don't call on the name of the Lord and ask Him to forgive us of sin, there's no other way to get to Heaven. It is a free-will choice we all should make before checking out of this world. You have a will; use it to save your life from spiritual death and eternal punishment. Yeah, it's that kind of message today. But at least you've been told the truth and have been given the opportunity. For those who have made the choice, stay woke. For those who haven't, wake up!

# *December 7*

# DO YOU TRUST HIM?

*Isaiah 26:4*

*So trust in the Lord (commit yourself to Him, lean on Him, hope confidently in Him) forever; for the Lord God is an everlasting Rock [the Rock of Ages].*

Trust in the Lord always. It takes time to trust someone, even Almighty God. If you don't know someone, how can you trust them? Trusting others without really knowing them isn't a natural thing for most of us. Getting to know God equals trust and faith and believing without seeing. Your relationship with God as a Christian is a reality, you are in His family. The next step once we've become a Christian is fellowship with Him. Spending time in prayer and worship with the Lord is a necessity for rich fellowship. It is in daily fellowship we learn about God. *"God is a rewarder of those who diligently seek Him."* (Hebrews 11:6) He doesn't have pressures like a man which could change His commitment to help us, He's a Rock that is never moved by circumstances. You can always count on God for help if you are trusting Him. *"Trust in the Lord with all your heart, and lean not unto your own understanding."* (Proverbs 3:5-6). As we do our part in trusting and believing, He'll do His part in helping.

# *December 8*

# THE GIFT THAT COUNTS

*Luke 11:13*

*If you then, evil as you are, know how to give good gifts
[gifts that are to their advantage] to your children,
how much more will your heavenly Father
give the Holy Spirit to those who ask
and continue to ask Him!*

Don't let evil people deceive you by giving you some sort of gift. It's most likely for their own gain. When God gives, it's usually like a domino effect. His gifts and blessings are more than what you may have been needing or desiring, but they will line up with what He's called you to do in life, toward your destiny and purpose. Most people never complete the original story for their lives because they don't include God who wrote the script. God has given the ultimate gift of His Son Jesus Christ, and we must choose Him as Lord, not just Savior.

# *December 9*

# STENCH IN GOD'S NOSTRILS

*1 John 2:15*

*Do not love or cherish the world or
the things that are in the world.
If anyone loves the world,
love for the Father is not in him.*

When we place our love totally on this world, or the things of this world, our love for God has been compromised. When your love for God is compromised, you are automatically in line for whatever defeat this world throws at you. You become unprotected (Deuteronomy 4:23-24). Being that faith works by love (Galatians 5:6), everything we are, and everything we receive from God, is by faith, including salvation. If your love-walk, and your love for God is now turned to love for this world, your faith is not what it should be, and you are flirting with idolatry (1 Corinthians 10:14). God does not like ugly, and that would be stench in His nostrils.

# December 10

# LIVE FOR GOD, SHAME THE DEVIL

*2 Peter 1:3*

*For His divine power has bestowed upon us all
things that [are requisite and suited]
to life and godliness, through the [full, personal]
knowledge of Him Who called us by and to
His own glory and excellence (virtue).*

All we need to live a godly and holy life is in the Bible. Living a holy and godly life isn't you being so heavenly minded that you're no Earthly good. It's really a basic way to live above evil in this world. As we line up with the character and integrity of Jesus, we bypass many pitfalls not otherwise realized. We become more sensitive to possible drama, insincerity, fake people, and the unseen presence of danger. Live it before you knock it. The wages of wrongdoing is death (Romans 6:23). Sometimes we play into the hands of trouble without even knowing it. Living for God brings benefits to your life you'd never experience otherwise. The favor and blessings of God will overtake you. He is a rewarder of those who diligently seek Him (Hebrews 11:6). The Life-Giver wants to give you the life you deserve. Live for God, shame the devil.

# December 11

# THE PURE IN HEART

*Matthew 5:8*

*Blessed (happy, enviably fortunate, and spiritually prosperous—
possessing the happiness produced by the experience of God's favor
and especially conditioned by the revelation of His grace, regardless
of their outward conditions) are the pure in heart, for they shall see
God!*

If we were to see God face to face in these human bodies, we would burn up because of the glory of His presence (Exodus 33:22-23). Pure in heart is when there's no guile found in your heart, there's no conniving, malicious intent, sly or cunning evil motive in you. Without humility, there can be no pure heart. Humility springs from understanding and understanding springs from love. The agape love of God working in a person's life is due to obedience to His commandments. The Bible says, to love God is to do His commandments (1 John 5:1-3), and Jesus summed them all up by giving a new commandment: love your neighbor as yourself. The pure heart has stated that he's all about Jesus. God has made Himself accessible in this life, but it will always be your choice to seek Him out for yourself, and not go by what others have told you about God.

# December 12

## GUILTY AS CHARGED

*1 John 1:7*

*But if we [really] are living and walking in the Light, as He [Himself] is in the Light, we have [true, unbroken] fellowship with one another, and the blood of Jesus Christ His Son cleanses (removes) us from all sin and guilt [keeps us cleansed from sin in all its forms and manifestations].*

Guilt can be annoying and can even keep us in bondage. If you feel guilty about something, and you're not convinced you're totally blameless, then that's conviction opposed to feeling condemned. There is therefore now no condemnation to those who walk after the dictates of the spirit, and not the flesh (Romans 8:1), your body's appetites. Conviction is when you know you messed up and now guilt is knocking at your door. We can feel the temptation of condemnation even when we've done no wrong, that's the evil in this world's job to make you think you did wrong (Revelations 12:10), when you didn't. Walking in the light as He is in the light, keeps us on the straight and narrow. There are less pitfalls, unnecessary troubles, and heartache when we walk in the light. Walking in the light is simply following the walk Jesus took while on the Earth. He followed God's plan for His life and was victorious on every side. Guilt can be a fork-in-the-road experience. Is it legitimate guilt because you messed up, or are you being tempted with condemnation to test your faith of being right with God.

# *December 13*

# WORDS OF COMFORT

*John 14:1-3*

*Do not let your hearts be troubled (distressed, agitated). You believe in and adhere to and trust in and rely on God; believe in and adhere to and trust in and rely also on Me.² In My Father's house there are many dwelling places (homes). If it were not so, I would have told you; for I am going away to prepare a place for you. ³ And when (if) I go and make ready a place for you, I will come back again and will take you to Myself, that where I am you may be also.*

As we believe in, adhere to, trust in, and rely on God, and the finished work at Calvary Jesus completed, the Prince of Peace (Jesus) will release His comfort from the Father of all comfort into your soul. Jesus does not want our hearts to be troubled. If He says don't let your heart be troubled, we can do just that. Keep your mind focused on Him and not all the drama and confusion of this world (Isaiah 26:3). We must position ourselves away from the things that would increase our heart trouble. Talking to people with the same issues can be good or bad. If there's no solution in the conversation, it could turn for the worse, and your heart is in the same place of trouble. Surround yourself with people you trust who can speak positively into your life words of comfort based on God's Word.

# *December 14*

# TIME TO COME OUT OF THE CLOSET

*1 Peter 4:16*

*But if [one is ill-treated and suffers] as a Christian [which he is contemptuously called], let him not be ashamed, but give glory to God that he is [deemed worthy to suffer] in this name.*

If you are ill-treated, suffer as a Christian, and are contemptuously called a Christian, do not be ashamed. When this happens, it lets you know your faith is shining through and you have been counted worthy to bear Jesus' name. All those choosing to live a godly life will suffer persecution (2 Timothy 3:12). That's right; stand up for God and show the world who you serve. It's time to come out of the closet of shame and be bold for the Lord in how we live, speak, and act. If you're ashamed of God in public, you have no real quality fellowship with Him in private. It's time for us to step up our prayer time and read His Word; the boldness will come automatically once your Christian lifestyle has matured.

# *December 15*

# A HEART CONDITION

*Ezekiel 36:26*

*A new heart will I give you and a new spirit will I put within you, and I will take away the stony heart out of your flesh and give you a heart of flesh.*

In His Word, God says, I will take out your stony stubborn heart and give you a tender responsive heart. From time to time, we can be stubborn for whatever reason. The headstrong person could use a more tender responsive heart, which will affect their stubborn headstrong attitude. Everyone has a different makeup, some of us are more naturally easy-going and more understanding. There are those of us that are go-getters, no-nonsense driven, which is great for certain situations. But to be hard-core 24/7 isn't a good idea for every area of your life. Being grounded in the things of God relaxes the tendency of always coming across like a drill sergeant. We have become hardened because of how this world is, but as Christians, we should be striving to live above this world's system and excel above the evil in it (John 17:15). The Lord will remove that stony, stubborn heart and replace it with a tender responsive heart if you come to Him. The body can only take so much stress and anxiety, we were never created to handle that, but God made a way, so take it.

# *December 16*

## EVERYONE IS CREATED BY GOD, BUT ALL AREN'T CHILDREN OF GOD

### *John 1:12*

*But to as many as did receive and welcome Him, He gave the authority (power, privilege, right) to become the children of God, that is, to those who believe in (adhere to, trust in, and rely on) His name—*

By believing in Jesus' name, we are given the right to become children of God. We must receive and welcome Him before being in the family of God. You may have heard it said we are all children of God. That is not true; the devil's children are not children of God, and if you haven't received Jesus Christ as Lord and Savior of your life, then it is impossible to be a child of God. Everything having to do with the Lord is of faith, dealing with the unseen but still trusting God's control. Everything in life that is dependent upon our five senses (our emotions) is Satan's territory of expertise. Without faith, there's no connection to God because you can't see Him with your eyes. Those who the Spirit of God leads are the true sons and daughters of God (Romans 8:14). So, if we live according to the flesh, our senses and emotions, we will die; but if by the Spirit, we will live a victorious life as children of God (Romans 8:13).

# *December 17*

# TRUST AND BE RENEWED

*Isaiah 40:31*

*But those who wait for the Lord [who expect, look for, and hope in Him] shall change and renew their strength and power; they shall lift their wings and mount up [close to God] as eagles [mount up to the sun]; they shall run and not be weary, they shall walk and not faint or become tired.*

Waiting on God is trusting Him. We often get ahead of the Lord while He's saying wait for Me. There are different seasons for different life events to occur (Ecclesiastes 3:1-8). We are taught to wait because patience and faith bring answered prayer. Waiting on and trusting in God for strength happens through perseverance in being steadfast in your belief. We are laborers together with God, and we need Him, but He needs us as well (1 Corinthians 3:9). Anything the Lord wants to do on Earth can only be carried out by a man or woman. We have dominion in the Earth, and God can only work through obedient saints faithful to His will. It's God's law and rule. He runs the universe, and we oversee the running of the Earth. We have not been doing such a great job at it because of the evil down here. To trust in someone invisible isn't the easiest thing, but it is possible through faith. Once you've decided to trust, no matter what the circumstances or what's been said about God in the past, it comes down to what you think and act on concerning the Lord. Those who trust will be renewed.

# *December 18*

# DON'T LET YOUR HEART BE TROUBLED

### *John 14:1*

*Do not let your hearts be troubled (distressed, agitated). You believe in and adhere to and trust in and rely on God; believe in and adhere to and trust in and rely also on Me.*

Let not your hearts be troubled. This is a statement Jesus made when He was teaching. If He's saying don't let your hearts be troubled, there must be the ability to do that, which goes along with the statement. Guarding our hearts is important (Proverbs 4:23). What goes into it can be very concerning. Out of the abundance of the heart, your mouth will leak, or speak (Luke 6:45). As we hear a thing over and over again, we develop faith in it, or you could say, spiritual muscle memory of what you've been hearing. As we believe a thing we've been hearing all the time, we begin to live that thing, or become it. You will speak, good or bad words based on what you've been hearing. As we confess something over and over, creativity develops, and it will manifest in time. Faith comes by hearing and hearing, and hearing (Romans 10:17). Whatever you're hearing all the time will affect you. To your ears, to your mind, then it drops down into your spirit, your heart.

# December 19

## OUR DAILY BREAD

*Matthew 6:11*
*Give us this day our daily bread.*

M ost of us are familiar with today's scripture. It is speaking of God supplying provisions for His people. He will supply as needed. Each day brings new insights into God's way of supplying our needs. He doesn't provide the same way every time. He may have provided for you one way in the past, but it may be coming a different way this time. When we look into the future wondering how the answer's going to come, we can easily miss God. The timing is always in His hands. Many times, we think, it's too late, God didn't come through. He can change the due date of the deadline you were given, if necessary. Staying in faith should be our focus, not figuring out how God's going to move on our behalf (2 Corinthians 5:7). The text reads, give us our daily bread, that's indicative of supplying as needed, each day, not a heap up for the future. God wants us depending on Him for each day's needs. God, give us this day, our daily bread.

# *December 20*

# TRUTH IS GREATER THAN FEAR

*Psalm 145:18*

*The Lord is near to all who call upon Him, to all who call upon Him sincerely and in truth.*

He is close by at all times, but to utilize God's help, we must come to Him the right way. He is a Holy God and should be approached in spirit and in truth, with no pretense or uncertainty. God is a God of faith and a rewarder of those who diligently seek Him (Hebrews 11:6). We are a spirit, we have a soul, and we live in a body. We are spirit beings; you have what it takes to ask God what you want and need. Being knowledgeable of His Word, the Bible gives you an advantage in receiving from God, and you're not just at His mercy all the time. Be on the offensive in this life, knowing God has your back. Go for that business that's been floating around in your thoughts. Go for that job you're afraid you won't get. Get to the point of going after something bigger than yourself, something that won't happen without God behind it. Now, you're living the supernatural lifestyle. Be who you are created to be; don't let fear take that from you. Truth is greater than fear.

# December 21

# WORSHIP, THE MISSING COMPONENT

*Psalm 95:6*

*O come, let us worship and bow down, let us kneel before the Lord our Maker [in reverent praise and supplication].*

To worship the Lord in spirit and in truth is God's desire for us. Many times, worship is spent on our knees. Bowing down in our hearts is as important as physically bowing down on our knees. Bowing down physically helps bring us to the surrender necessary to invoke God's manifested presence. Getting our minds quiet can take a little more time when we've had a busy day, but God eventually walks into the room as we stay put. You'll sense an unusual peace and sometimes a warmth in your soul that speaks loud and clear: the Lord is here. Bowing down in your spirit (your heart) comes after we've passed through the outer courts of His presence into the holy of holies (Psalm 100:4). Now you are totally engaged in worshiping the Lord, your spirit, soul, and body. We are three-part beings much like God but on a lower level. When we allow the hope of our calling to be enlightened, we know worship is a major part of it all. Remember, your feelings cannot decide whether you worship or not. It must become a lifestyle for each of us. Before you meet your maker, make Him proud.

# *December 22*

# BE KIND AND COMPASSIONATE

*Ephesians 4:32, NIV*

*Be kind and compassionate to one another, forgiving each other, just as in Christ God forgave you.*

We are to be kind and compassionate to one another, they go hand-in-hand. We can't be kind without being compassionate, and we can't be compassionate without being kind. You can't be kind or compassionate if there's unforgiveness in your heart. Holding an offense against someone takes you out of the kindness realm onto the dark side. Unforgiveness will eat you alive from the inside out if you don't rid yourself of it. We are to forgive others as Christ forgives us (Matthew 6:14). God never said, but since you committed that sin, I don't think I can forgive that. NO, the Lord forgives us of murder, theft, lying, adultery, fornication, conniving, malicious intent, etc. It's all under the precious blood of Jesus. Taking on the Lord's attitude of forgiving others puts us in the elite program of God. We are still prone to wrong-doings because of the appetites of our bodies which haven't changed. Only your human spirit has been reborn through the new birth. But the seed of kindness has been planted in you for growth. It needs development. When you allow the process of God to raise you, kindness and compassion will always be the plumbline to your success.

# *December 23*

# WHAT'S THAT ABOUT?

*Ephesians 6:18, NKJV*

*Praying always with all prayer and supplication in the Spirit, being watchful to this end with all perseverance and supplication for all the saints—*

P raying in the Spirit by speaking in tongues or unknown languages is a form of prayer. (Acts 2:4). It's praying God's perfect will back to Him. He is moved by faith on the lips of a believer confessing His Word back to Him in prayer. As we spend time alone with the Lord in prayer and reach that moment when we begin to feel His peace and comfort all around us and from inside, we're praying in the Spirit because He has now gotten involved with our prayer time. Getting started is always the most challenging part. We start by faith, feeling dry, or the day's stress is still on us. As we continue to pursue God, there will be a breakthrough, and praying becomes more fluid, easier. The more time we spend with God on a regular basis, the easier each time will be to get started. We can build up residuals from praying often, making it a more enjoyable and exciting time with the Lord.

# *December 24*

# TOUGHEN UP, BE THAT PERSON

*Romans 8:18*

*[But what of that?] For I consider that the sufferings of this present time (this present life) are not worth being compared with the glory that is about to be revealed to us and in us and for us and conferred on us!*

This life is the only hell a Christian will know and the only heaven a sinner will know. Suffering is a part of life if you haven't noticed yet. But what God is saying is what we suffer now is nothing compared to the glory He will reveal later. This peace, love, and glory of God will dominate our beings to a level of indescribable joy, safety, and comfort to our spirits, souls, and the new glorified bodies we'll have (Philippians 3:20-21). This will be obtained after the last day (the rapture). We are on testing grounds here on Earth to see who answers the call of God to be in His family after this world passes away as we know it (Matthew 24:35). Whatever troubles, storms, or crises you're experiencing now are ultimately for your development. Using God's Word to come against your enemy will never fail you. Once your thing with God is tight, you may fall from an attack, but you won't stay down, understanding your relationship and trusting your relationship with God, which holds you together. You are more than a conqueror through Christ Jesus. Toughen up, and be that person.

# December 25

# CONDEMNATION, THAT UNWANTED FEELING

*Romans 8:1*

*Therefore, [there is] now no condemnation (no adjudging guilty of wrong) for those who are in Christ Jesus, who live [and] walk not after the dictates of the flesh, but after the dictates of the Spirit.*

The Bible says, there is now no condemnation to those who are in Christ Jesus...but it goes on to say, for those who walk NOT after the dictates of the flesh. If you haven't renewed your mind with the Word of God, to start a new thought pattern in your thinking, and start to think like Jesus did walking the Earth, you're still going to mostly be just like you've always been with the same unwanted results you always get. Because you've always done things the way you have, doesn't mean God's in that way. God should have the final word before we make any major or minor moves in life (Proverbs 3:6). We are laborers together with God (1 Corinthians 3:9). When things don't turn out well because of our actions, maybe the Lord wasn't in the plan you came up with.

# December 26

# THE STEADFAST LOVE OF GOD

*Isaiah 54:10*

*For though the mountains should depart and the hills be shaken
or removed, yet My love and kindness shall not depart from you,
nor shall My covenant of peace and completeness be removed,
says the Lord, who has compassion on you.*

Here we see how much God loves His people. If the mountains should depart and the hills are shaken or removed, God's love and kindness will not leave us. His love is steadfast toward us. This means His love of correction, His love of comfort, His love which is connected to His kindness will be our portion in everyday living. Love is not letting someone do whatever they want to do. His love of comfort comes through His peace by which He anoints our human spirits to experience it. It's like a download from heaven, a direct connection into our hearts. When our hearts and minds are settled, peace comes in. The love of God has been shed abroad in our hearts by the Holy Spirit when we became Christians (Romans 5:5). As we develop that seed of agape love in us, (by loving others on purpose), that love grows, and comes into agreement with God's love, then we reap the benefits.

# *December 27*

## GOD'S WIFI

*Jeremiah 29:11*

*For I know the thoughts and plans that I have for you, says the Lord, thoughts and plans for welfare and peace and not for evil, to give you hope in your final outcome.*

God says He knows the plans He has for us, each of us. The plans are to prosper us and not to harm us, plans to give us hope, and a future. I think that's the main goal we all want in our lives, to live an abundant, prosperous life with hope. Since your life was already predestined by God when He made you, you just need to seek after the plan. How do we know the plan, by knowing God, which is the direct approach. Many of us walk in our destiny and purpose because we have a strong conviction of it in our heart and soul, we just do what our gut is suggesting. There are those of us that don't have it that easy. The plan for your life becomes clearer by spending time with the Lord. It's all connected once we're on God's WiFi.

# *December 28*

# TAKE YOUR PLACE NOW!

*Deuteronomy 6:5*

*And you shall love the Lord your God with all your [mind and] heart and with your entire being and with all your might.*

The distractions in this world are numerous, and all around us. To love the Lord with all your heart, mind, and soul, takes practice because of the evil distractions in the world. To love God with all your might is to obey His commandments (1 John 2:3-5). We must know the commandments in order to obey them. In a nutshell the commandments have come down to one that fulfills them all. Love your neighbor as yourself (John 13:34). Your neighbor is anyone you come into contact within your everyday life. Showing the love of God, which is selfless, especially to your brother or sister in Christ will develop your love expeditiously. If we love, we will not kill, steal, or destroy like the Devil (John 10:10). You are a love child of a loving God. Take your place now!

# December 29

# IT'S OKAY TO CRY, LET IT OUT

*Matthew 5:4*

*Blessed and enviably happy [with a happiness produced by the experience of God's favor and especially conditioned by the revelation of His matchless grace] are those who mourn, for they shall be comforted!*

If you are mourning right now, you shall be comforted, as per the Bible. When your trust and hope are in God, then comfort comes to you. The Word of God is and always has been conditional. If you obey His commandments, or at least are trying to, there's a grace and favor on your life. Once you understand the big picture of life under God's rule, there's a peace that follows you. Everything seems to line up more gracefully in our lives. Trouble in the world is what we all deal with from time to time. It either just left, or it's on its way to your front door. It's okay to mourn for a time, but joy comes in the morning, and you shall be comforted, as per God Himself.

# *December 30*

# TRUST HIM, WON'T HE DO IT?

*Psalms 119:114, NIV*
*You are my refuge and my shield;*
*I have put my hope in your word.*

Hoping in God's Word is a good hope. A hope that stays present and is attainable. Our confident, favorable expectation in and of the Lord's Words in our hearts and minds will produce a great harvest of victories. God's Word is Spirit and Life, and it will not return to God void of power or without accomplishment of what it was sent to do on our behalf. The Lord is our strength and shield; when our hearts trust Him, we are shielded and have refuge when we need it. We can't always trust everyone, but Jesus sticks closer than a brother. Trusting people isn't always easy because people tend to change under pressure or bad circumstances. The Lord is the same yesterday, today, and forever. We can totally trust in and rely on Him for everything; that's a comfort beyond compare. Sometimes, we must leave the battlefield of life to rest and refresh in the Lord. If you've tried everything else, it might be time to put the Lord's program for your life in motion. Trust Him, won't He do it?

# *December 31*

# Lord Have Mercy

*Matthew 5:7*

*Blessed (happy, to be envied, and spiritually prosperous—with life-joy and satisfaction in God's favor and salvation, regardless of their outward conditions) are the merciful, for they shall obtain mercy!*

If we want to be shown mercy, we must be merciful. The human race is flawed, and prone to eventually mess up, since we are not perfect. Mercy is a very valuable thing when needed. It is not a matter of *if* you mess up, it is a matter of when. When you do in today's world, people want to go right for the juggler to reprimand you. That is why mercy is so important. Some of us could use a little mercy in our lives right now. Show mercy, and mercy will be measured back to you again when you need it. God's mercy is so understanding, and measured out to the right amount we need at any given point. When you don't know what to do, ask God to have mercy on you.

# ABOUT THE AUTHOR

 Gioron T. Wilkins Sr. is a renowned musician with a rich history in the music industry. He is recognized for his exceptional talent as a guitarist and his profound ability to connect with people through music. Gioron's journey began in Manhattan, NY, and he later became a vital member of the music scene, touring with The Isley Brothers.

Gioron has embraced various roles throughout his life, including husband to Jill Wilkins and a loving father to three children and six grandchildren. His passion for music led him to join the Recording Academy for the Grammy's, where he learned to touch people's souls with his compositions, providing comfort and solace.

Gioron's spiritual journey has also been a significant part of his life. Raised in a church, he faced periods of doubt and strayed from his faith for a time. His diverse experiences have shaped his perspectives on life and spirituality. Today, he is an Ordained Minister and the CEO of Wilkins Ministries International.

Approaching his 70th birthday, Gioron has felt compelled to share his life's wisdom and biblical revelations with others. Although he had never initially planned to become an author, he believes that leaving behind a legacy of his life's experiences and insights can provide a valuable guide for others navigating their journey on Earth. Gioron remains open to the unexpected paths the future may hold, trusting in the higher purpose guiding his life.

# MUSIC BY GIORON T. WILKINS, SR.

Find on all streaming music platforms.

# CONNECT WITH AUTHOR

www.facebook.com/gioron
www.facebook.com/wilkinsministriesinternational

@gtwilkinsmusic
@wilkinsministries

www.wilkinsmi.org
www.gtwilkinsmusic.com

**Wilkins Ministries International Inc.**
Please join us on our TV Show "Keeping It Real". View
right here on this channel. Real Talk for real life issue...
YouTube

 WMI, PO Box 180, Circleville, NY 10919